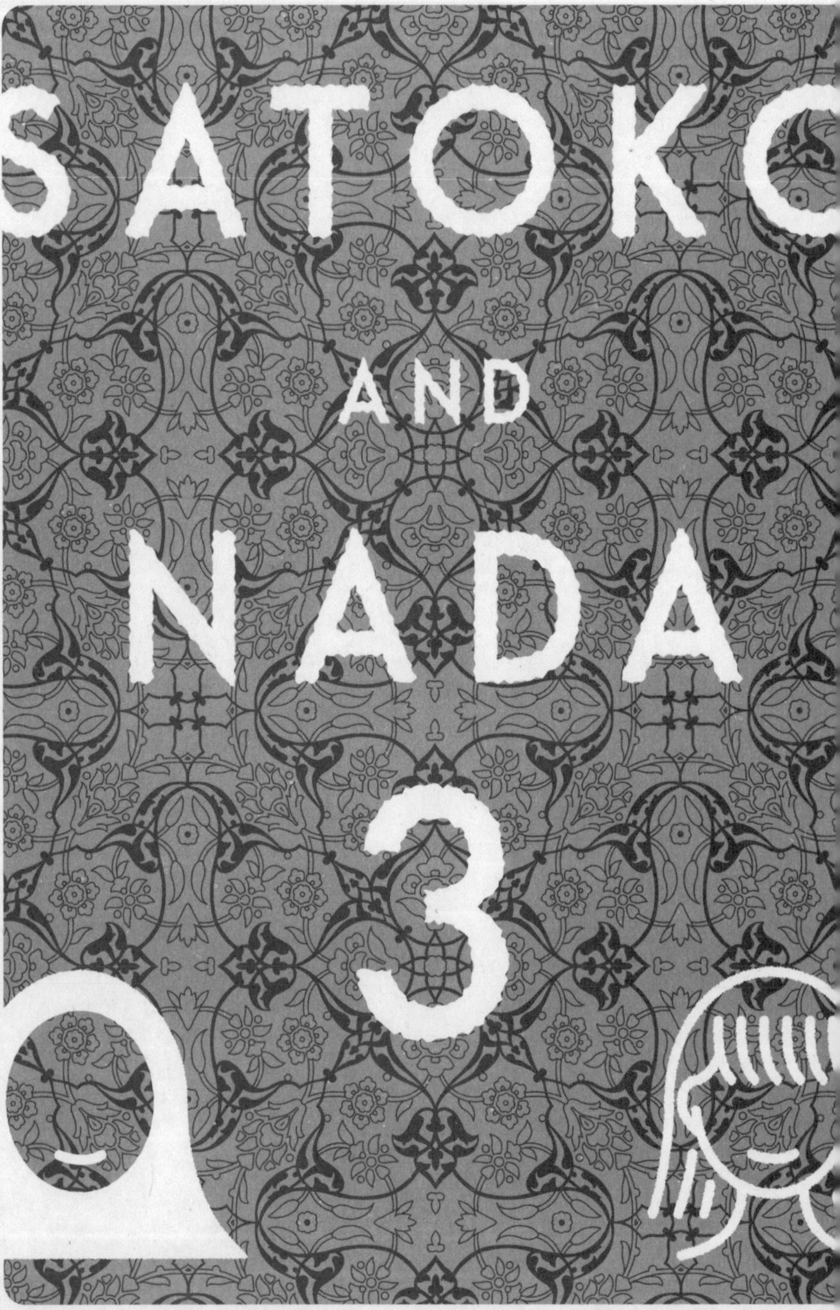
SATOKO
AND
NADA
3

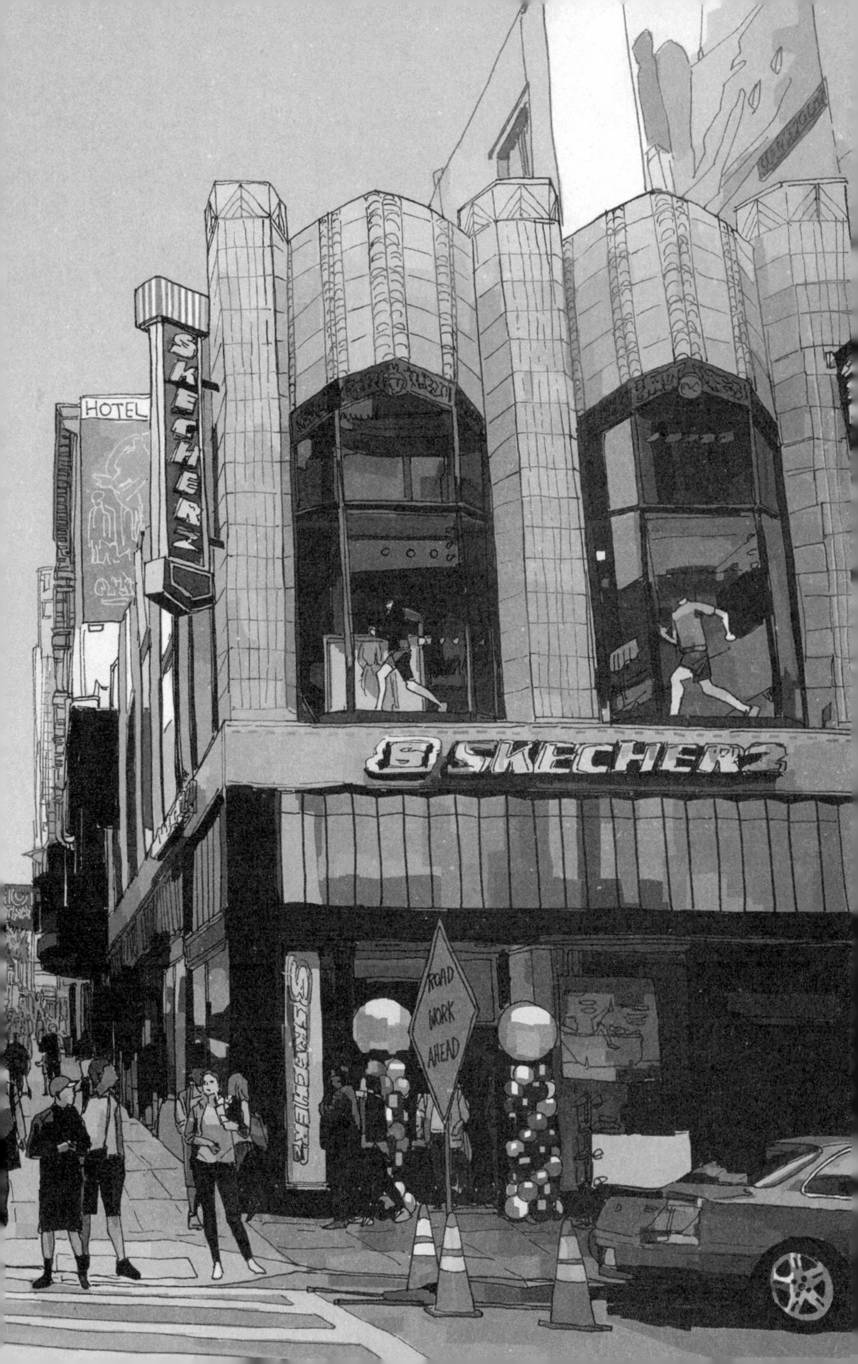
HOTEL
SKECHERS
SKECHERS
SKECHERS
ROAD WORK AHEAD

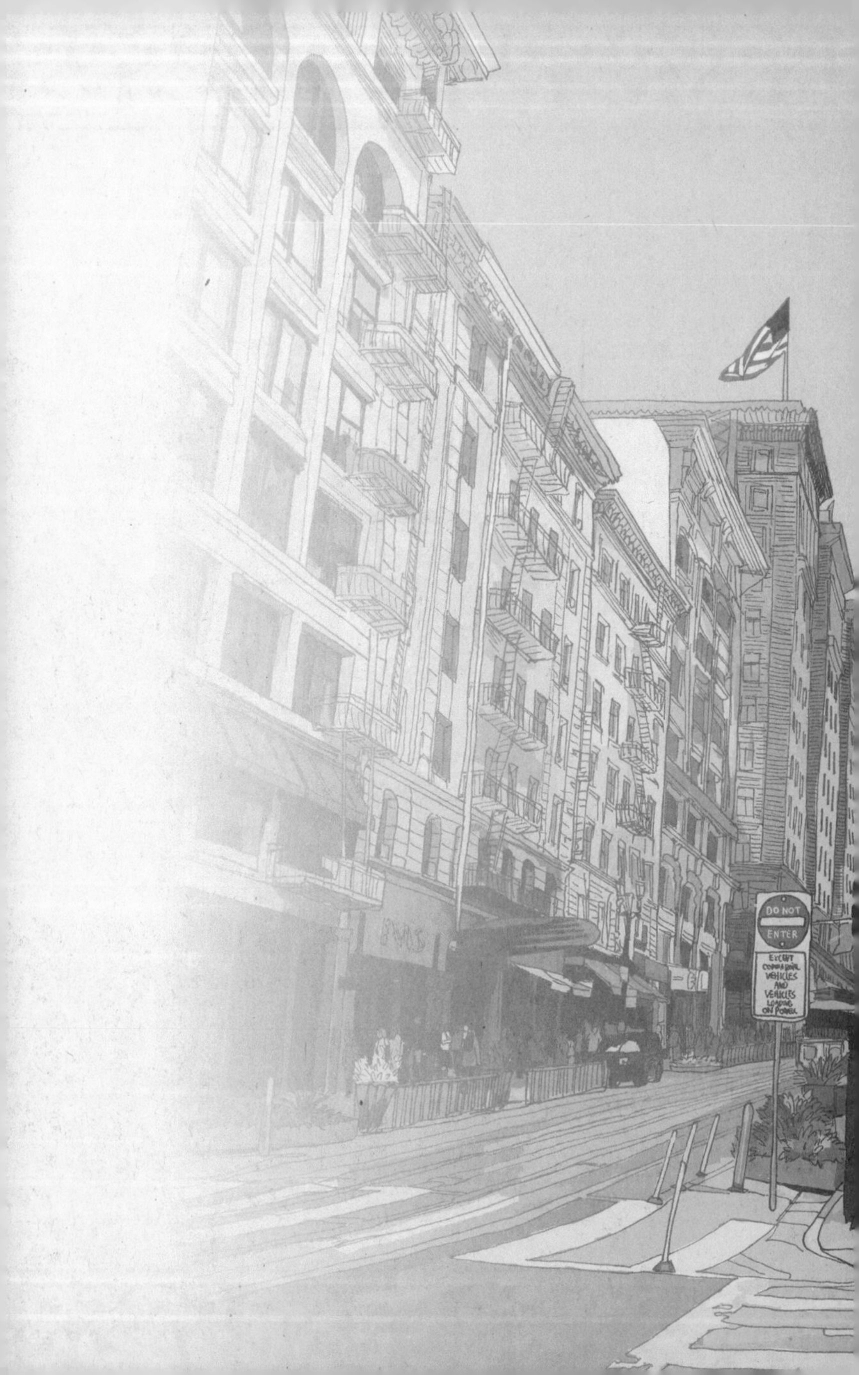
DO NOT
ENTER

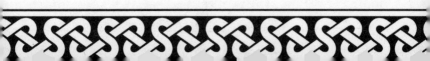

Previously in

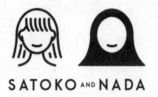

SATOKO AND NADA

Nada received word from her older
brother Rahman that her family found
her a fiancé. Will she marry someone
she's never met? What about her dream
of becoming a doctor? As Satoko and
friends worry about the shaken Nada,
the mysterious fiancé Abdullah suddenly
arrives from Saudi Arabia!

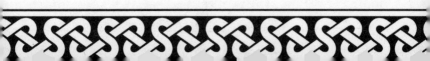

HE ACTUALLY CAME

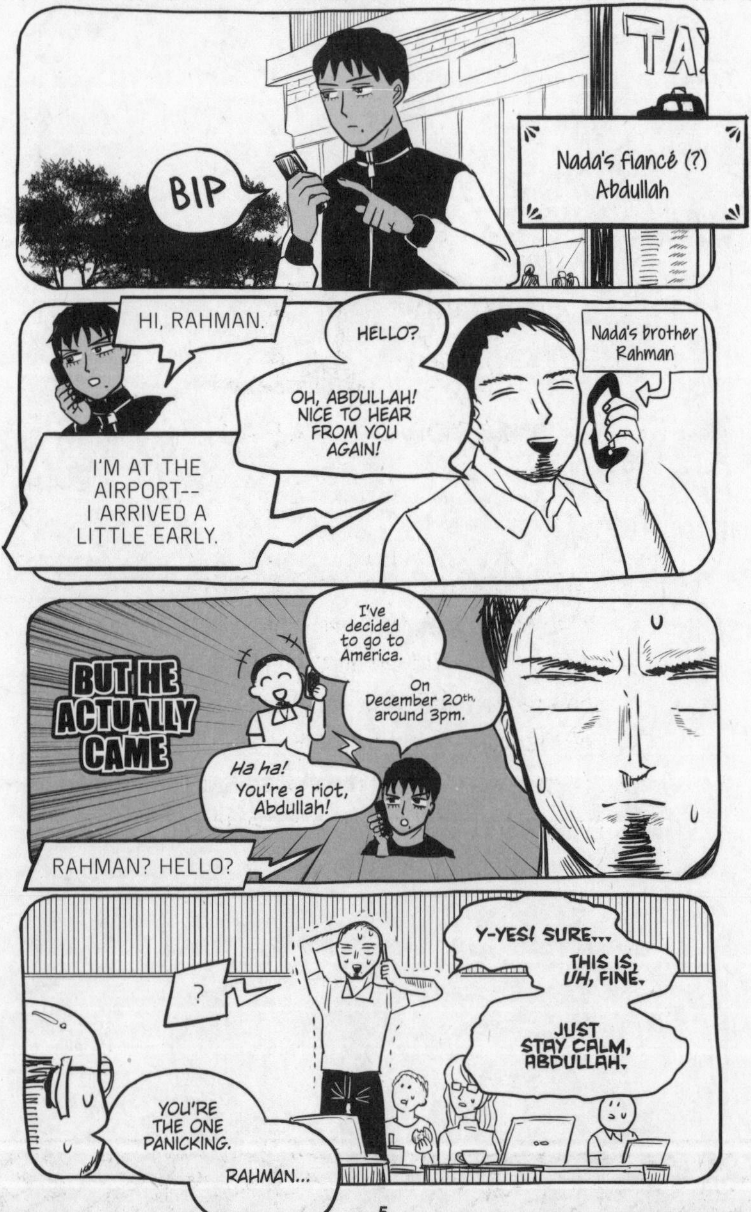
Nada's fiancé (?)
Abdullah
BIP
Nada's brother
Rahman
HELLO?
HI, RAHMAN.
OH, ABDULLAH! NICE TO HEAR FROM YOU AGAIN!
I'M AT THE AIRPORT-- I ARRIVED A LITTLE EARLY.
I've decided to go to America.
On December 20th, around 3pm.
BUT HE ACTUALLY CAME
Ha ha! You're a riot, Abdullah!
RAHMAN? HELLO?
Y-YES! SURE... THIS IS, UH, FINE.
JUST STAY CALM, ABDULLAH.
?
YOU'RE THE ONE PANICKING.
RAHMAN...

PANDEMONIUM

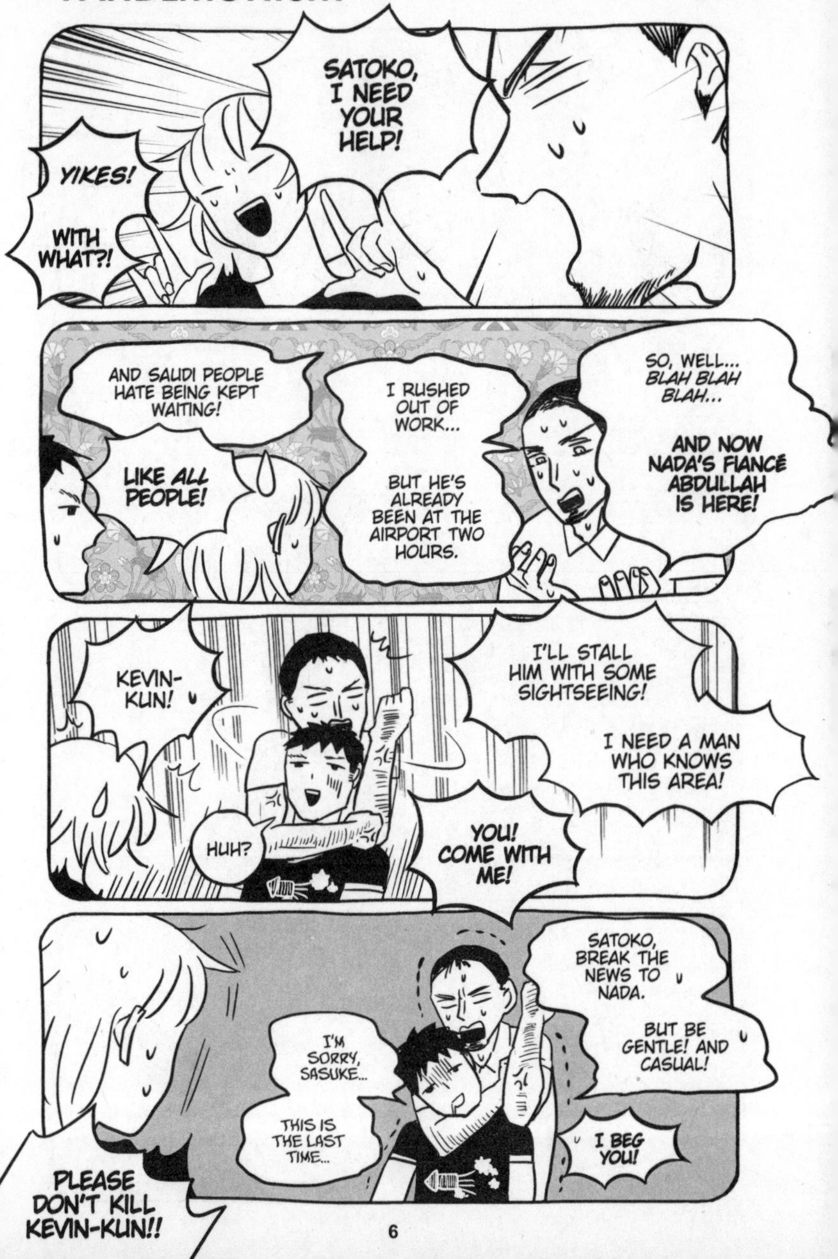
SATOKO, I NEED YOUR HELP!
YIKES!
WITH WHAT?!
SO, WELL... BLAH BLAH BLAH...
AND NOW NADA'S FIANCÉ ABDULLAH IS HERE!
I RUSHED OUT OF WORK...
BUT HE'S ALREADY BEEN AT THE AIRPORT TWO HOURS.
AND SAUDI PEOPLE HATE BEING KEPT WAITING!
LIKE ALL PEOPLE!
I'LL STALL HIM WITH SOME SIGHTSEEING!
I NEED A MAN WHO KNOWS THIS AREA!
YOU! COME WITH ME!
KEVIN-KUN!
HUH?
SATOKO, BREAK THE NEWS TO NADA.
BUT BE GENTLE! AND CASUAL!
I BEG YOU!
I'M SORRY, SASUKE...
THIS IS THE LAST TIME...
PLEASE DON'T KILL KEVIN-KUN!!

CAN'T SAY IT

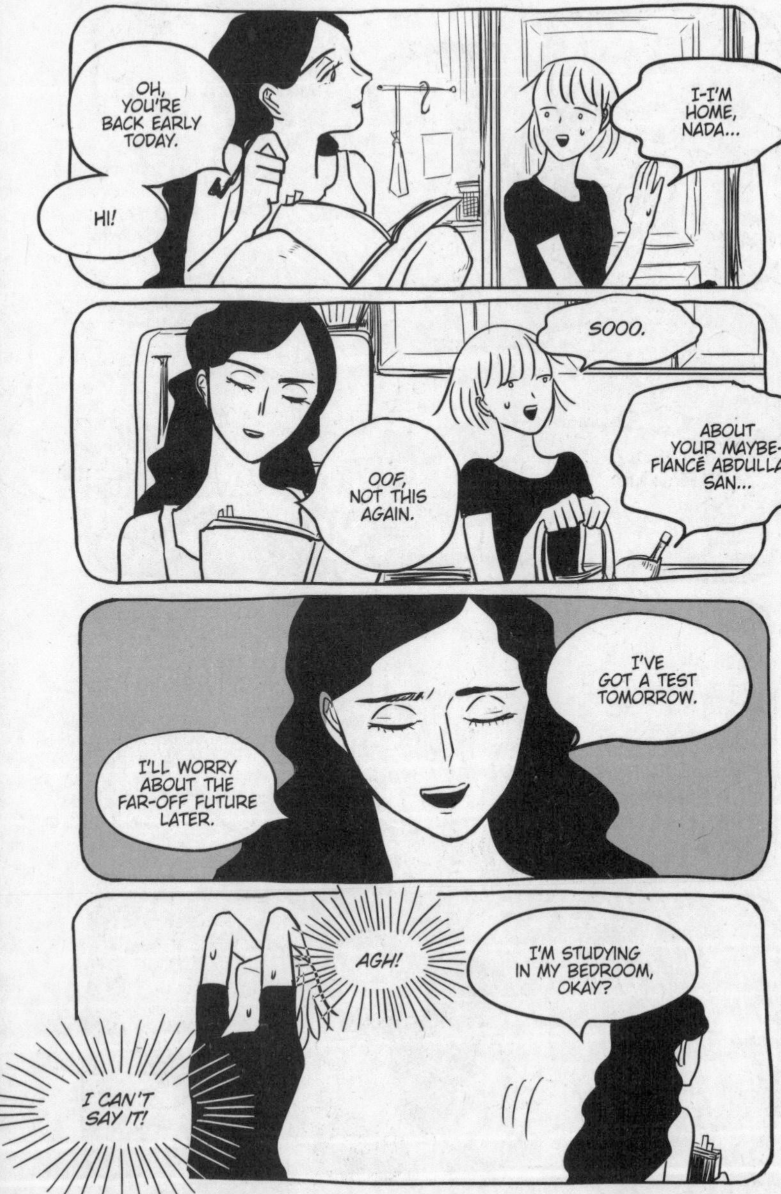
I-I'M HOME, NADA...
OH, YOU'RE BACK EARLY TODAY.
HI!
SOOO.
ABOUT YOUR MAYBE-FIANCÉ ABDULLAH-SAN...
OOF, NOT THIS AGAIN.
I'VE GOT A TEST TOMORROW.
I'LL WORRY ABOUT THE FAR-OFF FUTURE LATER.
I'M STUDYING IN MY BEDROOM, OKAY?
AGH!
I CAN'T SAY IT!

FAVOR

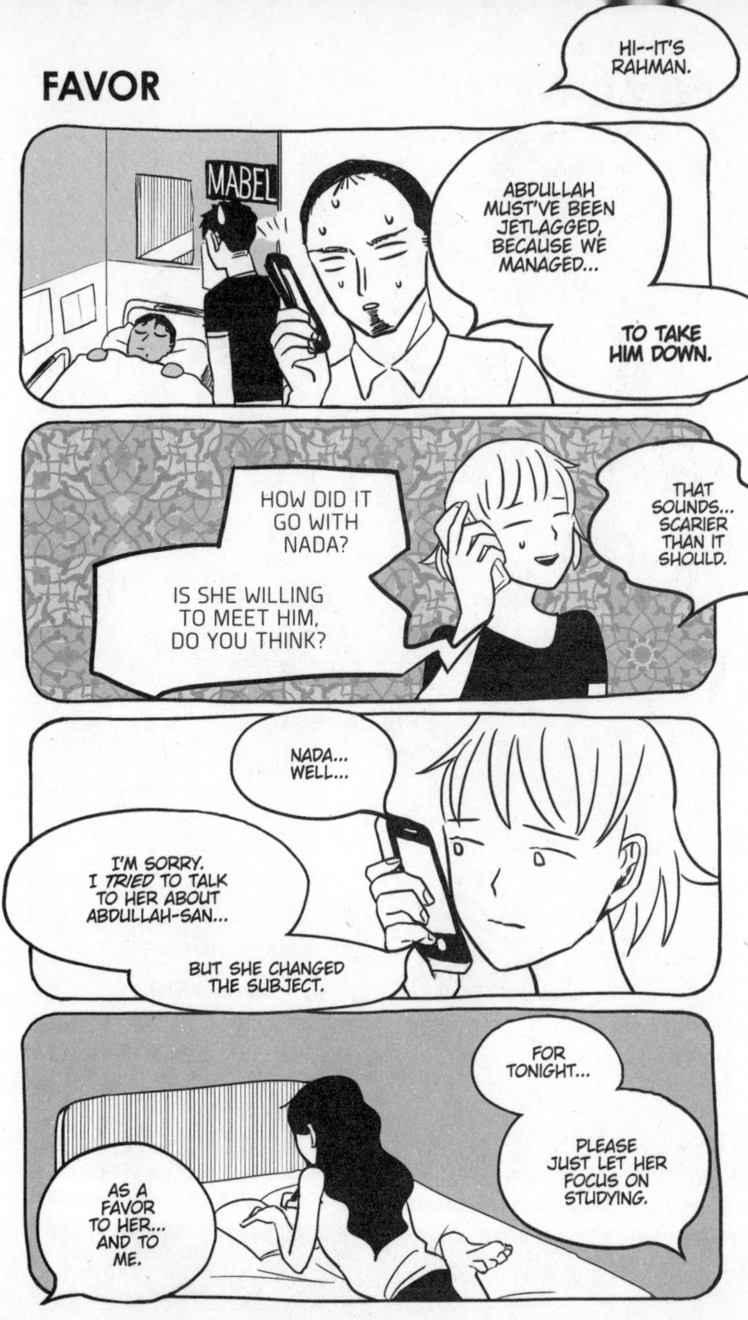
HI--IT'S RAHMAN.
MABEL
ABDULLAH MUST'VE BEEN JETLAGGED, BECAUSE WE MANAGED...
TO TAKE HIM DOWN.
THAT SOUNDS... SCARIER THAN IT SHOULD.
HOW DID IT GO WITH NADA?
IS SHE WILLING TO MEET HIM, DO YOU THINK?
NADA... WELL...
I'M SORRY. I *TRIED* TO TALK TO HER ABOUT ABDULLAH-SAN...
BUT SHE CHANGED THE SUBJECT.
FOR TONIGHT...
PLEASE JUST LET HER FOCUS ON STUDYING.
AS A FAVOR TO HER... AND TO ME.

PROACTIVE

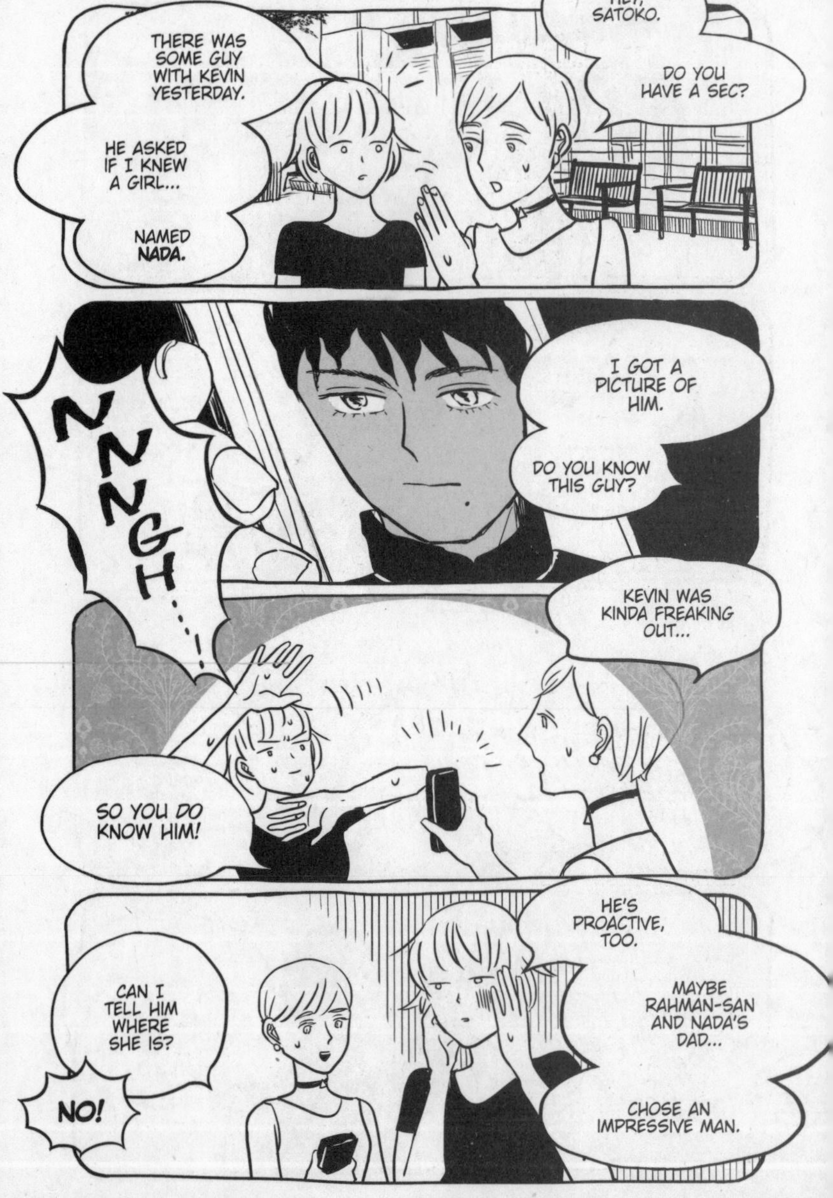
HEY, SATOKO.
DO YOU HAVE A SEC?
THERE WAS SOME GUY WITH KEVIN YESTERDAY.
HE ASKED IF I KNEW A GIRL...
NAMED NADA.
I GOT A PICTURE OF HIM.
DO YOU KNOW THIS GUY?
NNNGH...!
KEVIN WAS KINDA FREAKING OUT...
SO YOU DO KNOW HIM!
HE'S PROACTIVE, TOO.
MAYBE RAHMAN-SAN AND NADA'S DAD...
CHOSE AN IMPRESSIVE MAN.
CAN I TELL HIM WHERE SHE IS?
NO!

ENCOUNTER

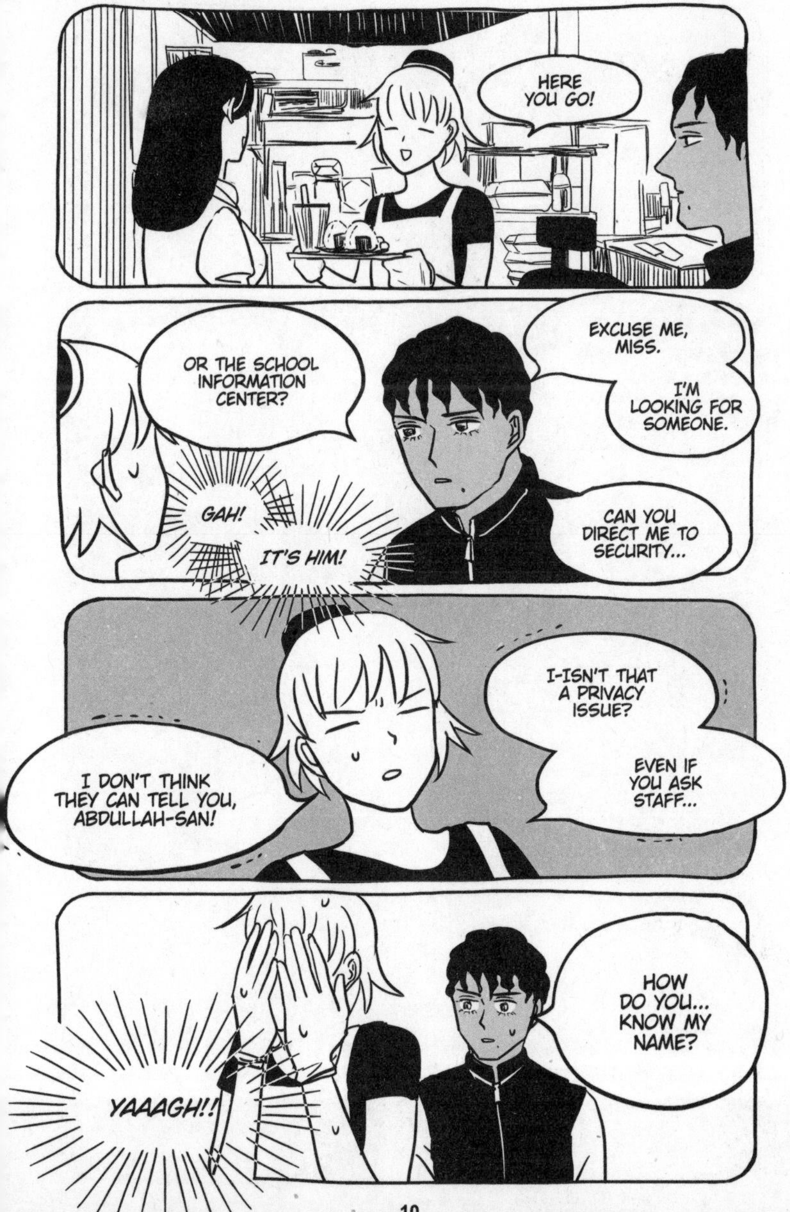
HERE YOU GO!
EXCUSE ME, MISS.
I'M LOOKING FOR SOMEONE.
CAN YOU DIRECT ME TO SECURITY...
OR THE SCHOOL INFORMATION CENTER?
GAH!
IT'S HIM!
I-ISN'T THAT A PRIVACY ISSUE?
EVEN IF YOU ASK STAFF...
I DON'T THINK THEY CAN TELL YOU, ABDULLAH-SAN!
HOW DO YOU... KNOW MY NAME?
YAAAGH!!

TRIAL

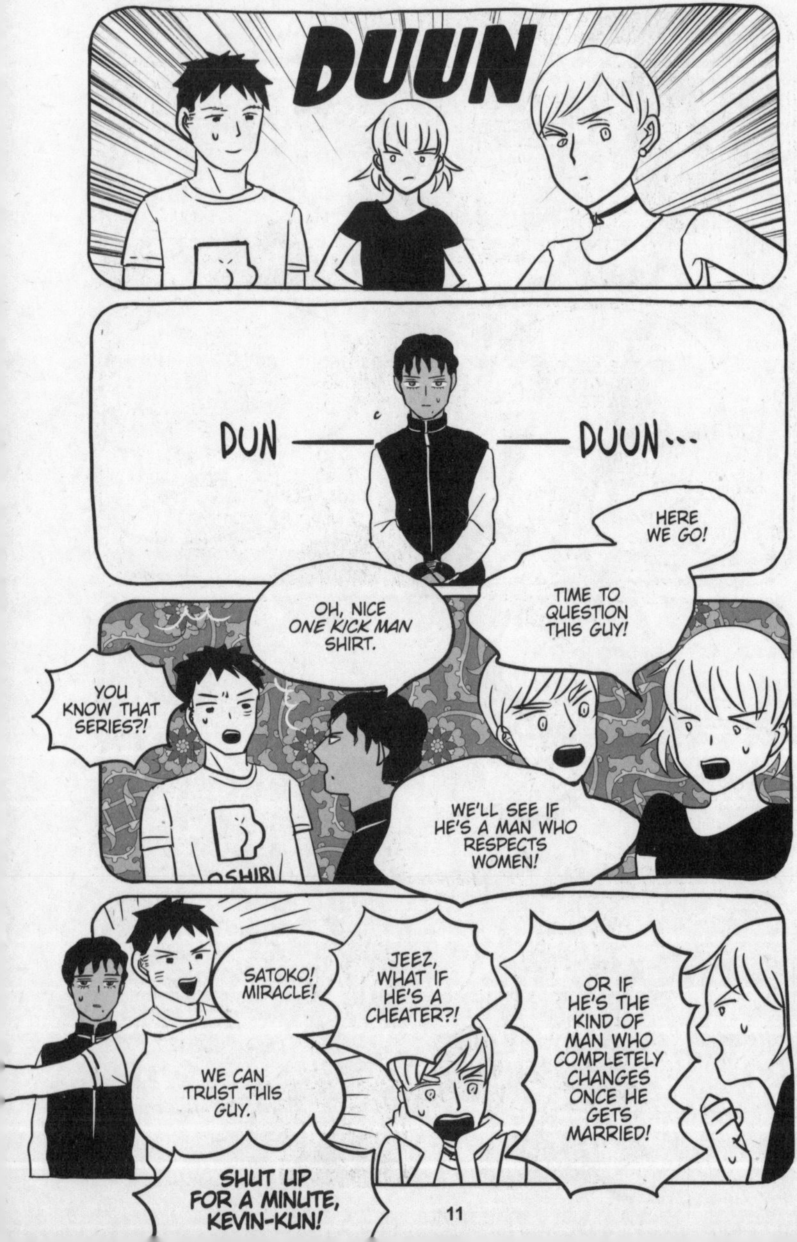
DUUN
DUN — — DUUN...
HERE WE GO!
TIME TO QUESTION THIS GUY!
OH, NICE *ONE KICK MAN* SHIRT.
YOU KNOW THAT SERIES?!
WE'LL SEE IF HE'S A MAN WHO RESPECTS WOMEN!
OR IF HE'S THE KIND OF MAN WHO COMPLETELY CHANGES ONCE HE GETS MARRIED!
JEEZ, WHAT IF HE'S A CHEATER?!
SATOKO! MIRACLE!
WE CAN TRUST THIS GUY.
SHUT UP FOR A MINUTE, KEVIN-KUN!

EXPLAIN YOURSELF

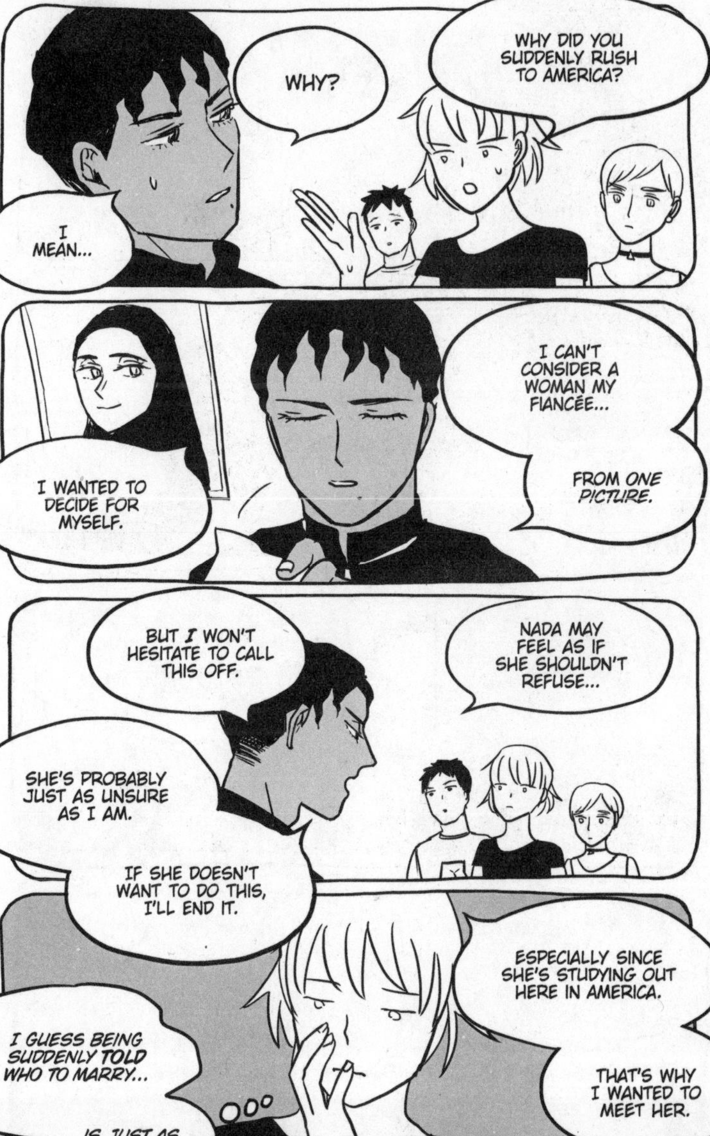
WHY DID YOU SUDDENLY RUSH TO AMERICA?
WHY?
I MEAN...
I CAN'T CONSIDER A WOMAN MY FIANCÉE...
FROM ONE PICTURE.
I WANTED TO DECIDE FOR MYSELF.
NADA MAY FEEL AS IF SHE SHOULDN'T REFUSE...
BUT I WON'T HESITATE TO CALL THIS OFF.
SHE'S PROBABLY JUST AS UNSURE AS I AM.
IF SHE DOESN'T WANT TO DO THIS, I'LL END IT.
ESPECIALLY SINCE SHE'S STUDYING OUT HERE IN AMERICA.
THAT'S WHY I WANTED TO MEET HER.
I GUESS BEING SUDDENLY TOLD WHO TO MARRY...
IS JUST AS TOUGH FOR MEN.

FEELINGS

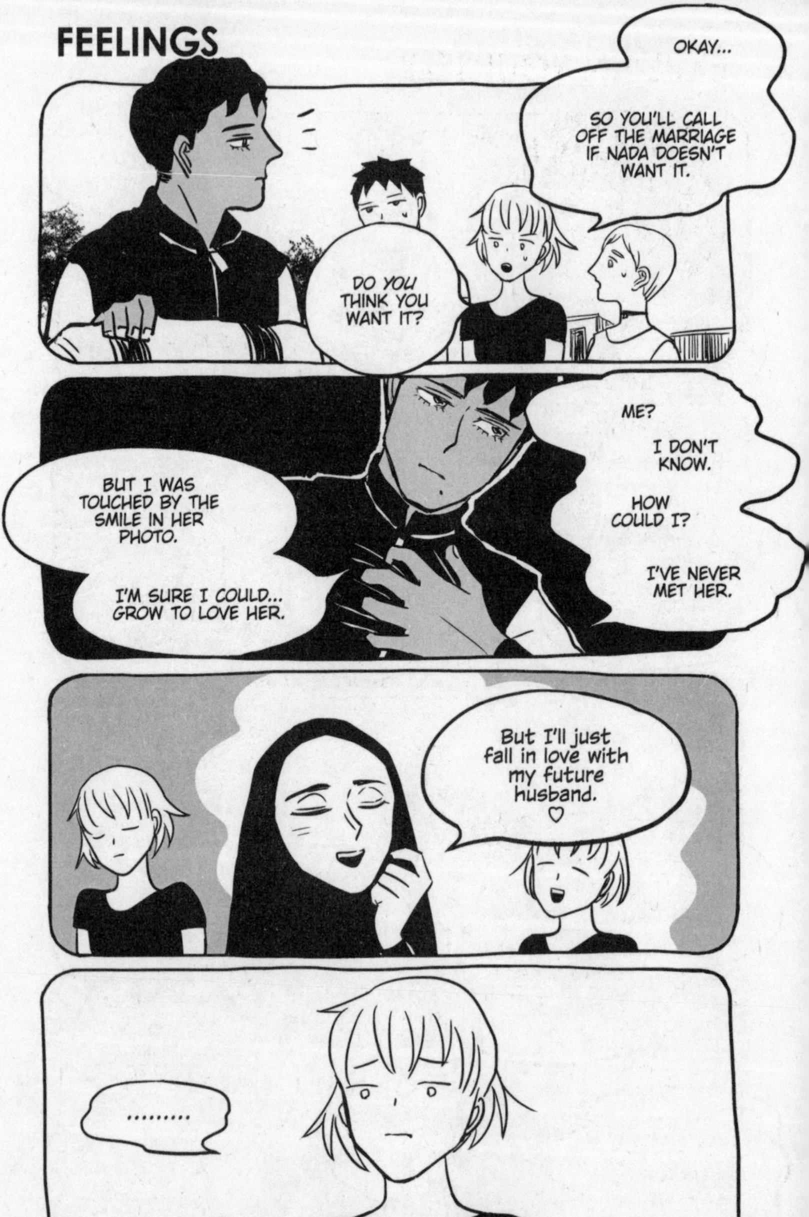

OKAY...
SO YOU'LL CALL OFF THE MARRIAGE IF NADA DOESN'T WANT IT.
DO YOU THINK YOU WANT IT?
ME?
I DON'T KNOW.
HOW COULD I?
I'VE NEVER MET HER.
BUT I WAS TOUCHED BY THE SMILE IN HER PHOTO.
I'M SURE I COULD... GROW TO LOVE HER.
But I'll just fall in love with my future husband. ♡
....

GOOD FRIENDS

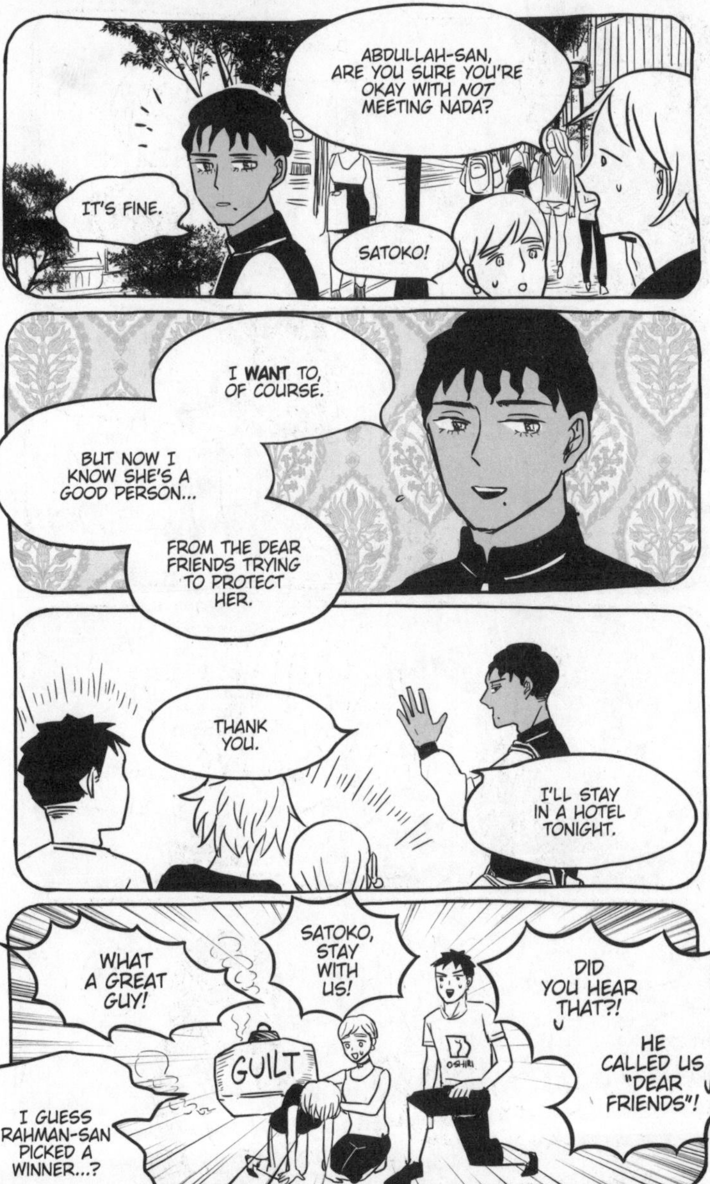
ABDULLAH-SAN, ARE YOU SURE YOU'RE OKAY WITH *NOT* MEETING NADA?
SATOKO!
IT'S FINE.
I **WANT** TO, OF COURSE.
BUT NOW I KNOW SHE'S A GOOD PERSON...
FROM THE DEAR FRIENDS TRYING TO PROTECT HER.
THANK YOU.
I'LL STAY IN A HOTEL TONIGHT.
DID YOU HEAR THAT?!
HE CALLED US "DEAR FRIENDS"!
OSHIRI
SATOKO, STAY WITH US!
WHAT A GREAT GUY!
GUILT
I GUESS RAHMAN-SAN PICKED A WINNER...?

HOME

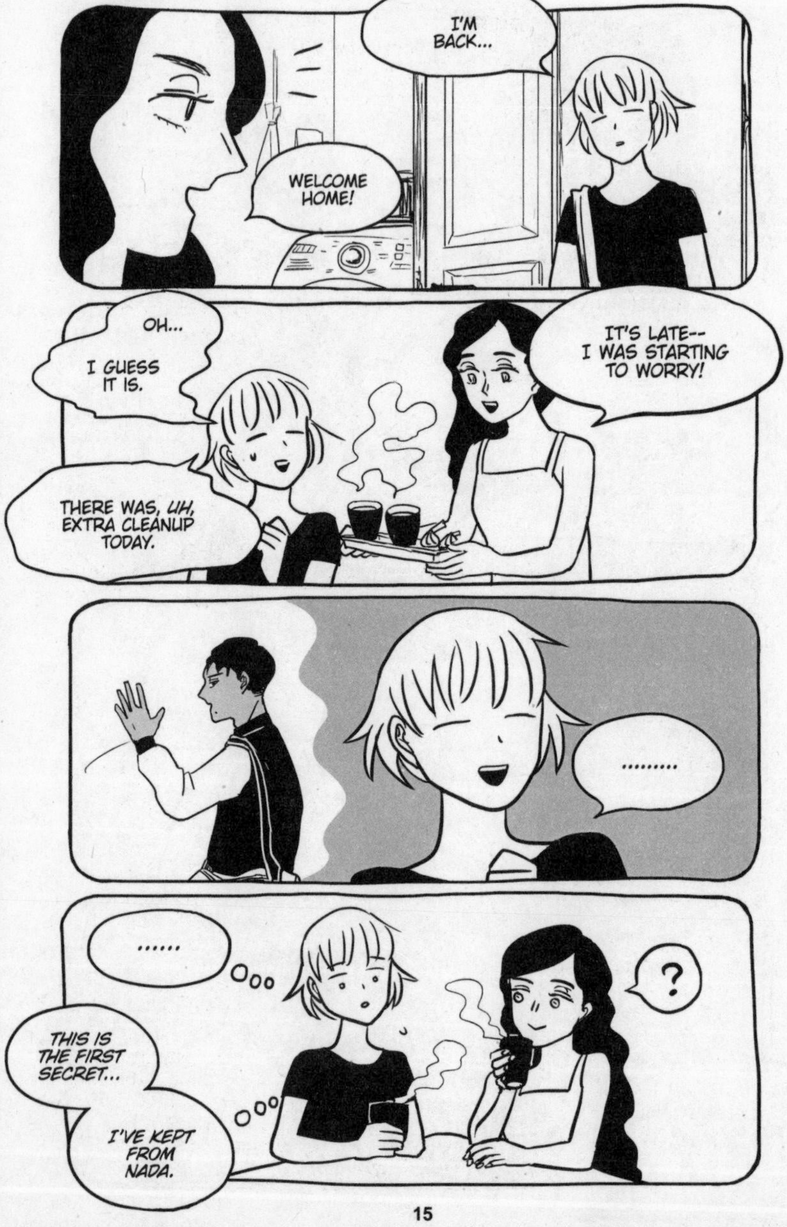
I'M BACK...
WELCOME HOME!
IT'S LATE-- I WAS STARTING TO WORRY!
OH... I GUESS IT IS.
THERE WAS, UH, EXTRA CLEANUP TODAY.
....
?
......
THIS IS THE FIRST SECRET...
I'VE KEPT FROM NADA.

ALL KINDS OF AGALS

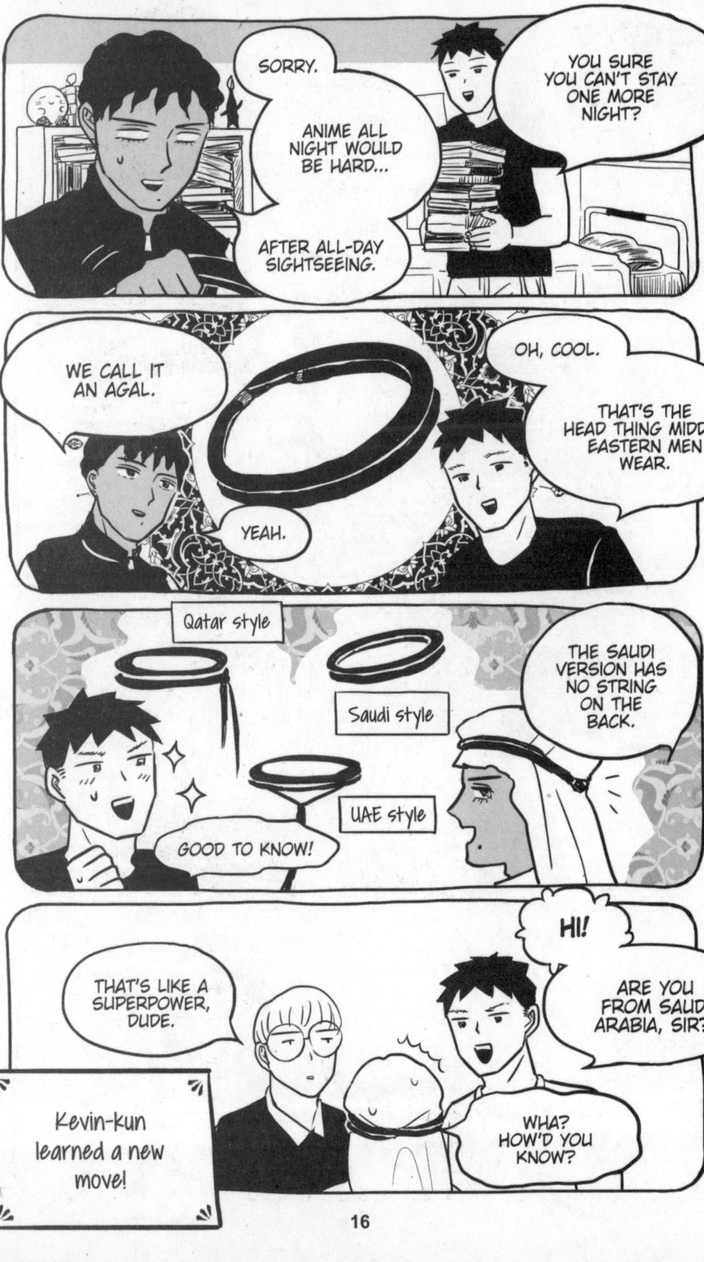
YOU SURE YOU CAN'T STAY ONE MORE NIGHT?
SORRY.
ANIME ALL NIGHT WOULD BE HARD...
AFTER ALL-DAY SIGHTSEEING.
OH, COOL.
THAT'S THE HEAD THING MIDDLE EASTERN MEN WEAR.
WE CALL IT AN AGAL.
YEAH.
THE SAUDI VERSION HAS NO STRING ON THE BACK.
Qatar style
Saudi style
UAE style
GOOD TO KNOW!
HI!
ARE YOU FROM SAUDI ARABIA, SIR?!
THAT'S LIKE A SUPERPOWER, DUDE.
WHA? HOW'D YOU KNOW?
Kevin-kun learned a new move!

ALL KINDS OF SHEMAGH

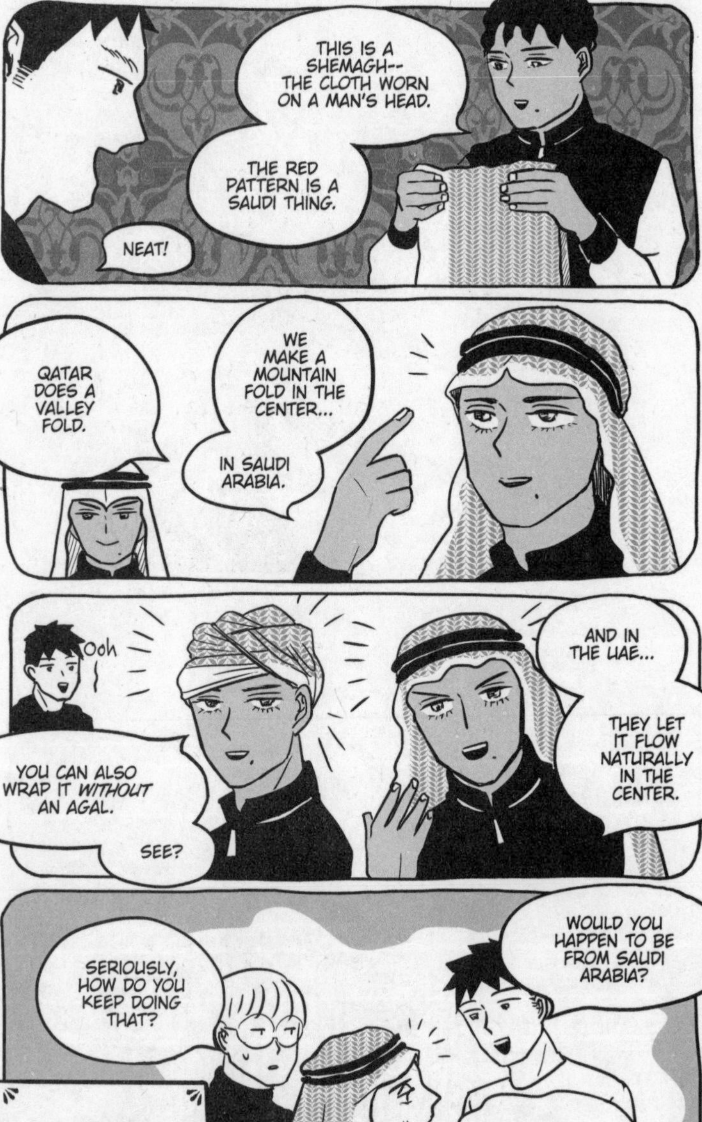
THIS IS A SHEMAGH-- THE CLOTH WORN ON A MAN'S HEAD.
THE RED PATTERN IS A SAUDI THING.
NEAT!
WE MAKE A MOUNTAIN FOLD IN THE CENTER...
IN SAUDI ARABIA.
QATAR DOES A VALLEY FOLD.
AND IN THE UAE...
THEY LET IT FLOW NATURALLY IN THE CENTER.
Ooh
YOU CAN ALSO WRAP IT *WITHOUT* AN AGAL.
SEE?
WOULD YOU HAPPEN TO BE FROM SAUDI ARABIA?
SERIOUSLY, HOW DO YOU KEEP DOING THAT?
HAVE WE... MET, KID?
XP UP

CONFLICTED

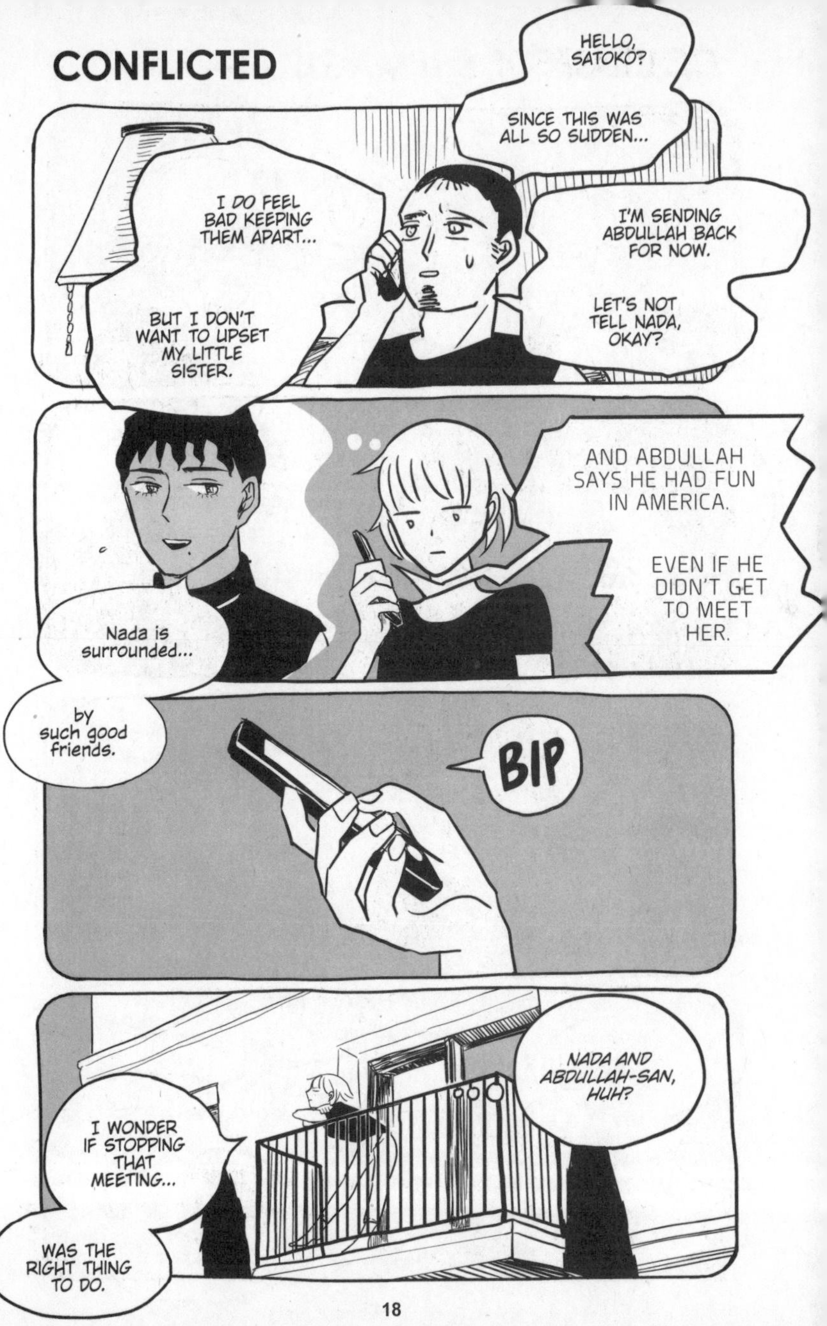
HELLO, SATOKO?
SINCE THIS WAS ALL SO SUDDEN...
I'M SENDING ABDULLAH BACK FOR NOW.
LET'S NOT TELL NADA, OKAY?
I DO FEEL BAD KEEPING THEM APART...
BUT I DON'T WANT TO UPSET MY LITTLE SISTER.
AND ABDULLAH SAYS HE HAD FUN IN AMERICA.
EVEN IF HE DIDN'T GET TO MEET HER.
Nada is surrounded...
by such good friends.
BIP
NADA AND ABDULLAH-SAN, HUH?
I WONDER IF STOPPING THAT MEETING...
WAS THE RIGHT THING TO DO.

COURAGE

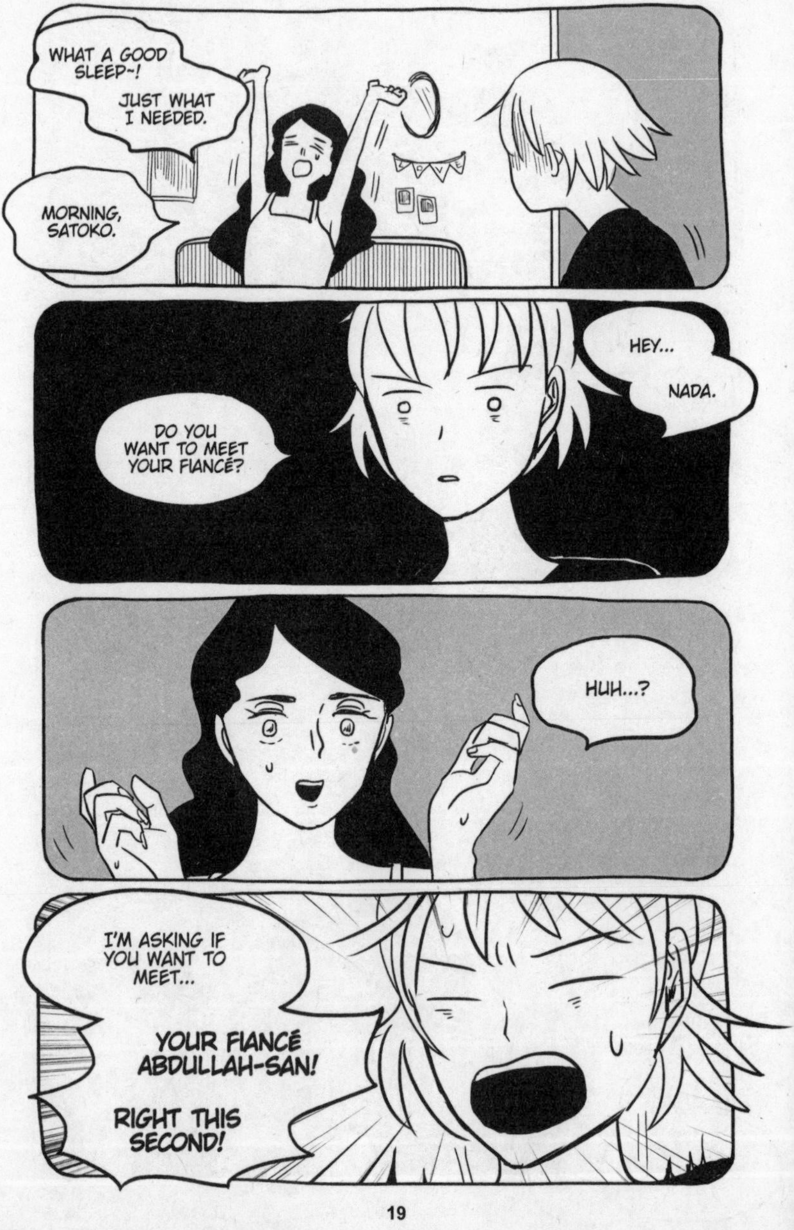
WHAT A GOOD SLEEP~! JUST WHAT I NEEDED.
MORNING, SATOKO.
HEY... NADA.
DO YOU WANT TO MEET YOUR FIANCÉ?
HUH...?
I'M ASKING IF YOU WANT TO MEET...
YOUR FIANCÉ ABDULLAH-SAN!
RIGHT THIS SECOND!

THE TRUTH

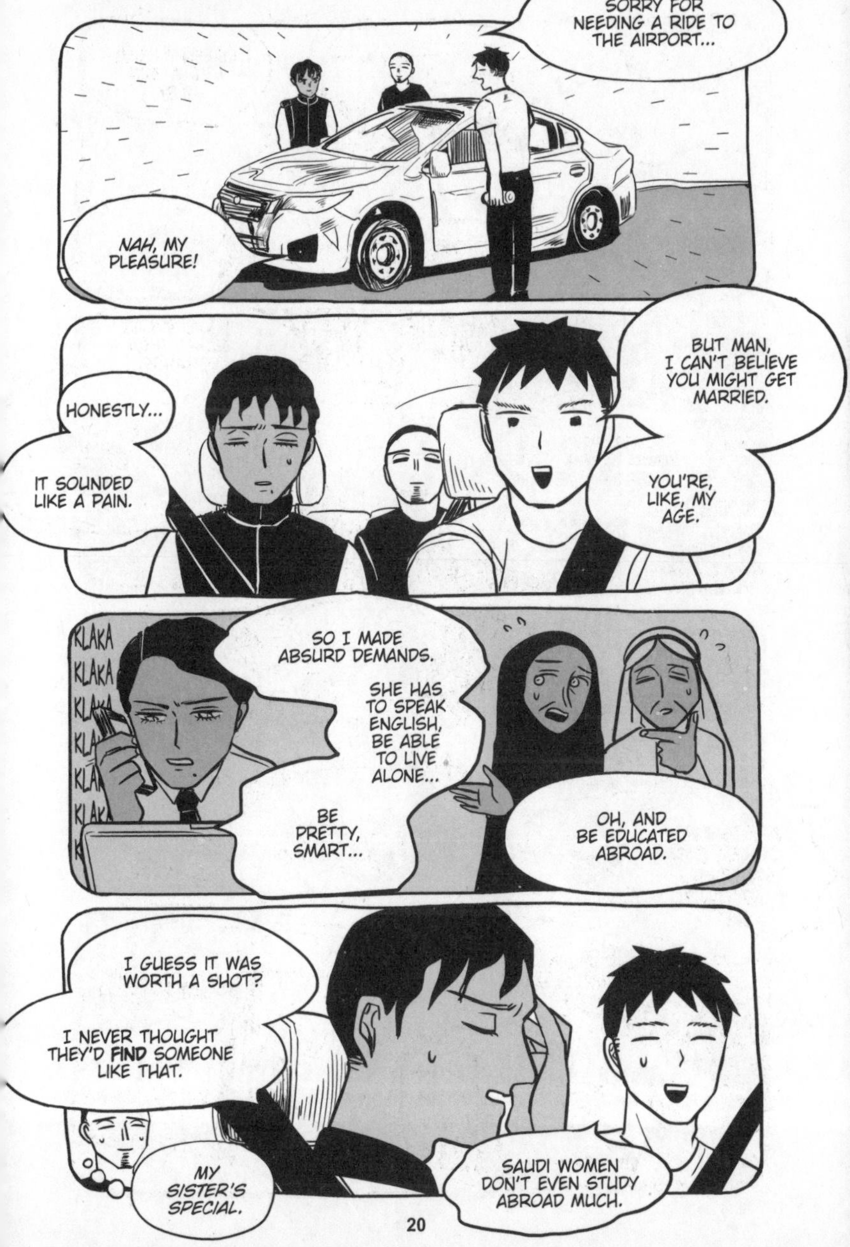

SORRY FOR NEEDING A RIDE TO THE AIRPORT...
NAH, MY PLEASURE!
BUT MAN, I CAN'T BELIEVE YOU MIGHT GET MARRIED.
YOU'RE, LIKE, MY AGE.
HONESTLY...
IT SOUNDED LIKE A PAIN.
SO I MADE ABSURD DEMANDS.
SHE HAS TO SPEAK ENGLISH, BE ABLE TO LIVE ALONE...
BE PRETTY, SMART...
OH, AND BE EDUCATED ABROAD.
KLAKA
KLAKA
I GUESS IT WAS WORTH A SHOT?
I NEVER THOUGHT THEY'D **FIND** SOMEONE LIKE THAT.
SAUDI WOMEN DON'T EVEN STUDY ABROAD MUCH.
MY SISTER'S SPECIAL.

HOW NICE

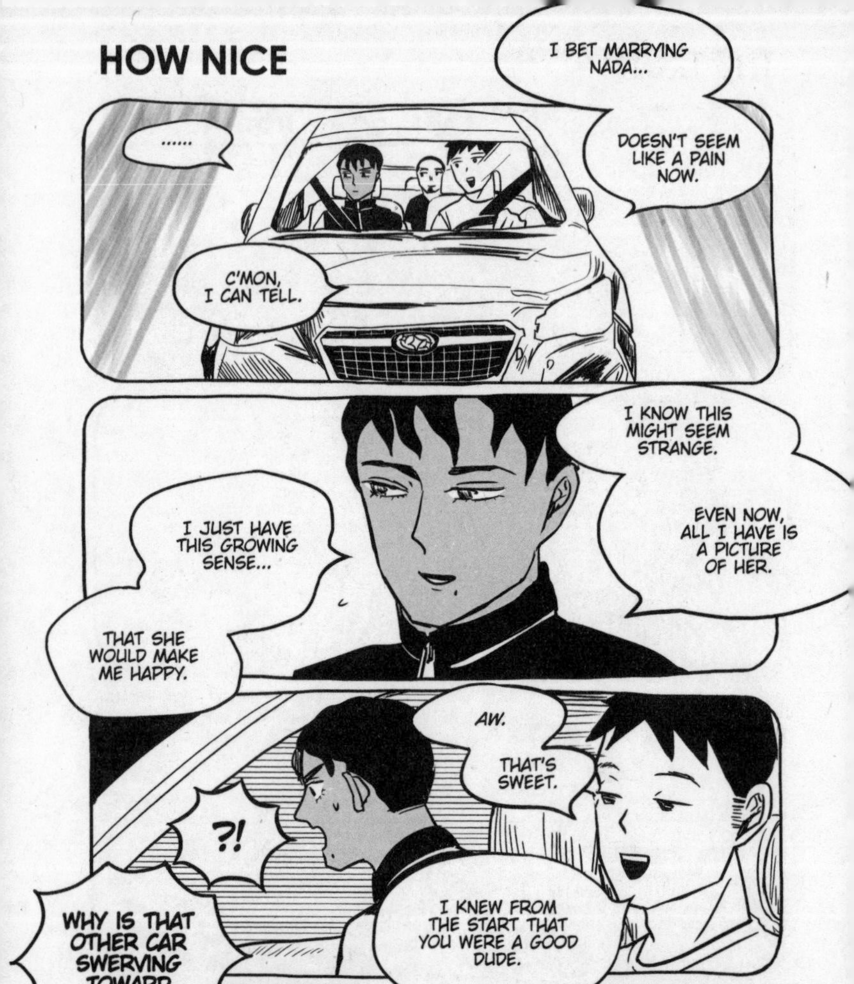
I BET MARRYING NADA...
DOESN'T SEEM LIKE A PAIN NOW.
......
C'MON, I CAN TELL.
I KNOW THIS MIGHT SEEM STRANGE.
EVEN NOW, ALL I HAVE IS A PICTURE OF HER.
I JUST HAVE THIS GROWING SENSE...
THAT SHE WOULD MAKE ME HAPPY.
AW.
THAT'S SWEET.
I KNEW FROM THE START THAT YOU WERE A GOOD DUDE.
?!
WHY IS THAT OTHER CAR SWERVING TOWARD US?!
?!

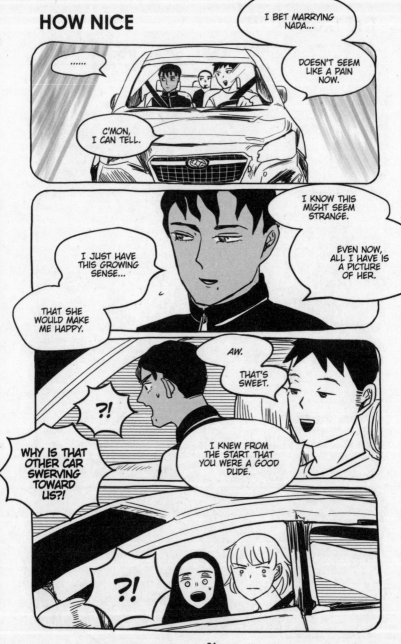

EYE CONTACT

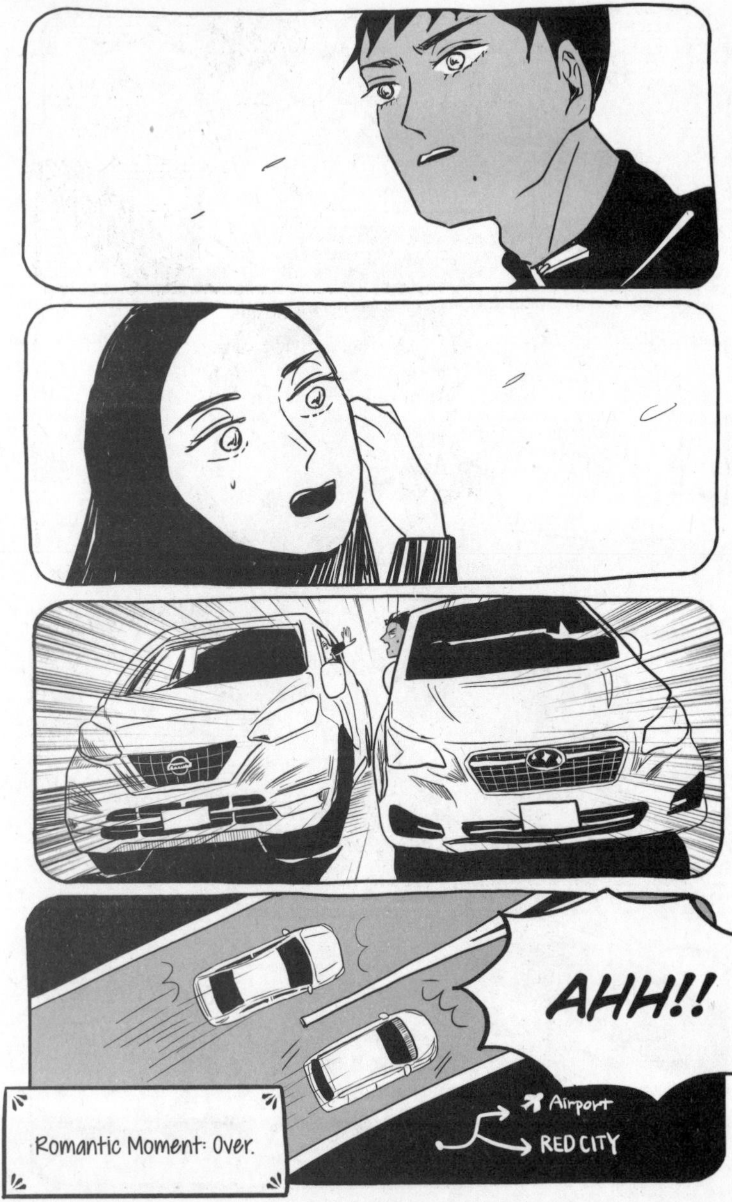
AHH!!
Airport
RED CITY
Romantic Moment: Over.

ENOUGH

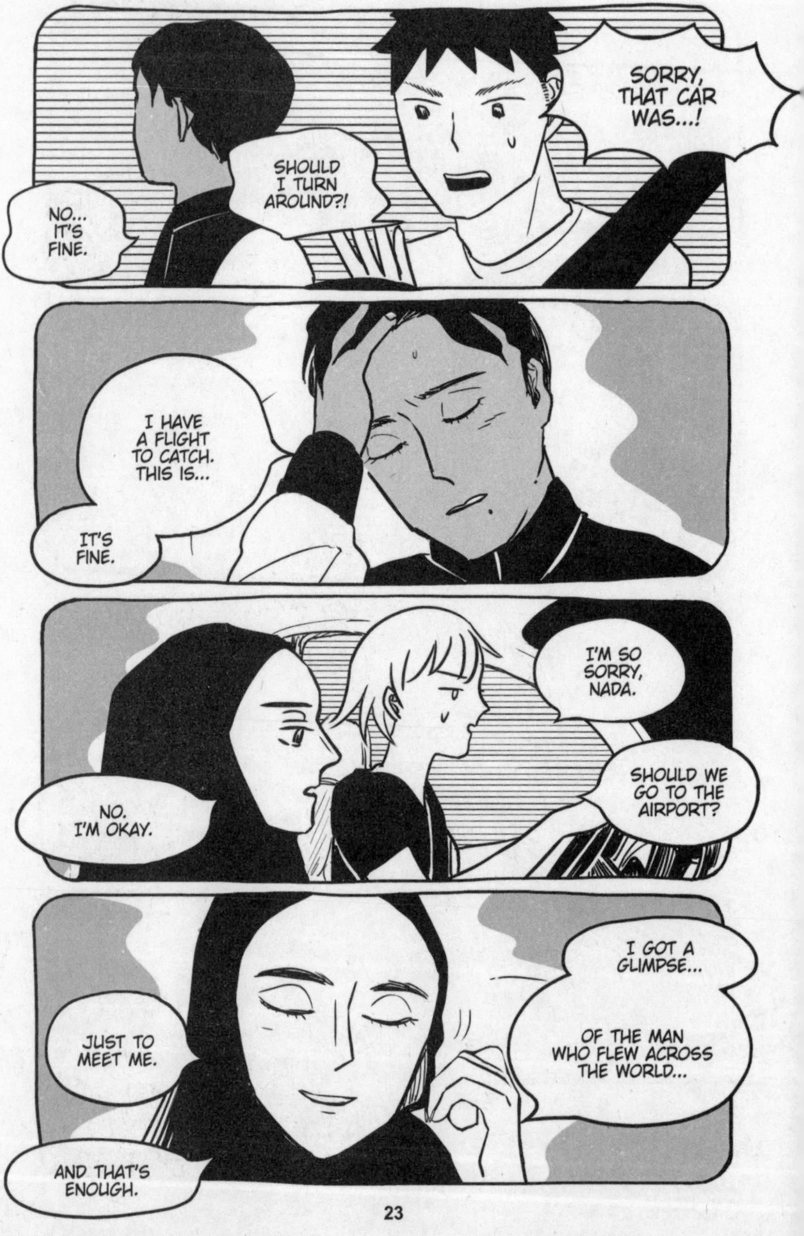
SORRY, THAT CAR WAS...!
SHOULD I TURN AROUND?!
NO... IT'S FINE.
I HAVE A FLIGHT TO CATCH. THIS IS...
IT'S FINE.
I'M SO SORRY, NADA.
SHOULD WE GO TO THE AIRPORT?
NO. I'M OKAY.
I GOT A GLIMPSE...
OF THE MAN WHO FLEW ACROSS THE WORLD...
JUST TO MEET ME.
AND THAT'S ENOUGH.

UNTIL NEXT TIME

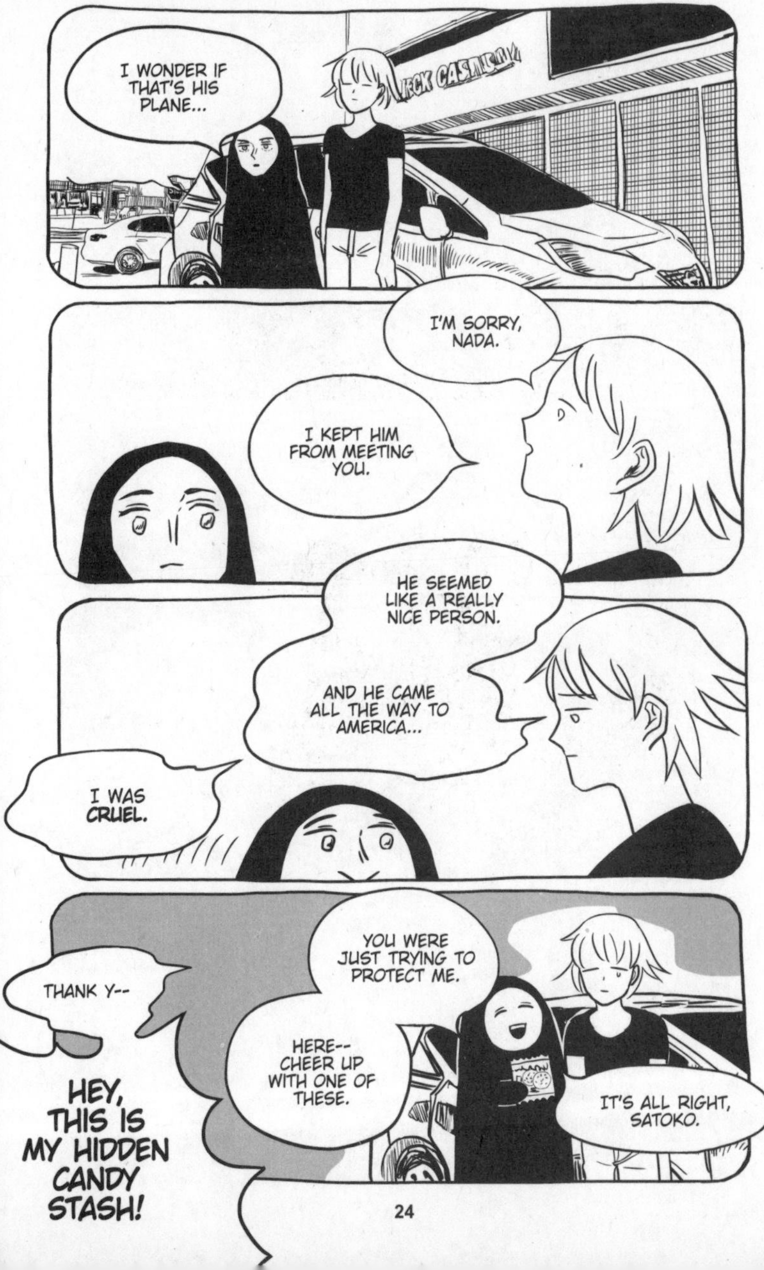
I WONDER IF THAT'S HIS PLANE...
I'M SORRY, NADA.
I KEPT HIM FROM MEETING YOU.
HE SEEMED LIKE A REALLY NICE PERSON.
AND HE CAME ALL THE WAY TO AMERICA...
I WAS CRUEL.
IT'S ALL RIGHT, SATOKO.
YOU WERE JUST TRYING TO PROTECT ME.
THANK Y--
HERE-- CHEER UP WITH ONE OF THESE.
HEY, THIS IS MY HIDDEN CANDY STASH!

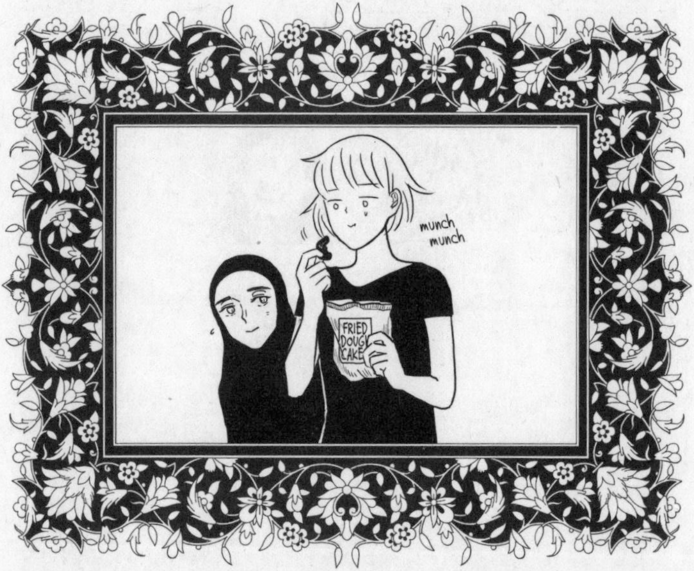
munch munch
FRIED DOUGH CAKE

SATOKO AND NADA

Presented by Yupechika

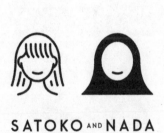

SATOKO AND NADA

Presented by Yupechika

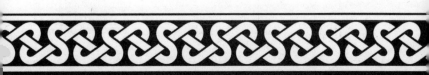

MAKE YOUR LIST

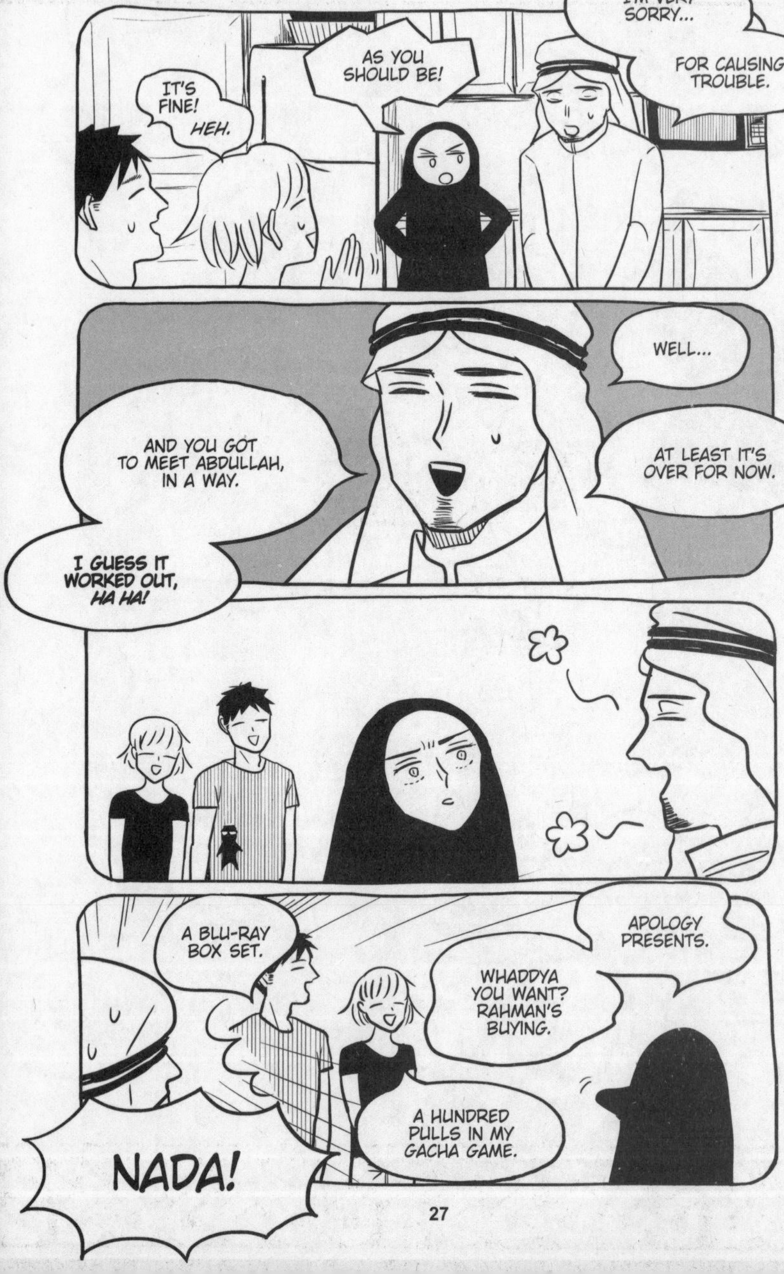
I'M VERY SORRY...
FOR CAUSING TROUBLE.
AS YOU SHOULD BE!
IT'S FINE! *HEH.*
WELL...
AT LEAST IT'S OVER FOR NOW.
AND YOU GOT TO MEET ABDULLAH, IN A WAY.
I GUESS IT WORKED OUT, *HA HA!*
APOLOGY PRESENTS.
WHADDYA YOU WANT? RAHMAN'S BUYING.
A BLU-RAY BOX SET.
A HUNDRED PULLS IN MY GACHA GAME.
NADA!

TERRIBLE

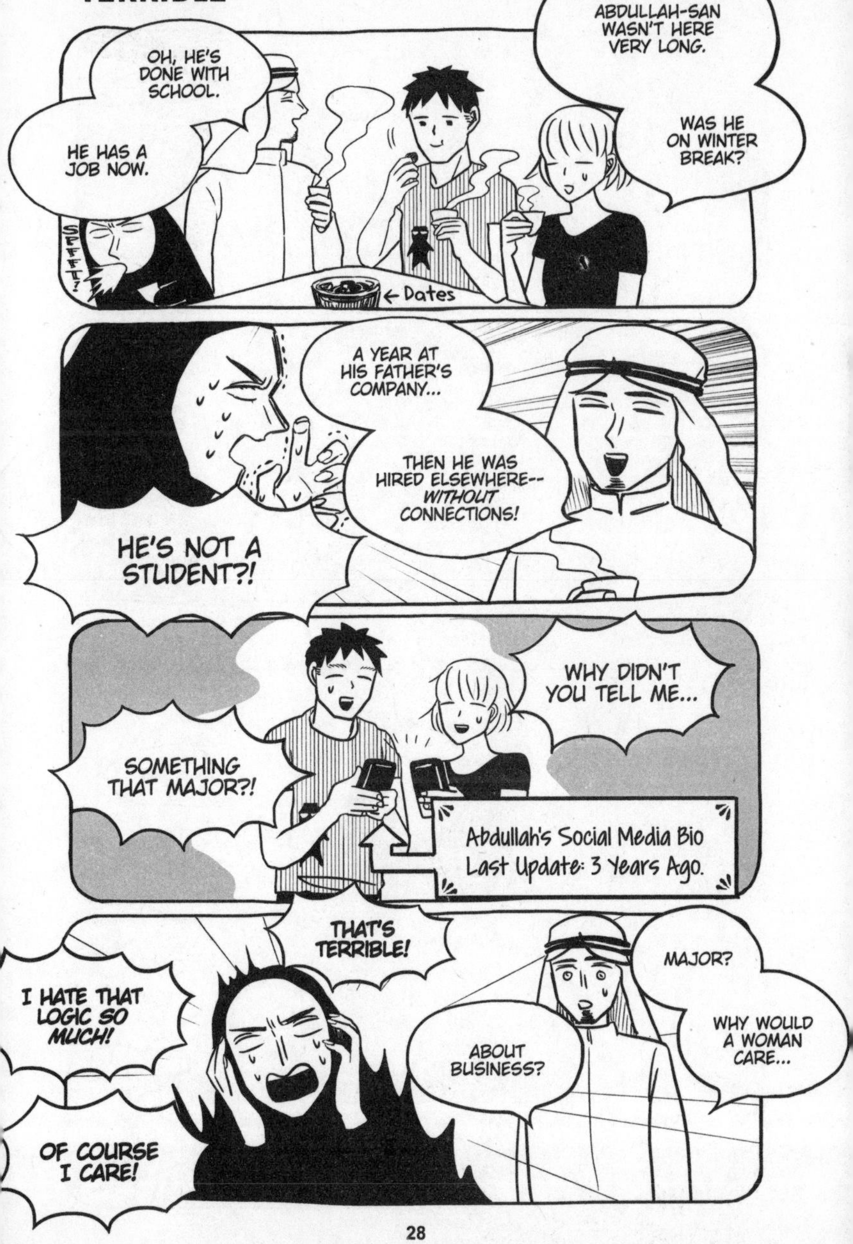

ABDULLAH-SAN WASN'T HERE VERY LONG.
WAS HE ON WINTER BREAK?
OH, HE'S DONE WITH SCHOOL.
HE HAS A JOB NOW.
SFFFT!
← Dates
A YEAR AT HIS FATHER'S COMPANY...
THEN HE WAS HIRED ELSEWHERE-- *WITHOUT* CONNECTIONS!
HE'S NOT A STUDENT?!
WHY DIDN'T YOU TELL ME...
SOMETHING THAT MAJOR?!
Abdullah's Social Media Bio
Last Update: 3 Years Ago.
MAJOR?
WHY WOULD A WOMAN CARE...
ABOUT BUSINESS?
THAT'S TERRIBLE!
I HATE THAT LOGIC SO *MUCH!*
OF COURSE I CARE!

DEAL MAKING

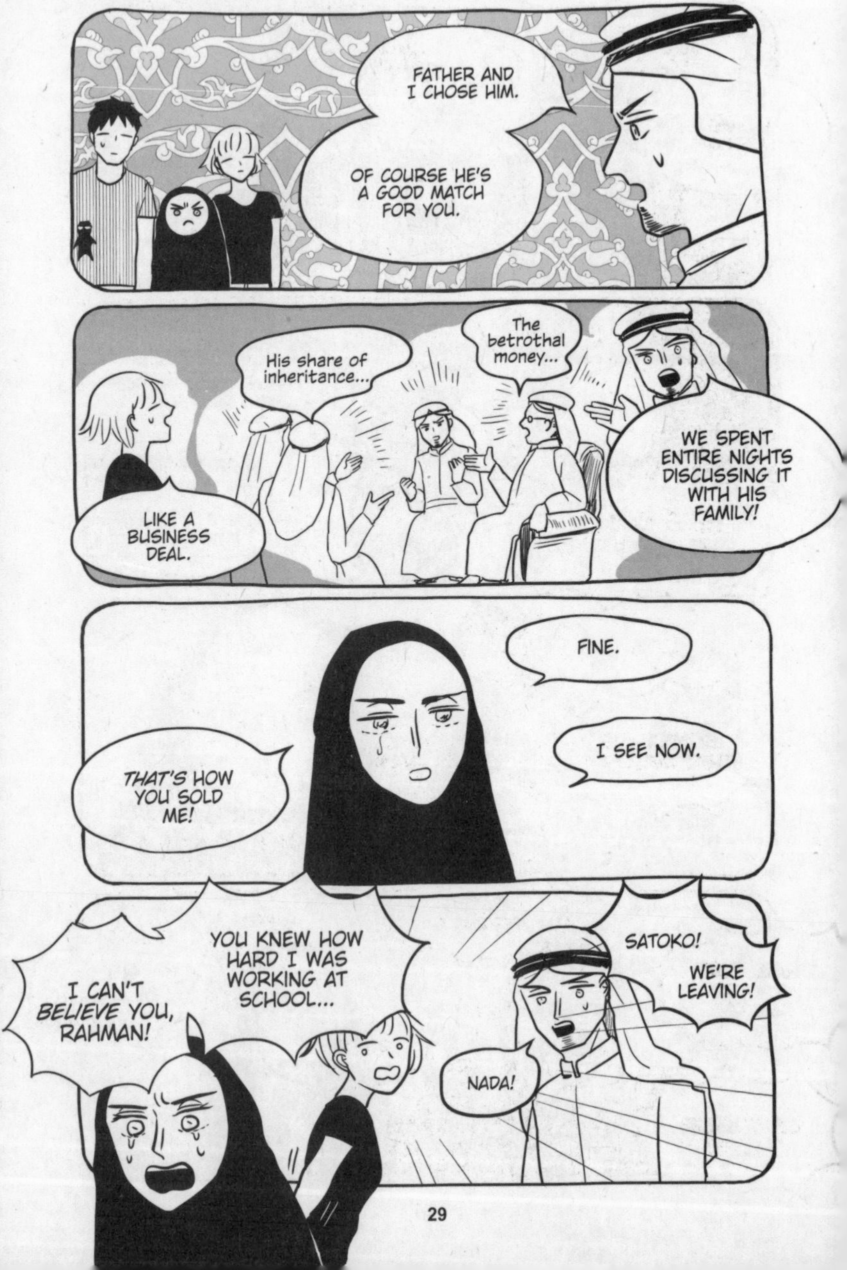
FATHER AND I CHOSE HIM.
OF COURSE HE'S A GOOD MATCH FOR YOU.
WE SPENT ENTIRE NIGHTS DISCUSSING IT WITH HIS FAMILY!
The betrothal money...
His share of inheritance...
LIKE A BUSINESS DEAL.
FINE.
I SEE NOW.
THAT'S HOW YOU SOLD ME!
SATOKO!
WE'RE LEAVING!
NADA!
YOU KNEW HOW HARD I WAS WORKING AT SCHOOL...
I CAN'T BELIEVE YOU, RAHMAN!

CHEER-UP GIFT

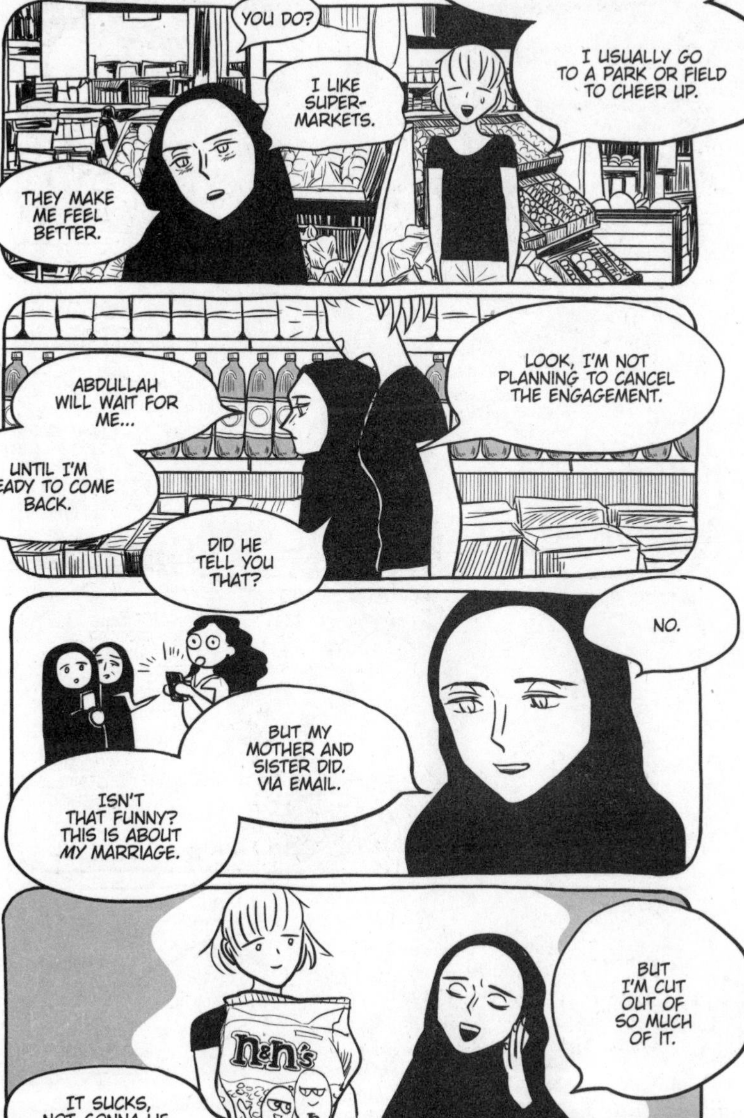

Y'KNOW, WHEN I'M IN A FIGHT WITH SOMEONE...
I USUALLY GO TO A PARK OR FIELD TO CHEER UP.
YOU DO?
I LIKE SUPER-MARKETS.
THEY MAKE ME FEEL BETTER.
LOOK, I'M NOT PLANNING TO CANCEL THE ENGAGEMENT.
ABDULLAH WILL WAIT FOR ME...
UNTIL I'M READY TO COME BACK.
DID HE TELL YOU THAT?
NO.
BUT MY MOTHER AND SISTER DID. VIA EMAIL.
ISN'T THAT FUNNY? THIS IS ABOUT MY MARRIAGE.
BUT I'M CUT OUT OF SO MUCH OF IT.
n&n's
IT SUCKS, NOT GONNA LIE.

VIDEO LECTURES

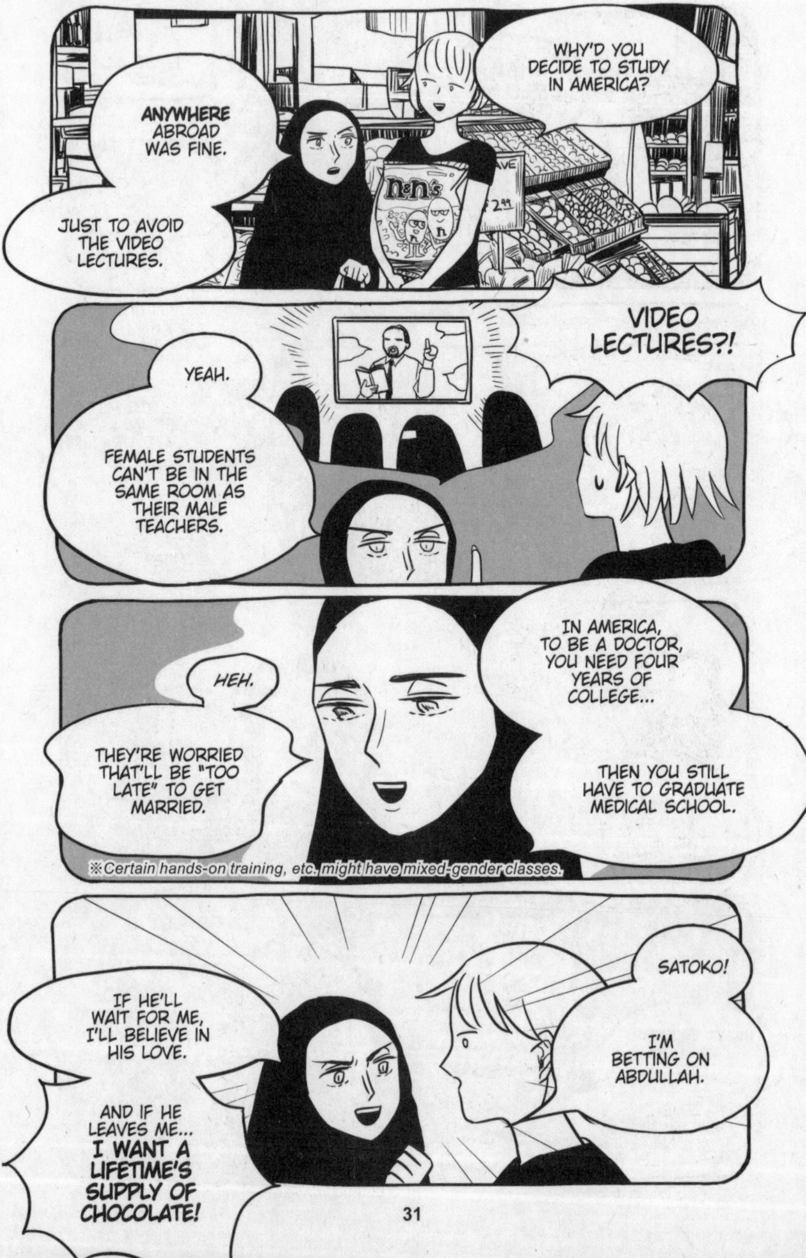
WHY'D YOU DECIDE TO STUDY IN AMERICA?
ANYWHERE ABROAD WAS FINE.
JUST TO AVOID THE VIDEO LECTURES.
VIDEO LECTURES?!
YEAH.
FEMALE STUDENTS CAN'T BE IN THE SAME ROOM AS THEIR MALE TEACHERS.
IN AMERICA, TO BE A DOCTOR, YOU NEED FOUR YEARS OF COLLEGE...
THEN YOU STILL HAVE TO GRADUATE MEDICAL SCHOOL.
HEH.
THEY'RE WORRIED THAT'LL BE "TOO LATE" TO GET MARRIED.
※Certain hands-on training, etc. might have mixed-gender classes.
SATOKO!
I'M BETTING ON ABDULLAH.
IF HE'LL WAIT FOR ME, I'LL BELIEVE IN HIS LOVE.
AND IF HE LEAVES ME... **I WANT A LIFETIME'S SUPPLY OF CHOCOLATE!**

ON HER SIDE

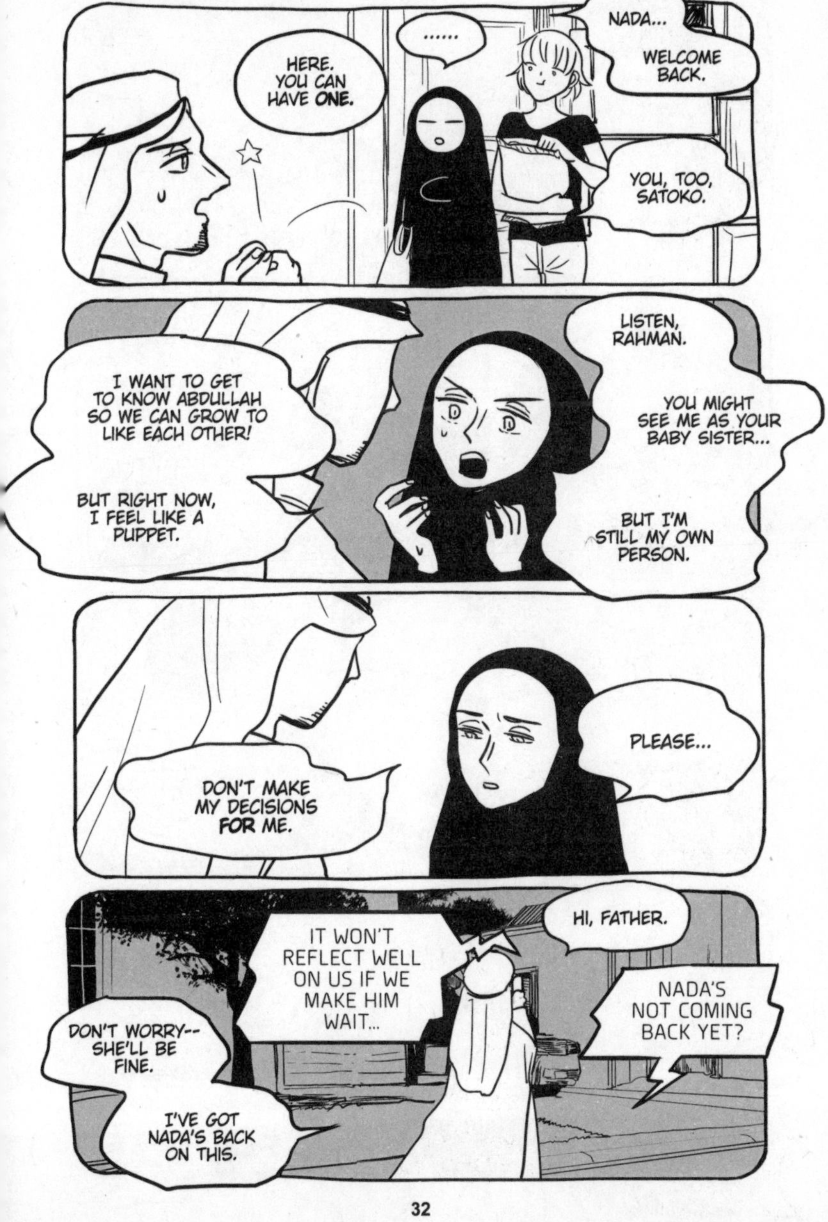
NADA...
WELCOME BACK.
YOU, TOO, SATOKO.
......
HERE. YOU CAN HAVE ONE.
LISTEN, RAHMAN.
YOU MIGHT SEE ME AS YOUR BABY SISTER...
BUT I'M STILL MY OWN PERSON.
I WANT TO GET TO KNOW ABDULLAH SO WE CAN GROW TO LIKE EACH OTHER!
BUT RIGHT NOW, I FEEL LIKE A PUPPET.
PLEASE...
DON'T MAKE MY DECISIONS FOR ME.
HI, FATHER.
NADA'S NOT COMING BACK YET?
IT WON'T REFLECT WELL ON US IF WE MAKE HIM WAIT...
DON'T WORRY-- SHE'LL BE FINE.
I'VE GOT NADA'S BACK ON THIS.

CONTACT INFO

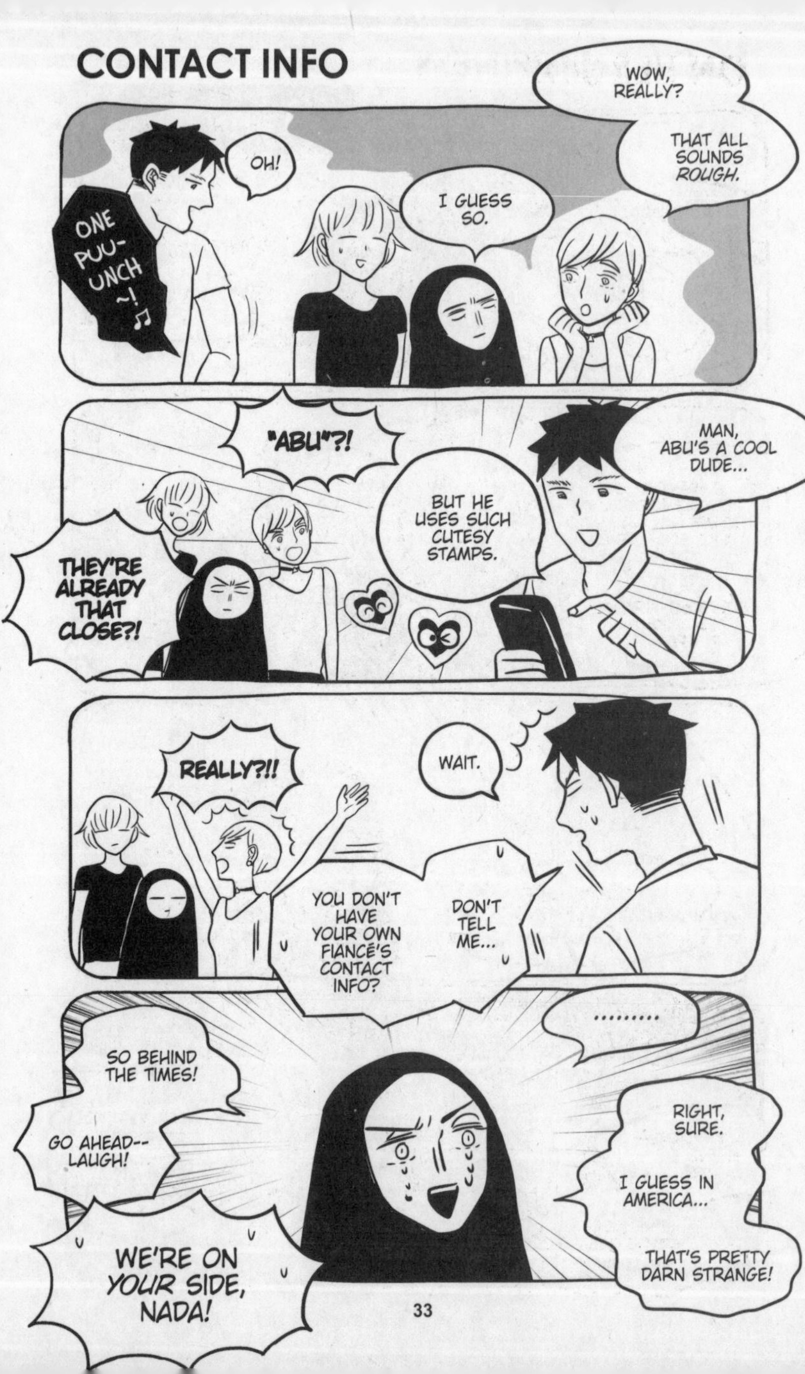
WOW, REALLY?
THAT ALL SOUNDS *ROUGH.*
I GUESS SO.
OH!
ONE PUU-UNCH ~! ♫
MAN, ABU'S A COOL DUDE...
BUT HE USES SUCH CUTESY STAMPS.
"ABU"?!
THEY'RE ALREADY THAT CLOSE?!
WAIT.
DON'T TELL ME...
YOU DON'T HAVE YOUR OWN FIANCÉ'S CONTACT INFO?
REALLY?!!
....
RIGHT, SURE.
I GUESS IN AMERICA...
THAT'S PRETTY DARN STRANGE!
SO BEHIND THE TIMES!
GO AHEAD--LAUGH!
WE'RE ON *YOUR* SIDE, NADA!

NADA'S HAPPINESS

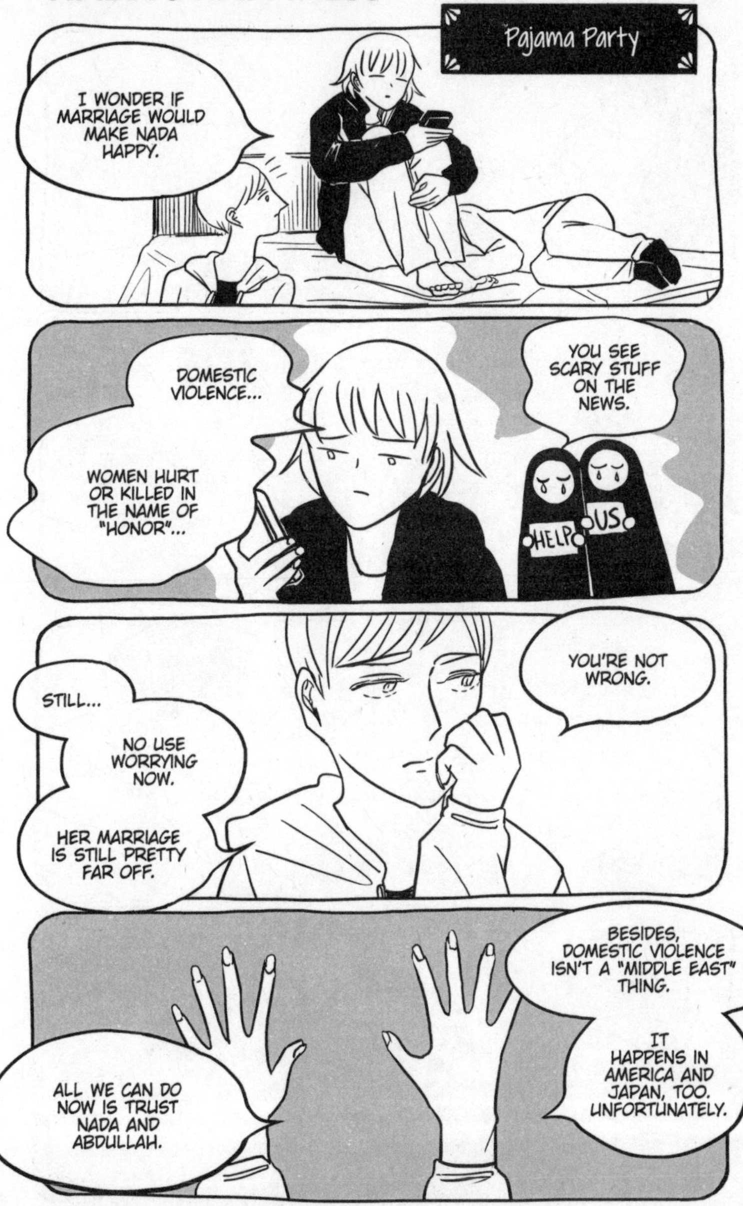
Pajama Party
I WONDER IF MARRIAGE WOULD MAKE NADA HAPPY.
YOU SEE SCARY STUFF ON THE NEWS.
DOMESTIC VIOLENCE...
US
HELP
WOMEN HURT OR KILLED IN THE NAME OF "HONOR"...
YOU'RE NOT WRONG.
STILL...
NO USE WORRYING NOW.
HER MARRIAGE IS STILL PRETTY FAR OFF.
BESIDES, DOMESTIC VIOLENCE ISN'T A "MIDDLE EAST" THING.
IT HAPPENS IN AMERICA AND JAPAN, TOO. UNFORTUNATELY.
ALL WE CAN DO NOW IS TRUST NADA AND ABDULLAH.

SOMEONE TO RELY ON

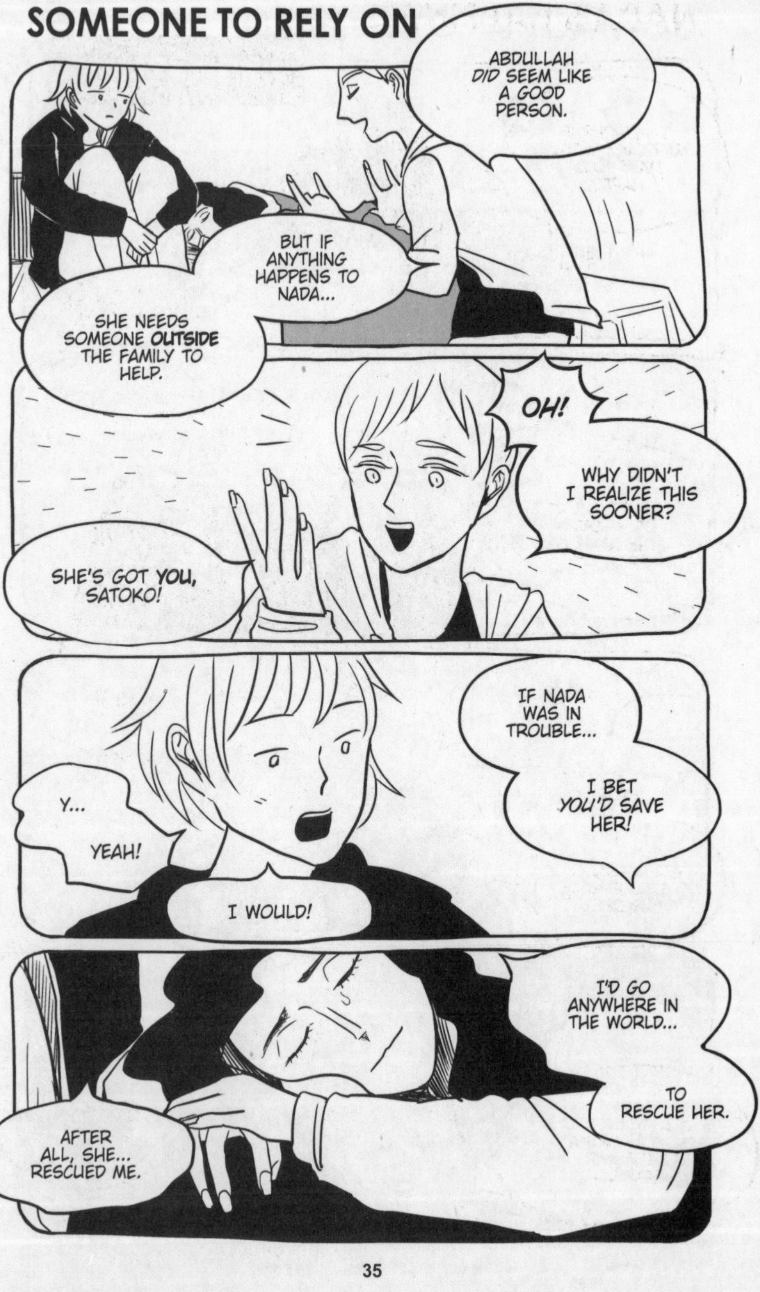
...ABDULLAH *DID* SEEM LIKE A GOOD PERSON.
BUT IF ANYTHING HAPPENS TO NADA...
SHE NEEDS SOMEONE **OUTSIDE** THE FAMILY TO HELP.
OH!
WHY DIDN'T I REALIZE THIS SOONER?
SHE'S GOT **YOU**, SATOKO!
IF NADA WAS IN TROUBLE...
I BET *YOU'D* SAVE HER!
Y...
YEAH!
I WOULD!
I'D GO ANYWHERE IN THE WORLD...
TO RESCUE HER.
AFTER ALL, SHE... RESCUED ME.

CONTACT INFO ACQUIRED

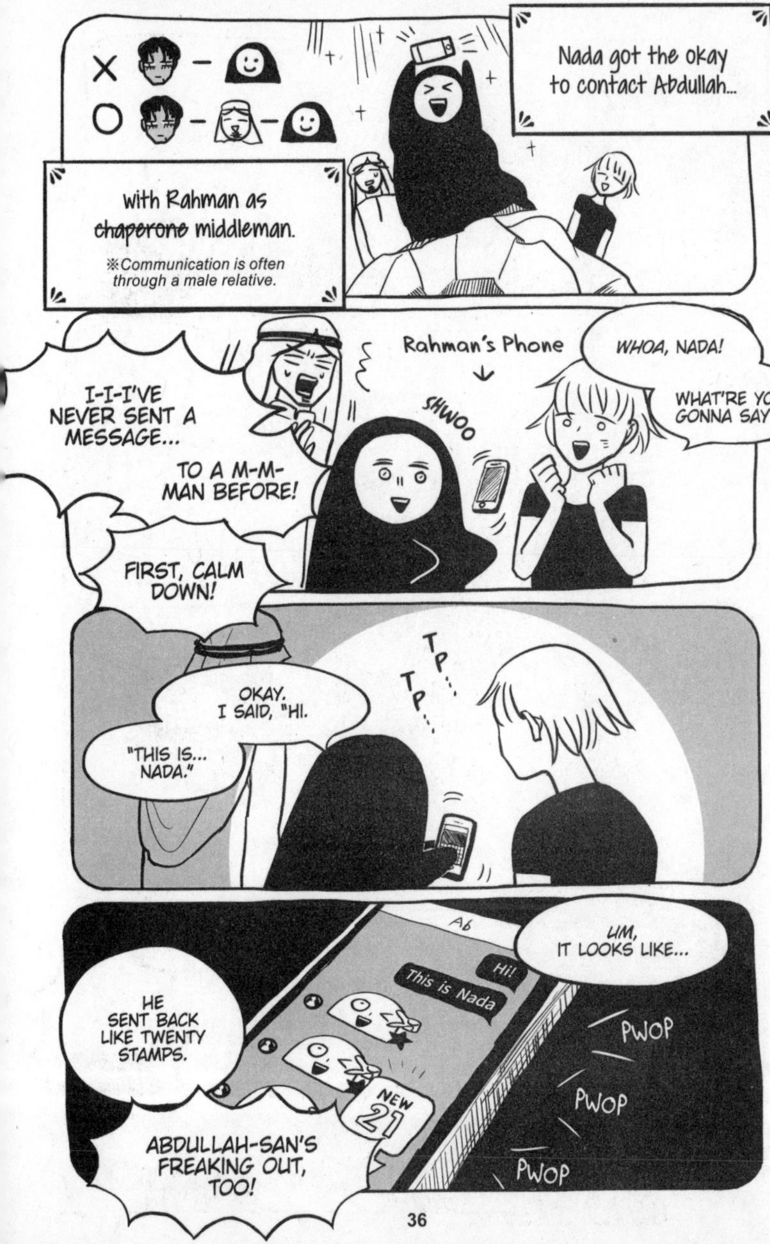
Nada got the okay to contact Abdullah...
with Rahman as ~~chaperone~~ middleman.
※Communication is often through a male relative.
Rahman's Phone
WHOA, NADA!
WHAT'RE YOU GONNA SAY?!
SHWOO
I-I-I'VE NEVER SENT A MESSAGE...
TO A M-M-MAN BEFORE!
FIRST, CALM DOWN!
TP... TP...
OKAY. I SAID, "HI.
"THIS IS... NADA."
Ab
UM, IT LOOKS LIKE...
Hi!
This is Nada
HE SENT BACK LIKE TWENTY STAMPS.
PWOP
PWOP
PWOP
NEW 21
ABDULLAH-SAN'S FREAKING OUT, TOO!

ACCIDENT

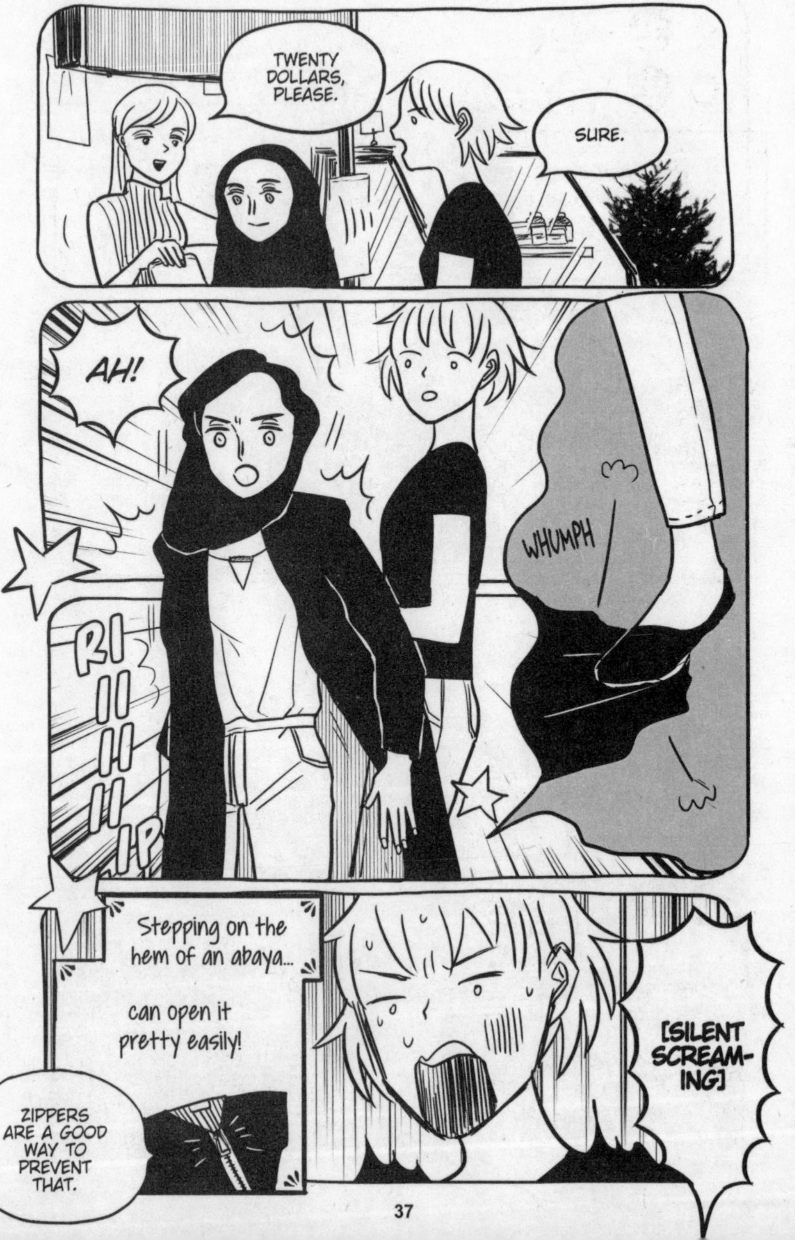

TWENTY DOLLARS, PLEASE.
SURE.
WHUMPH
AH!
RIIIIIIIIP
[SILENT SCREAMING]
Stepping on the hem of an abaya...
can open it pretty easily!
ZIPPERS ARE A GOOD WAY TO PREVENT THAT.

ABAYA

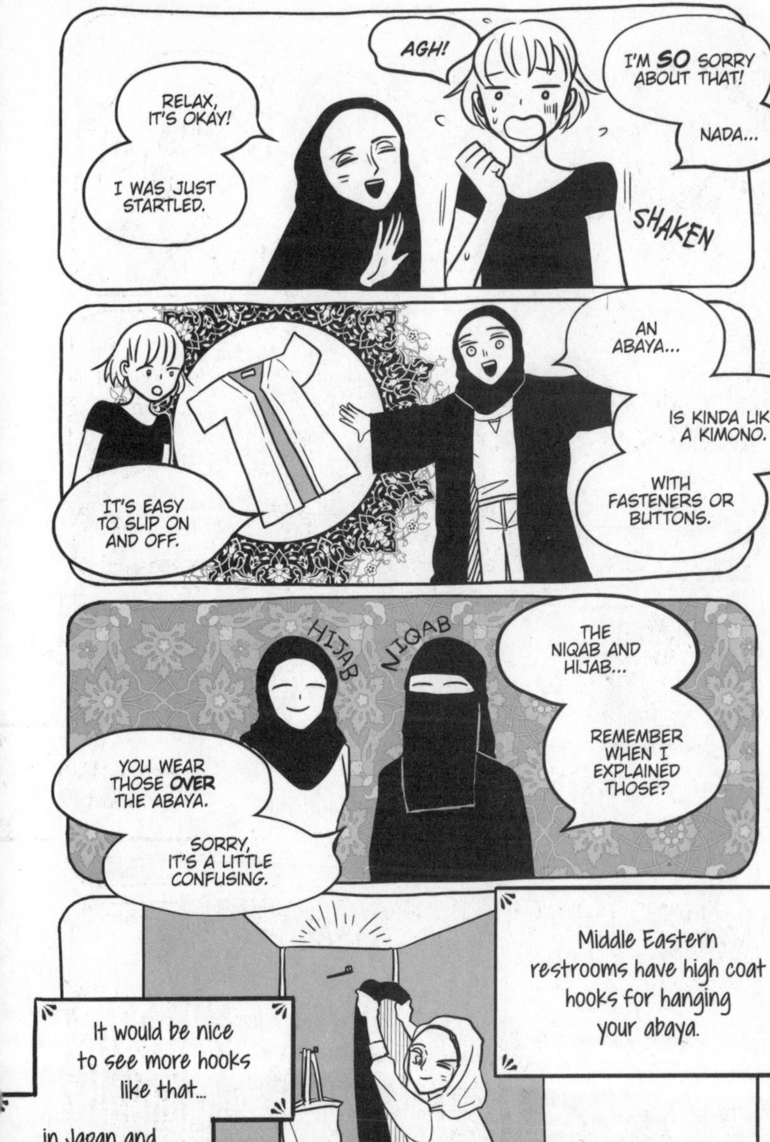

AGH!
I'M **SO** SORRY ABOUT THAT!
NADA...
SHAKEN
RELAX, IT'S OKAY!
I WAS JUST STARTLED.
AN ABAYA...
IS KINDA LIKE A KIMONO.
WITH FASTENERS OR BUTTONS.
IT'S EASY TO SLIP ON AND OFF.
THE NIQAB AND HIJAB...
REMEMBER WHEN I EXPLAINED THOSE?
NIQAB
HIJAB
YOU WEAR THOSE **OVER** THE ABAYA.
SORRY, IT'S A LITTLE CONFUSING.
Middle Eastern restrooms have high coat hooks for hanging your abaya.
It would be nice to see more hooks like that...
in Japan and America, too.

ABAYA CARE

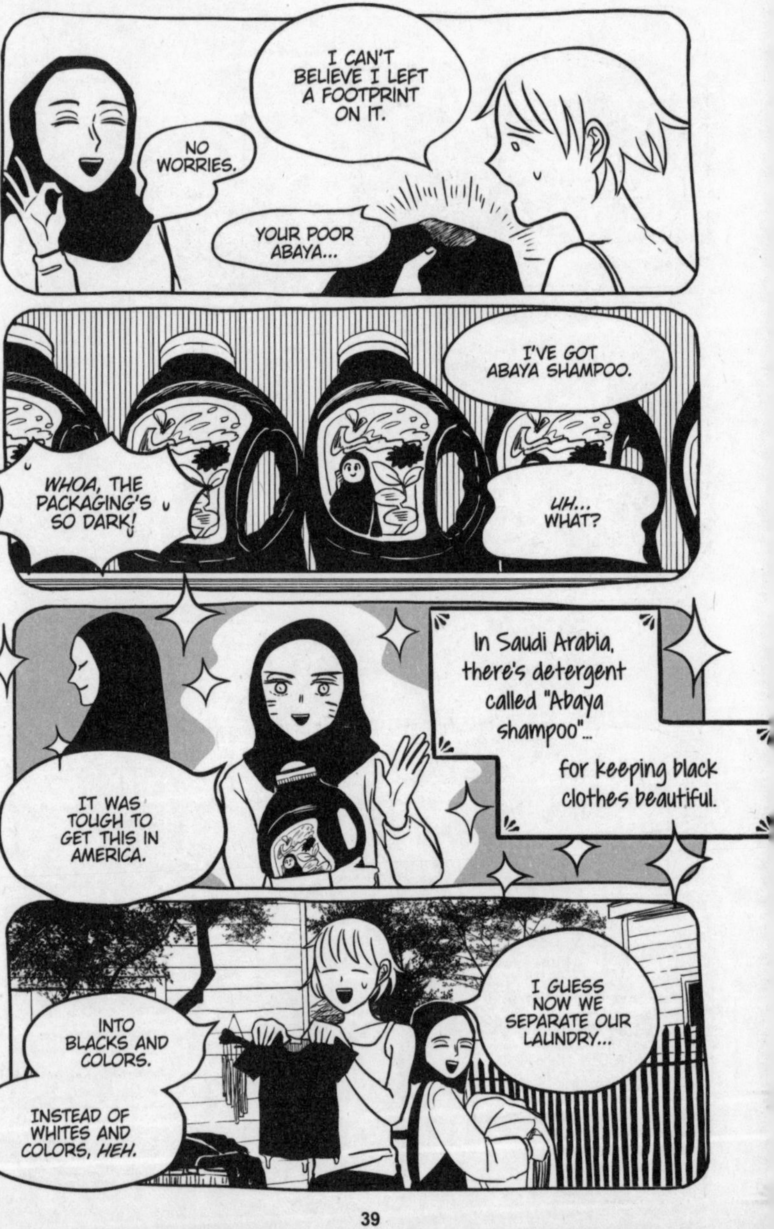
I CAN'T BELIEVE I LEFT A FOOTPRINT ON IT.
YOUR POOR ABAYA...
NO WORRIES.
I'VE GOT ABAYA SHAMPOO.
UH... WHAT?
WHOA, THE PACKAGING'S SO DARK!
In Saudi Arabia, there's detergent called "Abaya shampoo"...
for keeping black clothes beautiful.
IT WAS TOUGH TO GET THIS IN AMERICA.
I GUESS NOW WE SEPARATE OUR LAUNDRY...
INTO BLACKS AND COLORS.
INSTEAD OF WHITES AND COLORS, *HEH*.

UNDERWEAR

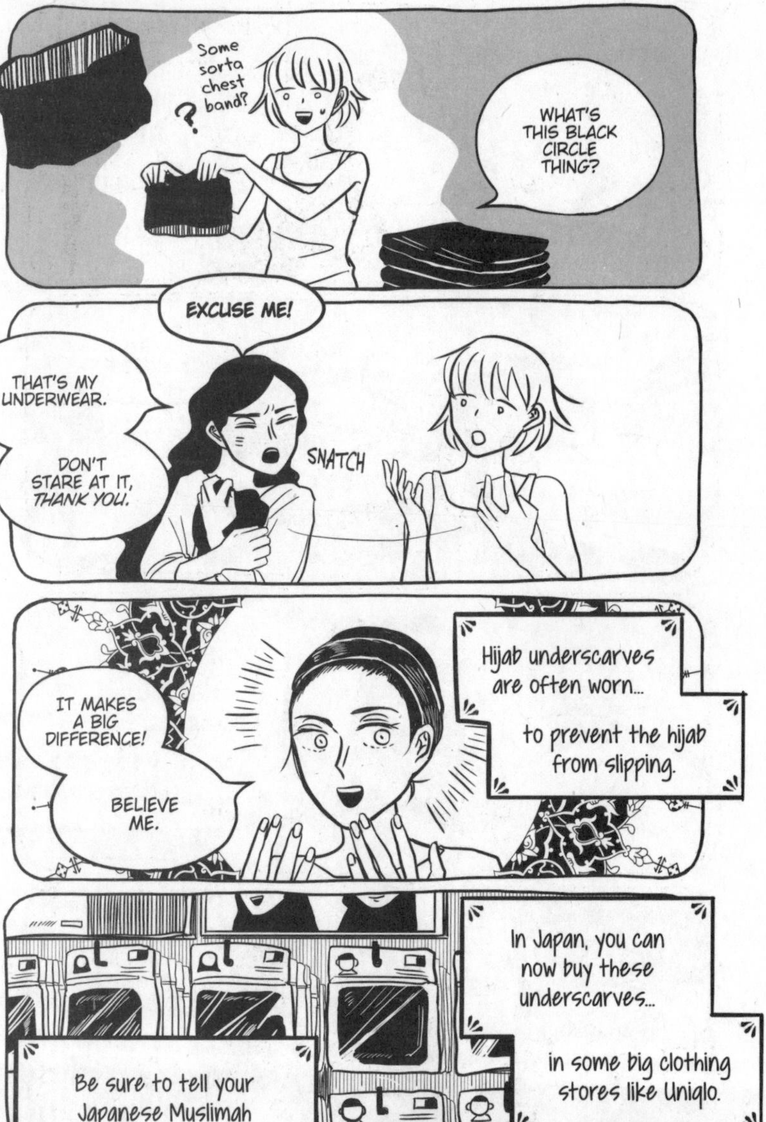
WHAT'S THIS BLACK CIRCLE THING?
Some sorta chest band?
EXCUSE ME!
THAT'S MY UNDERWEAR.
SNATCH
DON'T STARE AT IT, *THANK YOU.*
Hijab underscarves are often worn...
to prevent the hijab from slipping.
IT MAKES A BIG DIFFERENCE!
BELIEVE ME.
In Japan, you can now buy these underscarves...
in some big clothing stores like Uniqlo.
Be sure to tell your Japanese Muslimah friends!

DID I PRAY?

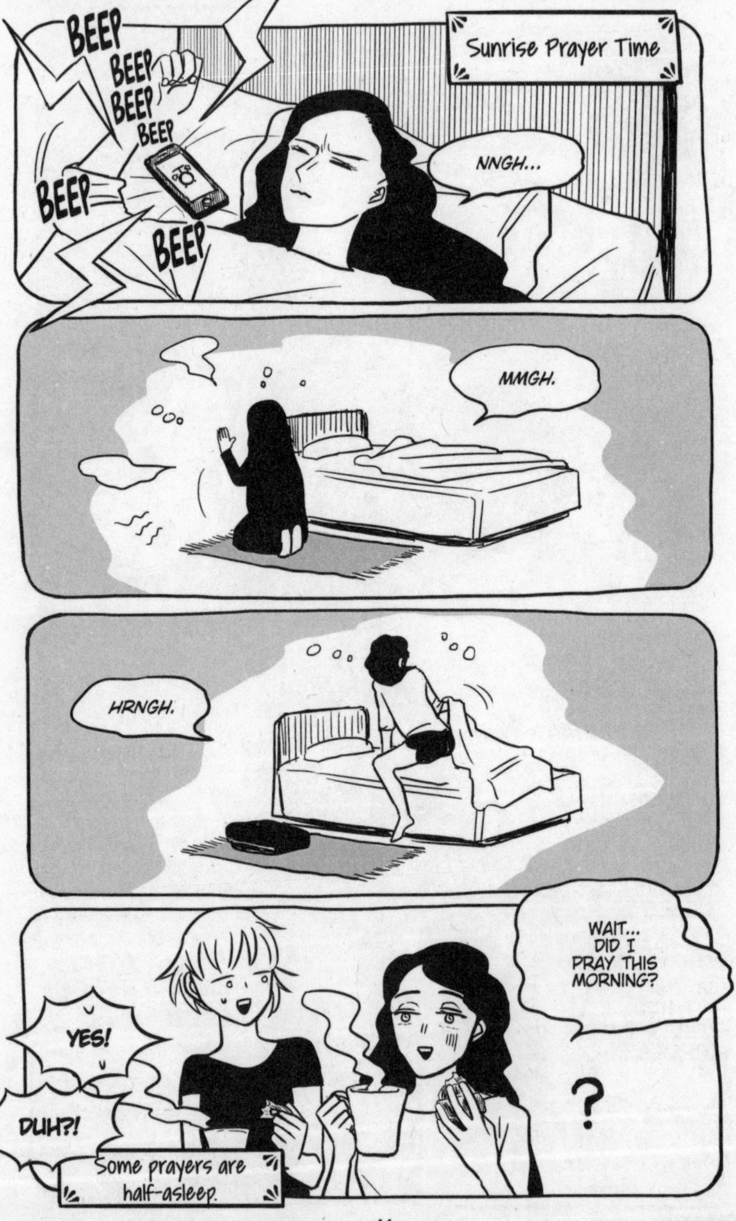

Sunrise Prayer Time
NNGH...
BEEP
BEEP
BEEP
BEEP
BEEP
BEEP
MMGH.
HRNGH.
WAIT... DID I PRAY THIS MORNING?
?
YES!
DUH?!
Some prayers are half-asleep.

DID I PRAY? PART 2

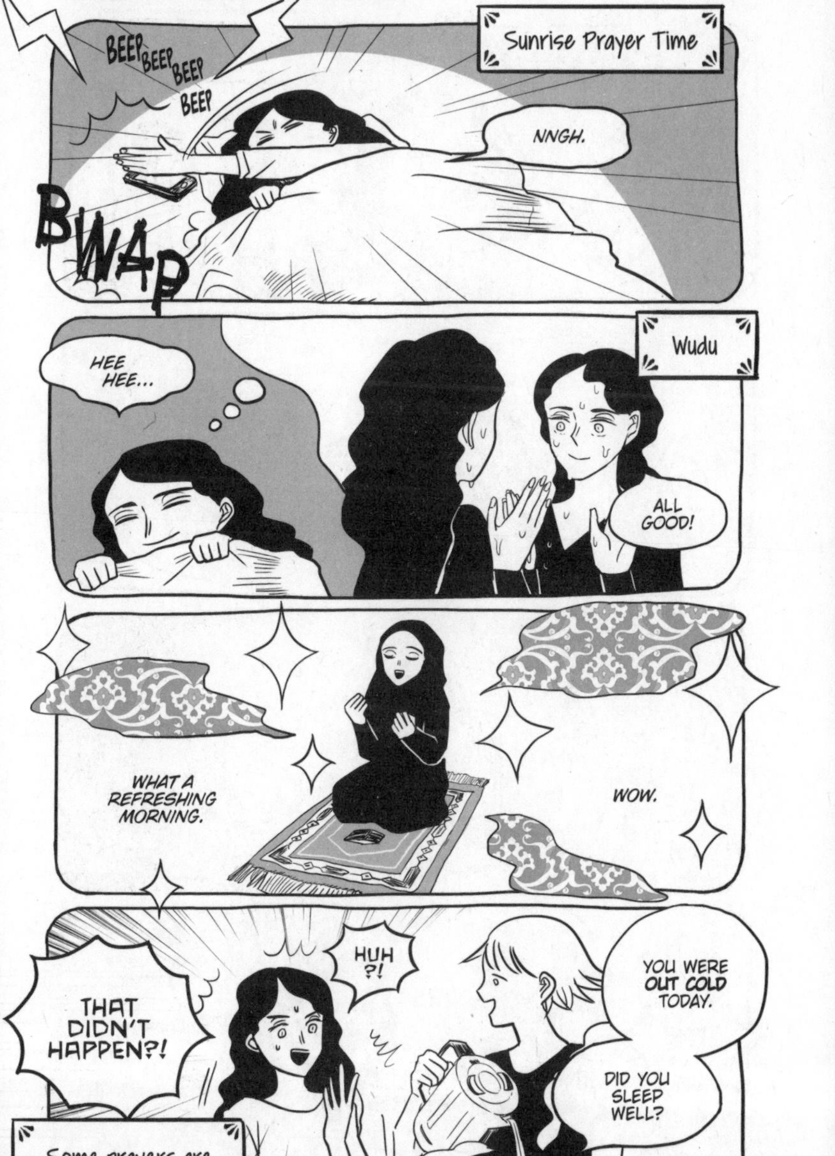
Sunrise Prayer Time
NNGH.
BEEP BEEP BEEP BEEP
BWAP
Wudu
ALL GOOD!
HEE HEE...
WOW.
WHAT A REFRESHING MORNING.
YOU WERE OUT COLD TODAY.
DID YOU SLEEP WELL?
HUH ?!
THAT DIDN'T HAPPEN?!
Some prayers are just dreams.

DAILY ROUTINE

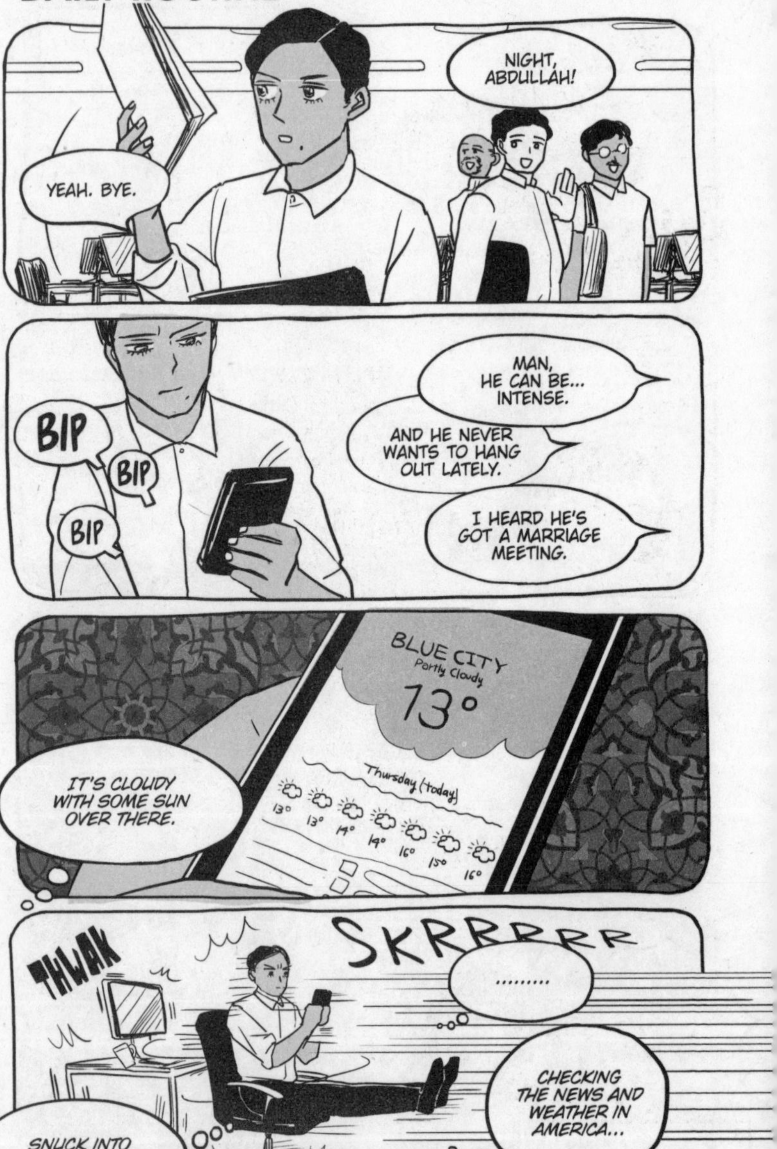
NIGHT, ABDULLAH!
YEAH. BYE.
MAN, HE CAN BE... INTENSE.
AND HE NEVER WANTS TO HANG OUT LATELY.
I HEARD HE'S GOT A MARRIAGE MEETING.
BIP
BIP
BIP
BLUE CITY
Partly Cloudy
73°
Thursday (today)
13° 13° 14° 14° 16° 15° 16°
IT'S CLOUDY WITH SOME SUN OVER THERE.
SKRRRRRR
....
CHECKING THE NEWS AND WEATHER IN AMERICA...
THWAK
SNUCK INTO MY DAILY ROUTINE.

LIFETIME

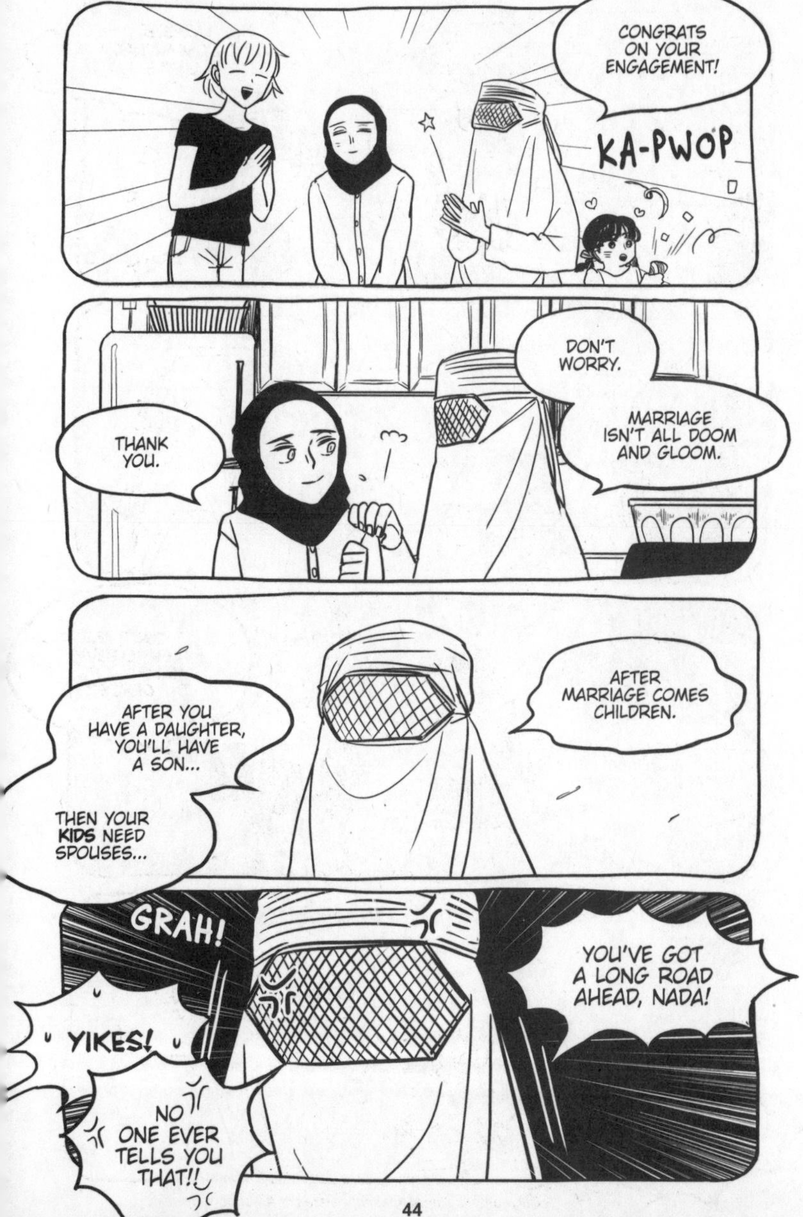

CONGRATS ON YOUR ENGAGEMENT!
KA-PWOP
DON'T WORRY.
MARRIAGE ISN'T ALL DOOM AND GLOOM.
THANK YOU.
AFTER MARRIAGE COMES CHILDREN.
AFTER YOU HAVE A DAUGHTER, YOU'LL HAVE A SON...
THEN YOUR **KIDS** NEED SPOUSES...
YOU'VE GOT A LONG ROAD AHEAD, NADA!
GRAH!
YIKES!
NO ONE EVER TELLS YOU THAT!!

ADVICE

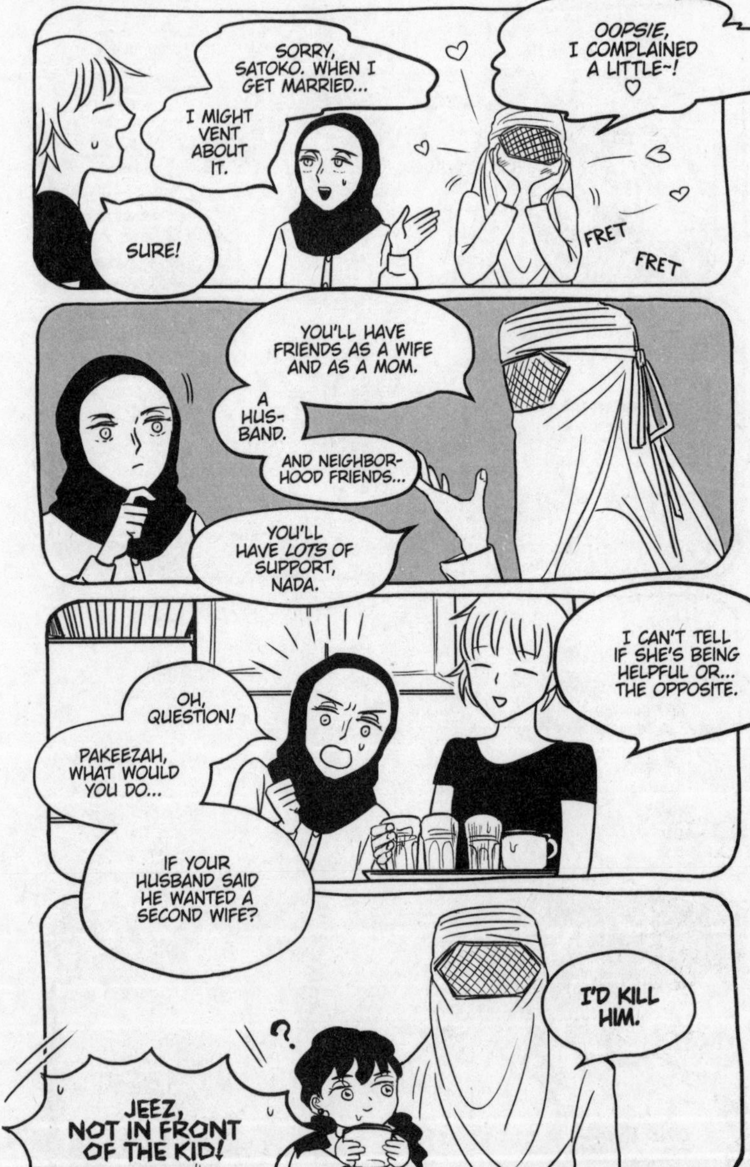
OOPSIE, I COMPLAINED A LITTLE~!
SORRY, SATOKO. WHEN I GET MARRIED...
I MIGHT VENT ABOUT IT.
FRET
FRET
SURE!
YOU'LL HAVE FRIENDS AS A WIFE AND AS A MOM.
A HUS- BAND.
AND NEIGHBOR- HOOD FRIENDS...
YOU'LL HAVE *LOTS* OF SUPPORT, NADA.
I CAN'T TELL IF SHE'S BEING HELPFUL OR... THE OPPOSITE.
OH, QUESTION!
PAKEEZAH, WHAT WOULD YOU DO...
IF YOUR HUSBAND SAID HE WANTED A SECOND WIFE?
I'D KILL HIM.
?
JEEZ, NOT IN FRONT OF THE KID!

※ *Polygamy is illegal in all fifty states in America, anyway.*

PREPARE YOURSELF!

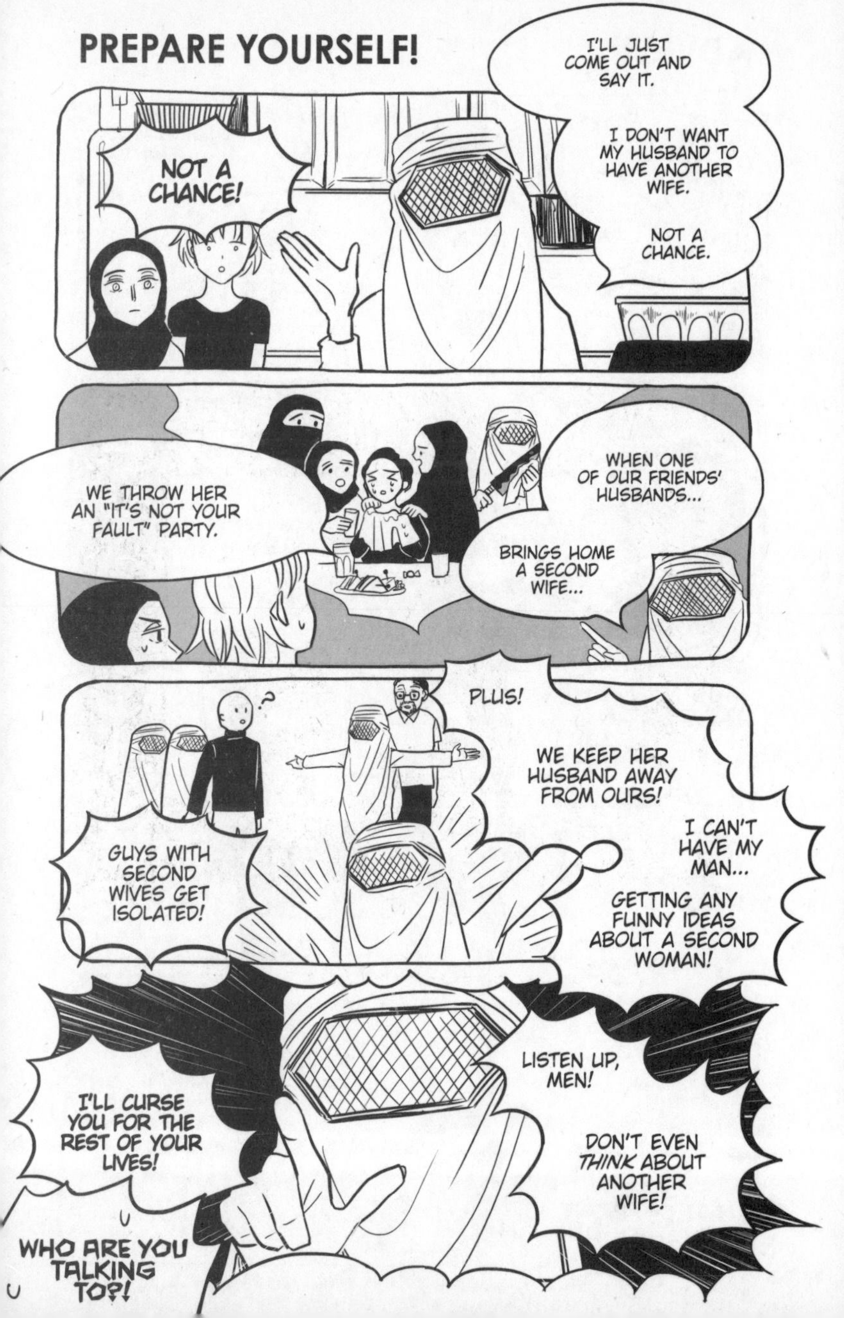
I'LL JUST COME OUT AND SAY IT.
I DON'T WANT MY HUSBAND TO HAVE ANOTHER WIFE.
NOT A CHANCE.
NOT A CHANCE!
WHEN ONE OF OUR FRIENDS' HUSBANDS...
BRINGS HOME A SECOND WIFE...
WE THROW HER AN "IT'S NOT YOUR FAULT" PARTY.
PLUS!
WE KEEP HER HUSBAND AWAY FROM OURS!
I CAN'T HAVE MY MAN...
GETTING ANY FUNNY IDEAS ABOUT A SECOND WOMAN!
GUYS WITH SECOND WIVES GET ISOLATED!
LISTEN UP, MEN!
DON'T EVEN *THINK* ABOUT ANOTHER WIFE!
I'LL CURSE YOU FOR THE REST OF YOUR LIVES!
WHO ARE YOU TALKING TO?!

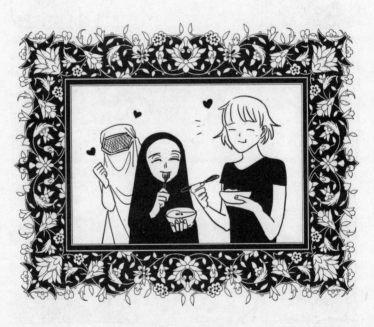

SATOKO AND NADA

Presented by Yupechika

MANICURES

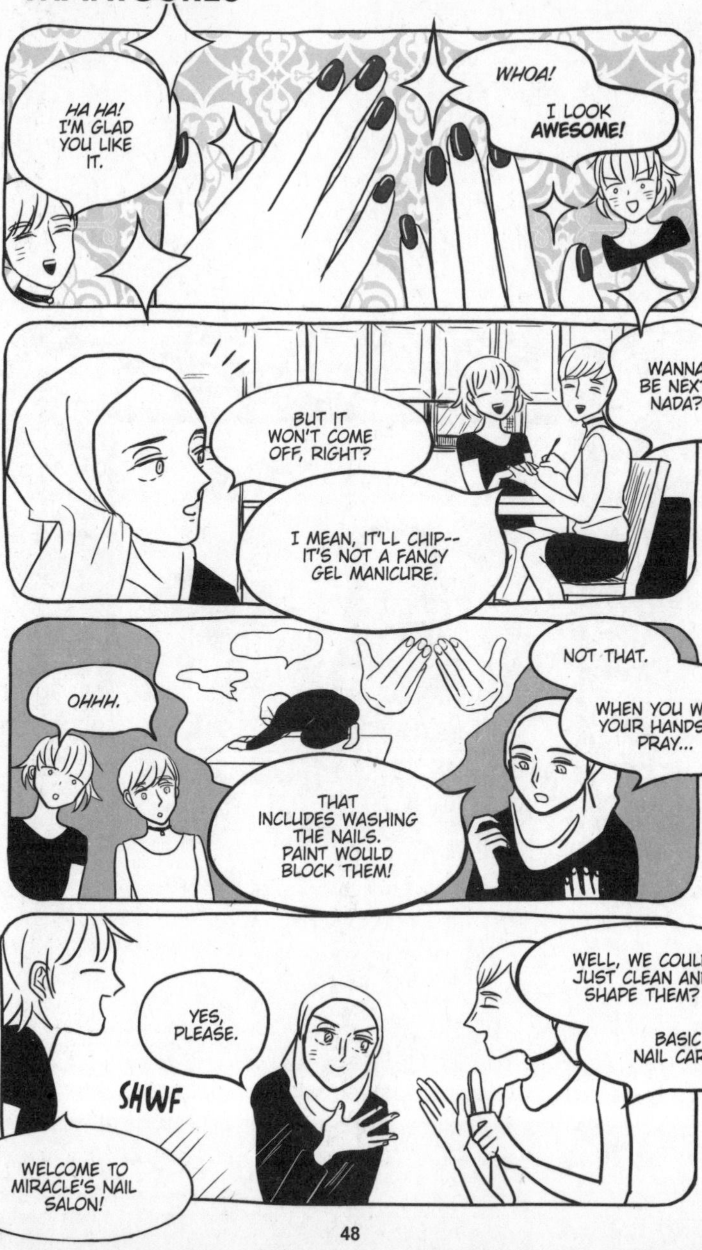

WHOA!
I LOOK **AWESOME!**
HA HA! I'M GLAD YOU LIKE IT.
WANNA BE NEXT, NADA?
BUT IT WON'T COME OFF, RIGHT?
I MEAN, IT'LL CHIP-- IT'S NOT A FANCY GEL MANICURE.
NOT THAT.
WHEN YOU WASH YOUR HANDS TO PRAY...
THAT INCLUDES WASHING THE NAILS. PAINT WOULD BLOCK THEM!
OHHH.
WELL, WE COULD JUST CLEAN AND SHAPE THEM?
BASIC NAIL CARE.
YES, PLEASE.
SHWF
WELCOME TO MIRACLE'S NAIL SALON!

HENNA NAILS

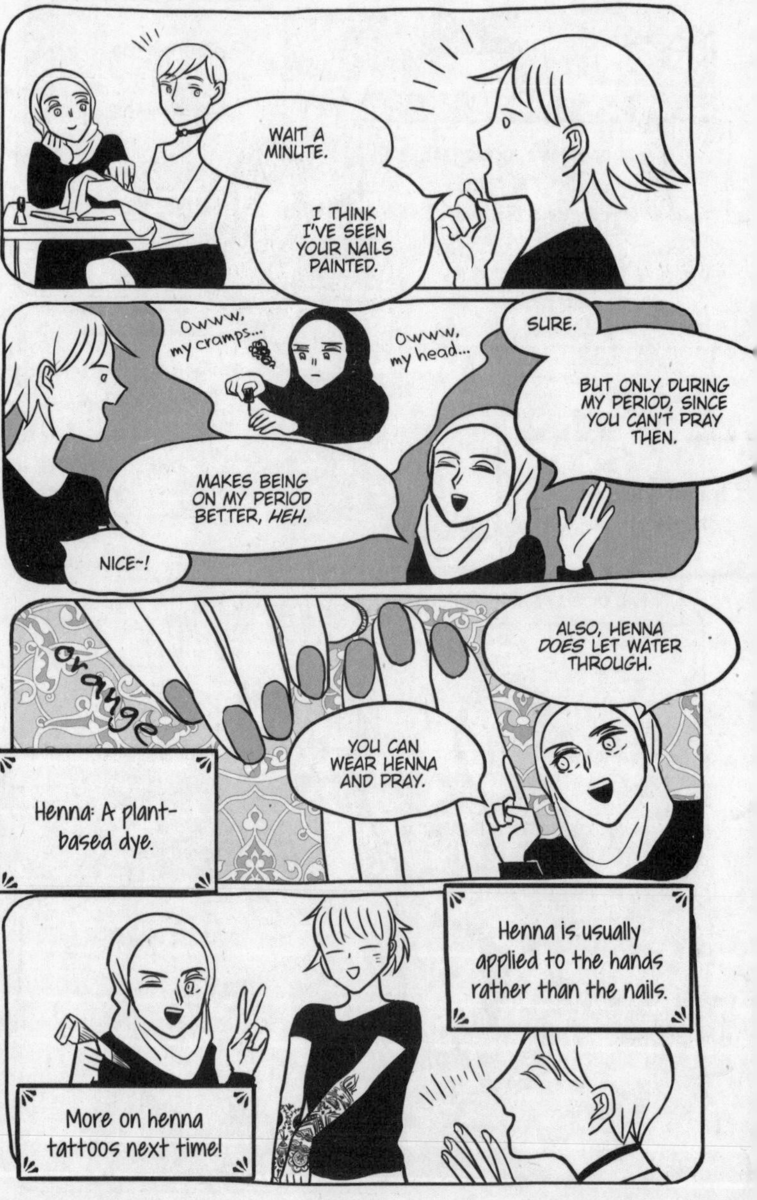
WAIT A MINUTE.
I THINK I'VE SEEN YOUR NAILS PAINTED.
SURE.
BUT ONLY DURING MY PERIOD, SINCE YOU CAN'T PRAY THEN.
Owww, my head...
Owww, my cramps...
MAKES BEING ON MY PERIOD BETTER, *HEH*.
NICE~!
ALSO, HENNA *DOES* LET WATER THROUGH.
YOU CAN WEAR HENNA AND PRAY.
orange
Henna: A plant-based dye.
Henna is usually applied to the hands rather than the nails.
More on henna tattoos next time!

HENNA TATTOOS

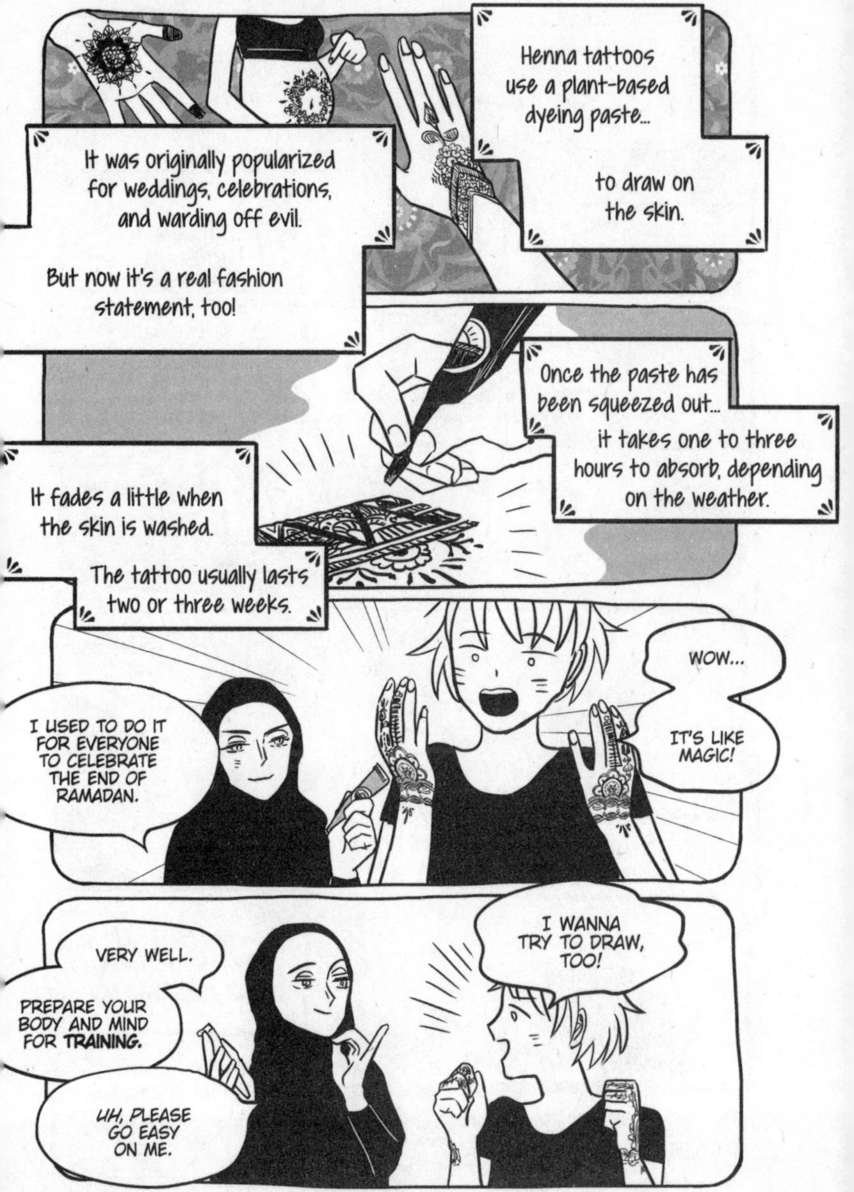
Henna tattoos use a plant-based dyeing paste...
to draw on the skin.
It was originally popularized for weddings, celebrations, and warding off evil.
But now it's a real fashion statement, too!
Once the paste has been squeezed out...
it takes one to three hours to absorb, depending on the weather.
It fades a little when the skin is washed.
The tattoo usually lasts two or three weeks.
WOW...
IT'S LIKE MAGIC!
I USED TO DO IT FOR EVERYONE TO CELEBRATE THE END OF RAMADAN.
I WANNA TRY TO DRAW, TOO!
VERY WELL.
PREPARE YOUR BODY AND MIND FOR **TRAINING.**
UH, PLEASE GO EASY ON ME.

HENNA PATTERNS

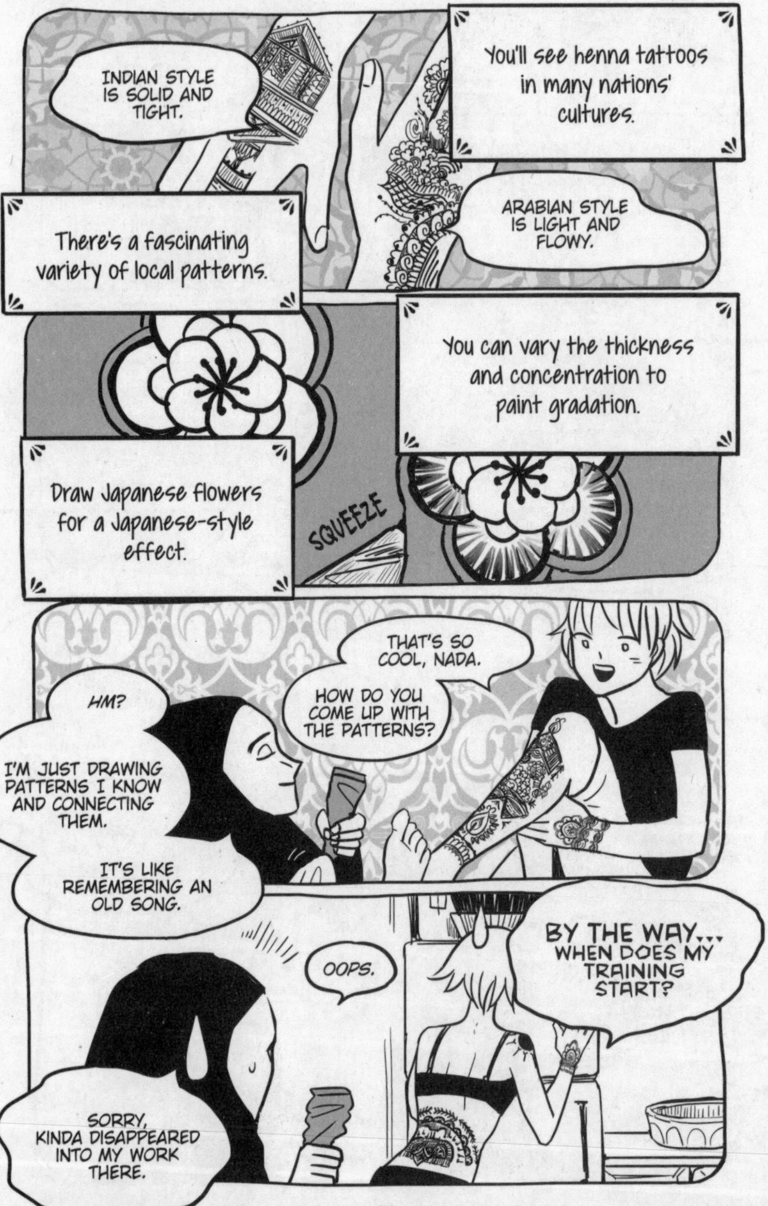
You'll see henna tattoos in many nations' cultures.
INDIAN STYLE IS SOLID AND TIGHT.
ARABIAN STYLE IS LIGHT AND FLOWY.
There's a fascinating variety of local patterns.
You can vary the thickness and concentration to paint gradation.
SQUEEZE
Draw Japanese flowers for a Japanese-style effect.
THAT'S SO COOL, NADA.
HOW DO YOU COME UP WITH THE PATTERNS?
HM?
I'M JUST DRAWING PATTERNS I KNOW AND CONNECTING THEM.
IT'S LIKE REMEMBERING AN OLD SONG.
BY THE WAY... WHEN DOES MY TRAINING START?
OOPS.
SORRY, KINDA DISAPPEARED INTO MY WORK THERE.

KA-BOOM

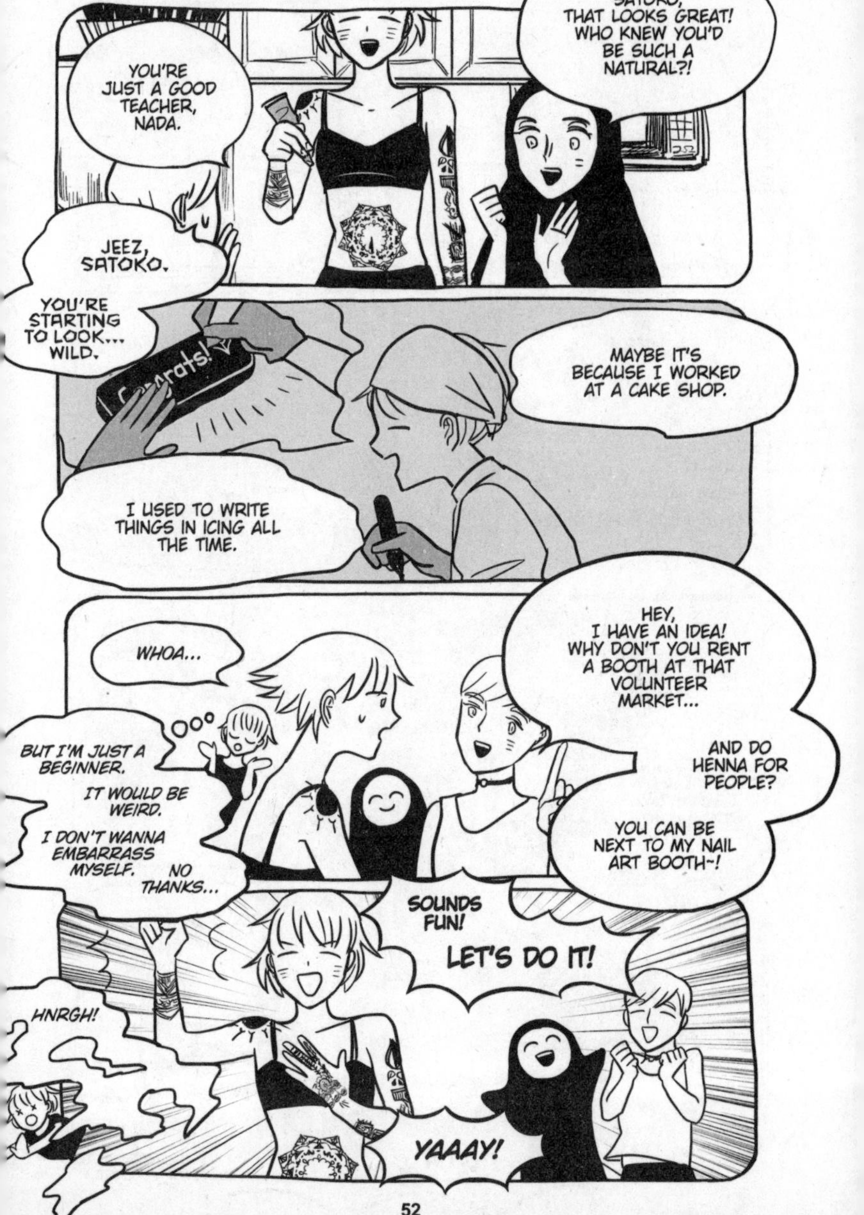
SATOKO, THAT LOOKS GREAT! WHO KNEW YOU'D BE SUCH A NATURAL?!
YOU'RE JUST A GOOD TEACHER, NADA.
JEEZ, SATOKO.
YOU'RE STARTING TO LOOK... WILD.
MAYBE IT'S BECAUSE I WORKED AT A CAKE SHOP.
I USED TO WRITE THINGS IN ICING ALL THE TIME.
HEY, I HAVE AN IDEA! WHY DON'T YOU RENT A BOOTH AT THAT VOLUNTEER MARKET...
AND DO HENNA FOR PEOPLE?
YOU CAN BE NEXT TO MY NAIL ART BOOTH~!
WHOA...
OOO
BUT I'M JUST A BEGINNER.
IT WOULD BE WEIRD.
I DON'T WANNA EMBARRASS MYSELF.
NO THANKS...
SOUNDS FUN!
LET'S DO IT!
YAAAY!
HNRGH!

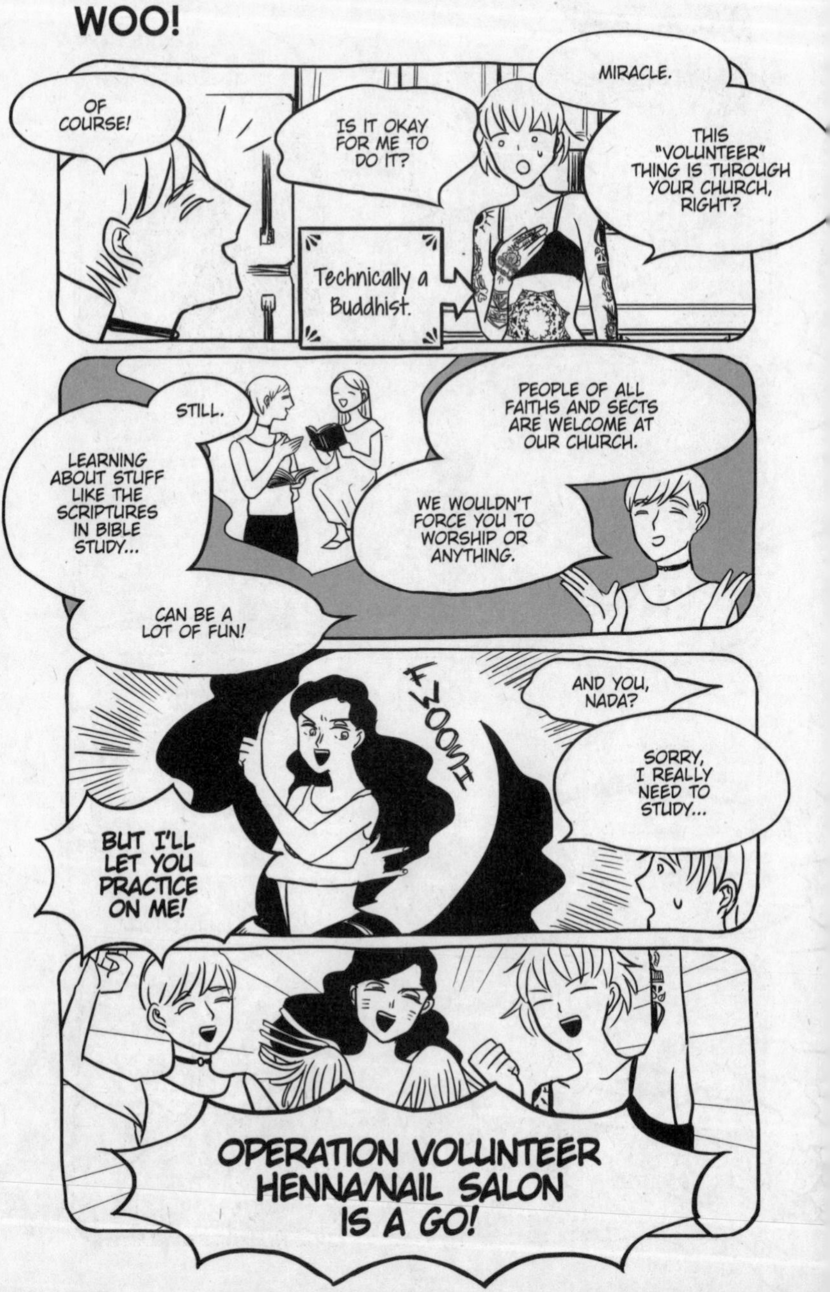
WOO!
MIRACLE.
THIS "VOLUNTEER" THING IS THROUGH YOUR CHURCH, RIGHT?
IS IT OKAY FOR ME TO DO IT?
Technically a Buddhist.
OF COURSE!
PEOPLE OF ALL FAITHS AND SECTS ARE WELCOME AT OUR CHURCH.
WE WOULDN'T FORCE YOU TO WORSHIP OR ANYTHING.
STILL.
LEARNING ABOUT STUFF LIKE THE SCRIPTURES IN BIBLE STUDY...
CAN BE A LOT OF FUN!
AND YOU, NADA?
SORRY, I REALLY NEED TO STUDY...
FWOOSH
BUT I'LL LET YOU PRACTICE ON ME!
OPERATION VOLUNTEER HENNA/NAIL SALON IS A GO!

IT'S A TRAP

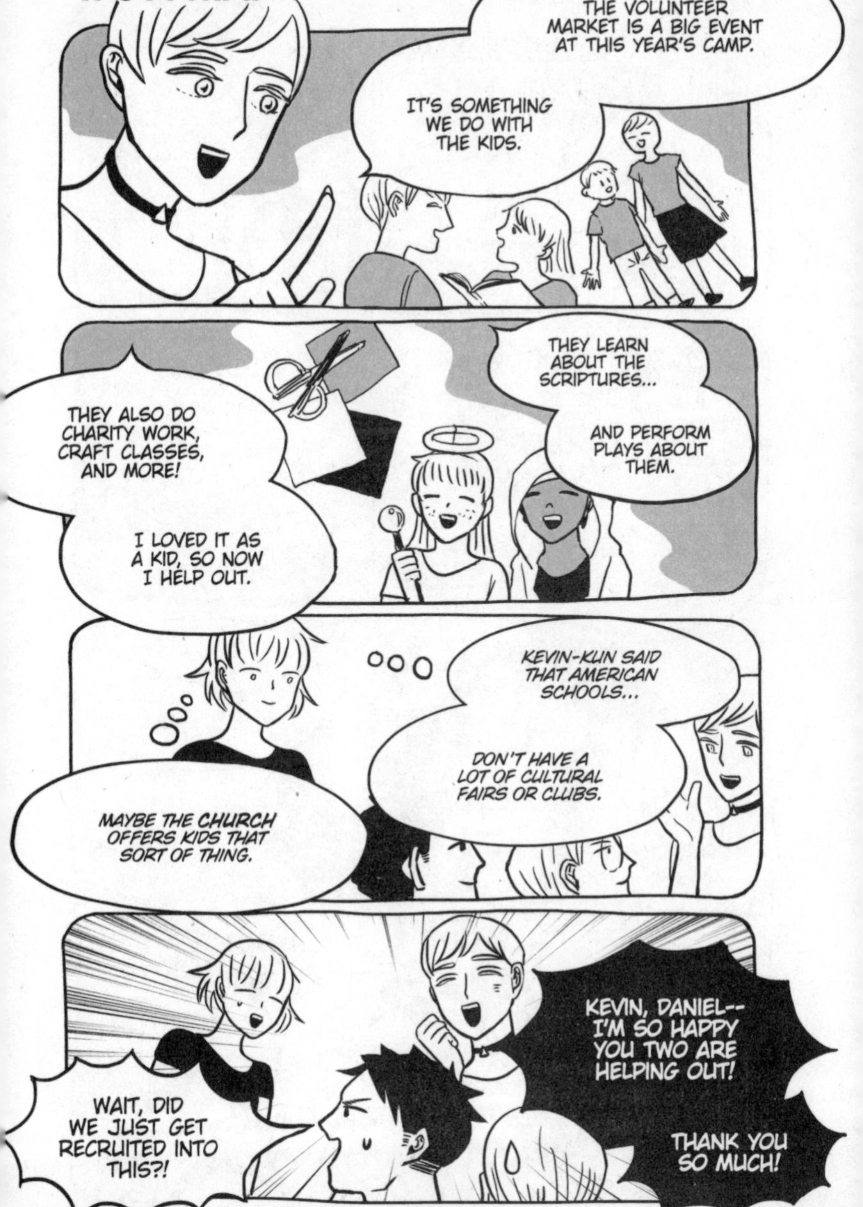
THE VOLUNTEER MARKET IS A BIG EVENT AT THIS YEAR'S CAMP.
IT'S SOMETHING WE DO WITH THE KIDS.
THEY LEARN ABOUT THE SCRIPTURES...
AND PERFORM PLAYS ABOUT THEM.
THEY ALSO DO CHARITY WORK, CRAFT CLASSES, AND MORE!
I LOVED IT AS A KID, SO NOW I HELP OUT.
KEVIN-KUN SAID THAT AMERICAN SCHOOLS...
DON'T HAVE A LOT OF CULTURAL FAIRS OR CLUBS.
MAYBE THE CHURCH OFFERS KIDS THAT SORT OF THING.
KEVIN, DANIEL-- I'M SO HAPPY YOU TWO ARE HELPING OUT!
THANK YOU SO MUCH!
WAIT, DID WE JUST GET RECRUITED INTO THIS?!

TAKE A BREAK!

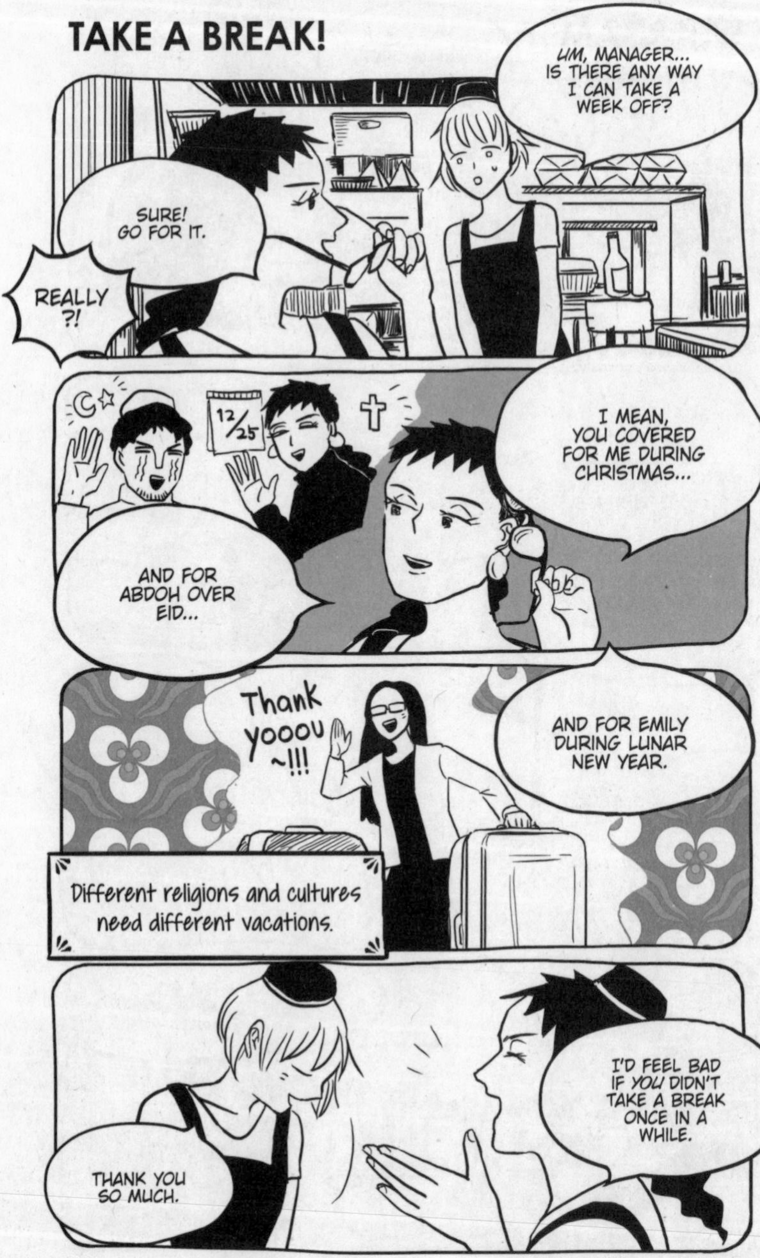
UM, MANAGER... IS THERE ANY WAY I CAN TAKE A WEEK OFF?
SURE! GO FOR IT.
REALLY ?!
I MEAN, YOU COVERED FOR ME DURING CHRISTMAS...
12/25
AND FOR ABDOH OVER EID...
AND FOR EMILY DURING LUNAR NEW YEAR.
Thank yooou ~!!!
Different religions and cultures need different vacations.
I'D FEEL BAD IF *YOU* DIDN'T TAKE A BREAK ONCE IN A WHILE.
THANK YOU SO MUCH.

WHERE AM I?

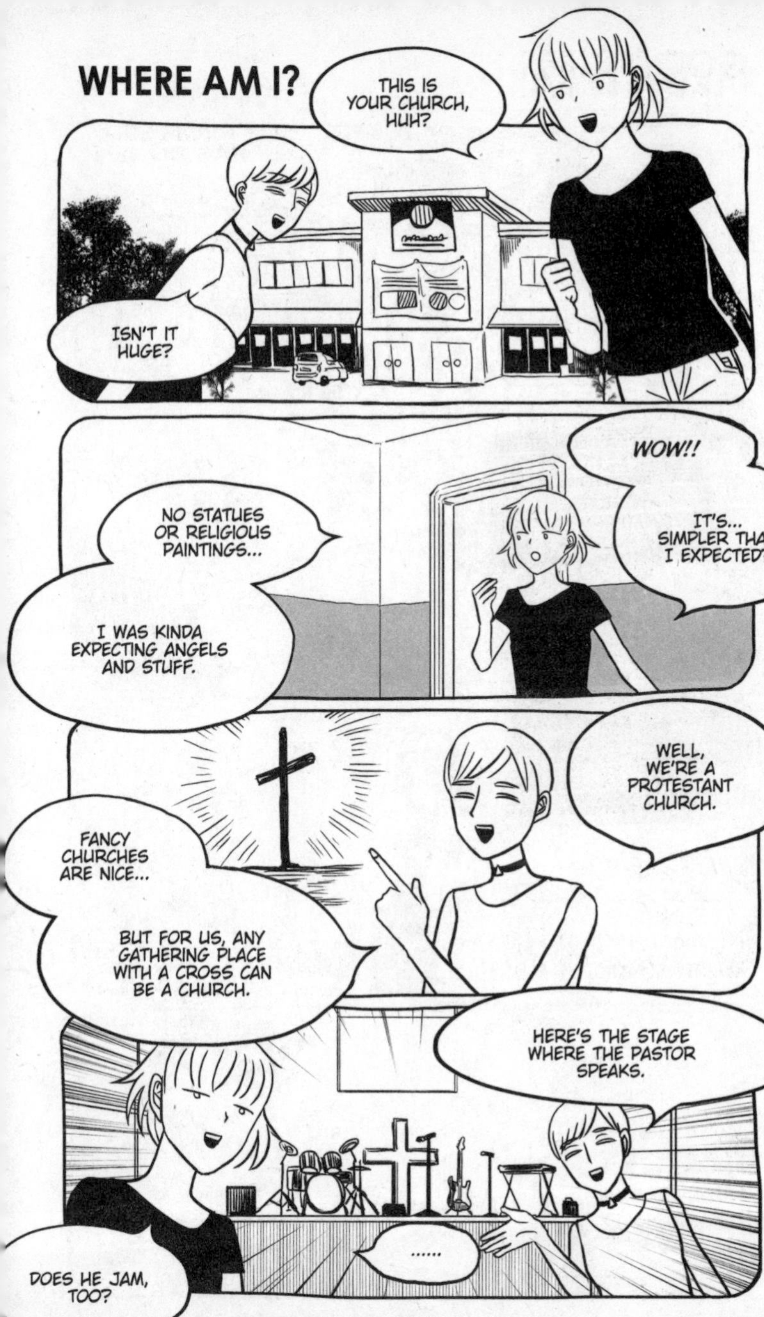
THIS IS YOUR CHURCH, HUH?
ISN'T IT HUGE?
WOW!!
IT'S... SIMPLER THAN I EXPECTED?
NO STATUES OR RELIGIOUS PAINTINGS...
I WAS KINDA EXPECTING ANGELS AND STUFF.
WELL, WE'RE A PROTESTANT CHURCH.
FANCY CHURCHES ARE NICE...
BUT FOR US, ANY GATHERING PLACE WITH A CROSS CAN BE A CHURCH.
HERE'S THE STAGE WHERE THE PASTOR SPEAKS.
......
DOES HE JAM, TOO?

GOOD VIBES

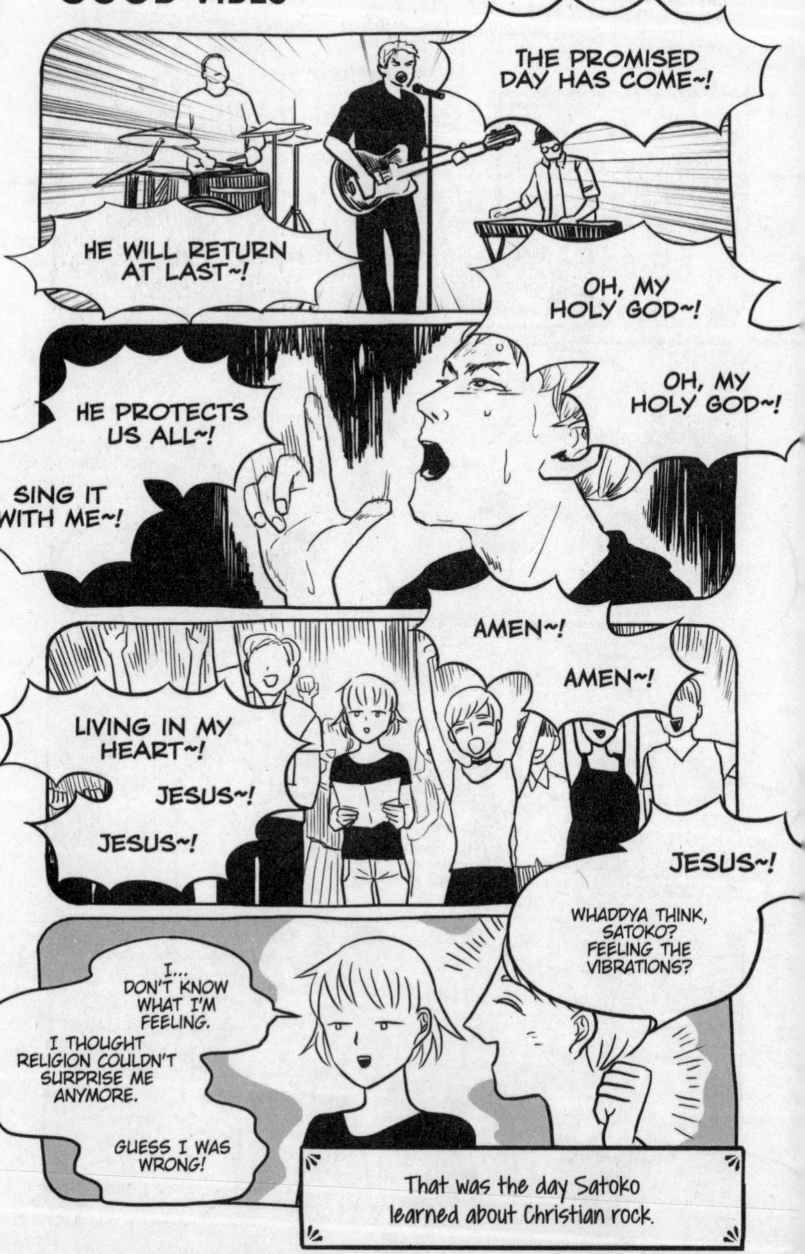

THE PROMISED DAY HAS COME~!
HE WILL RETURN AT LAST~!
OH, MY HOLY GOD~!
OH, MY HOLY GOD~!
HE PROTECTS US ALL~!
SING IT WITH ME~!
AMEN~!
AMEN~!
LIVING IN MY HEART~!
JESUS~!
JESUS~!
JESUS~!
WHADDYA THINK, SATOKO? FEELING THE VIBRATIONS?
I... DON'T KNOW WHAT I'M FEELING.
I THOUGHT RELIGION COULDN'T SURPRISE ME ANYMORE.
GUESS I WAS WRONG!
That was the day Satoko learned about Christian rock.

MANY FORMS

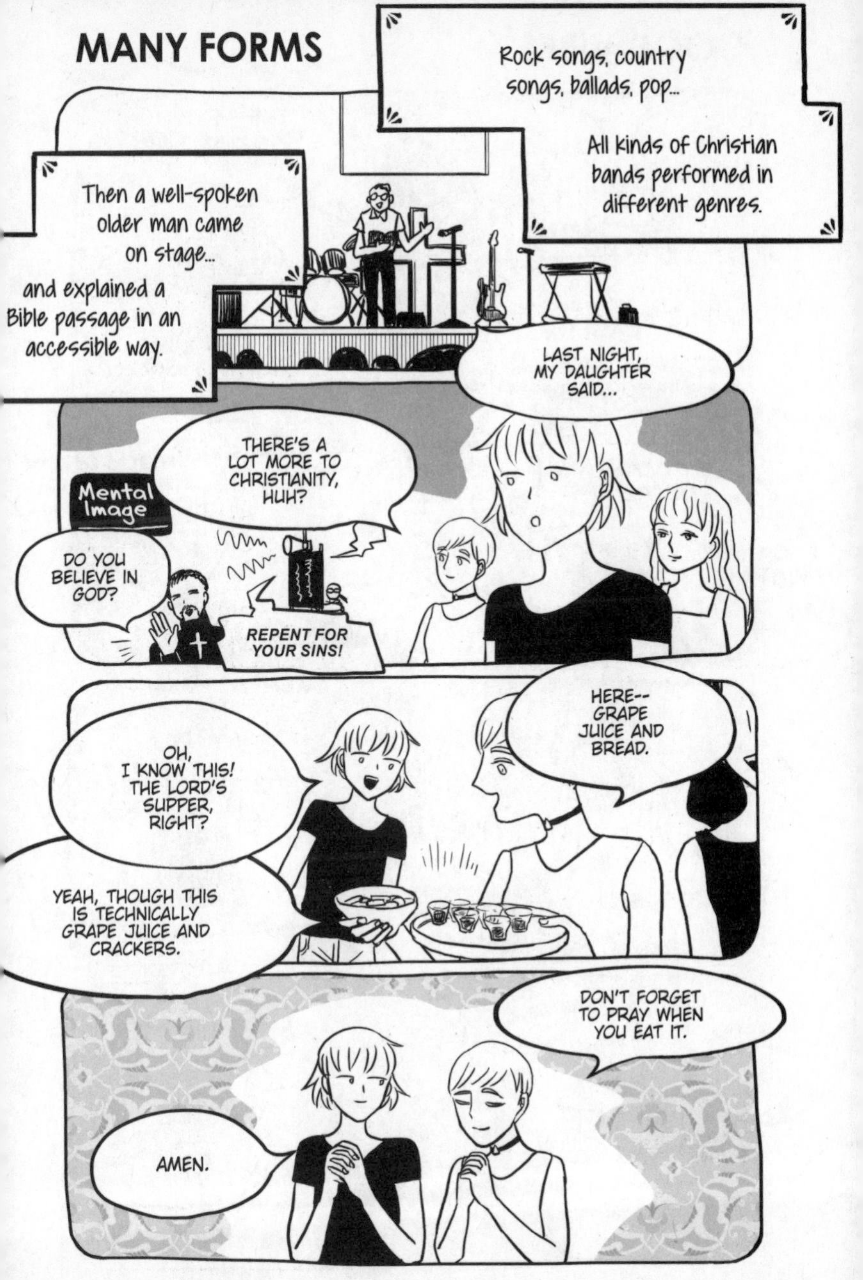
Rock songs, country songs, ballads, pop...
All kinds of Christian bands performed in different genres.
Then a well-spoken older man came on stage...
and explained a Bible passage in an accessible way.
LAST NIGHT, MY DAUGHTER SAID...
THERE'S A LOT MORE TO CHRISTIANITY, HUH?
Mental Image
REPENT FOR YOUR SINS!
DO YOU BELIEVE IN GOD?
HERE-- GRAPE JUICE AND BREAD.
OH, I KNOW THIS! THE LORD'S SUPPER, RIGHT?
YEAH, THOUGH THIS IS TECHNICALLY GRAPE JUICE AND CRACKERS.
DON'T FORGET TO PRAY WHEN YOU EAT IT.
AMEN.

GRRR

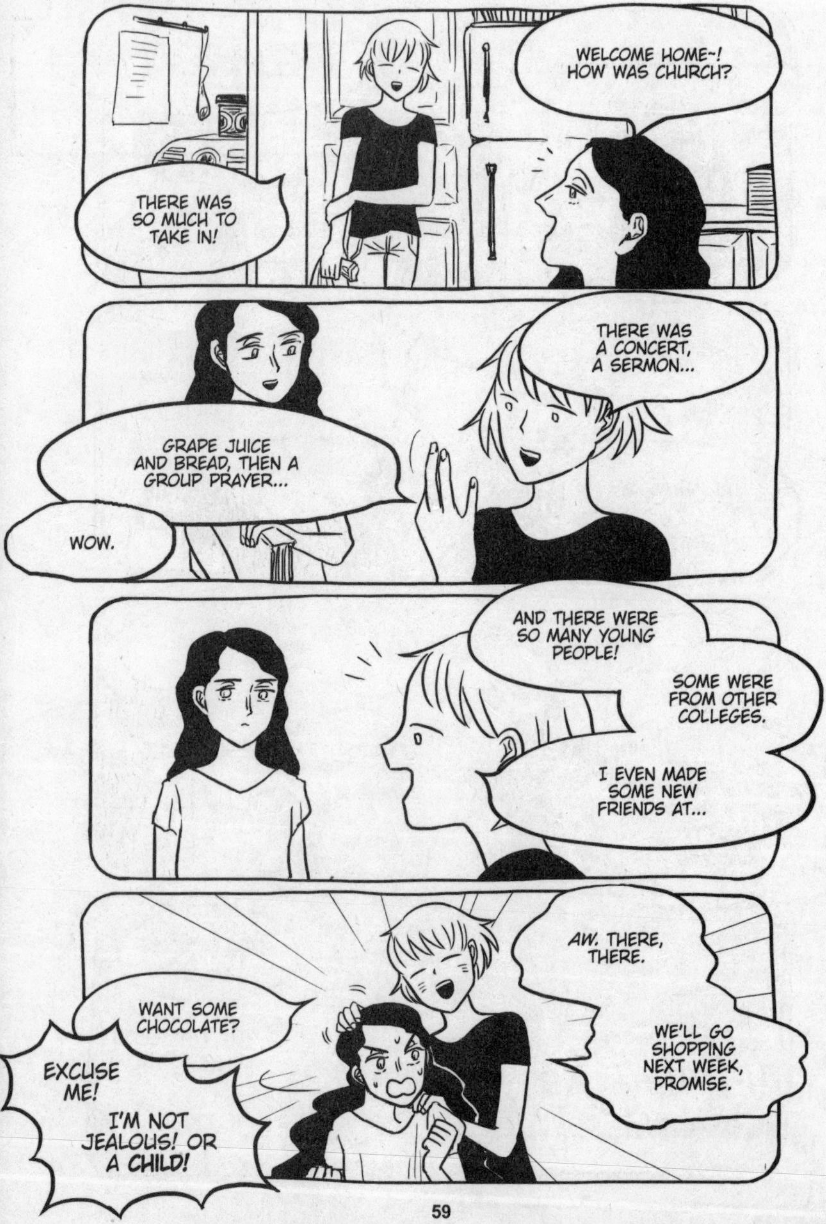
WELCOME HOME~! HOW WAS CHURCH?
THERE WAS SO MUCH TO TAKE IN!
THERE WAS A CONCERT, A SERMON...
GRAPE JUICE AND BREAD, THEN A GROUP PRAYER...
WOW.
AND THERE WERE SO MANY YOUNG PEOPLE!
SOME WERE FROM OTHER COLLEGES.
I EVEN MADE SOME NEW FRIENDS AT...
AW. THERE, THERE.
WE'LL GO SHOPPING NEXT WEEK, PROMISE.
WANT SOME CHOCOLATE?
EXCUSE ME!
I'M NOT JEALOUS! OR A CHILD!

PREPARATIONS

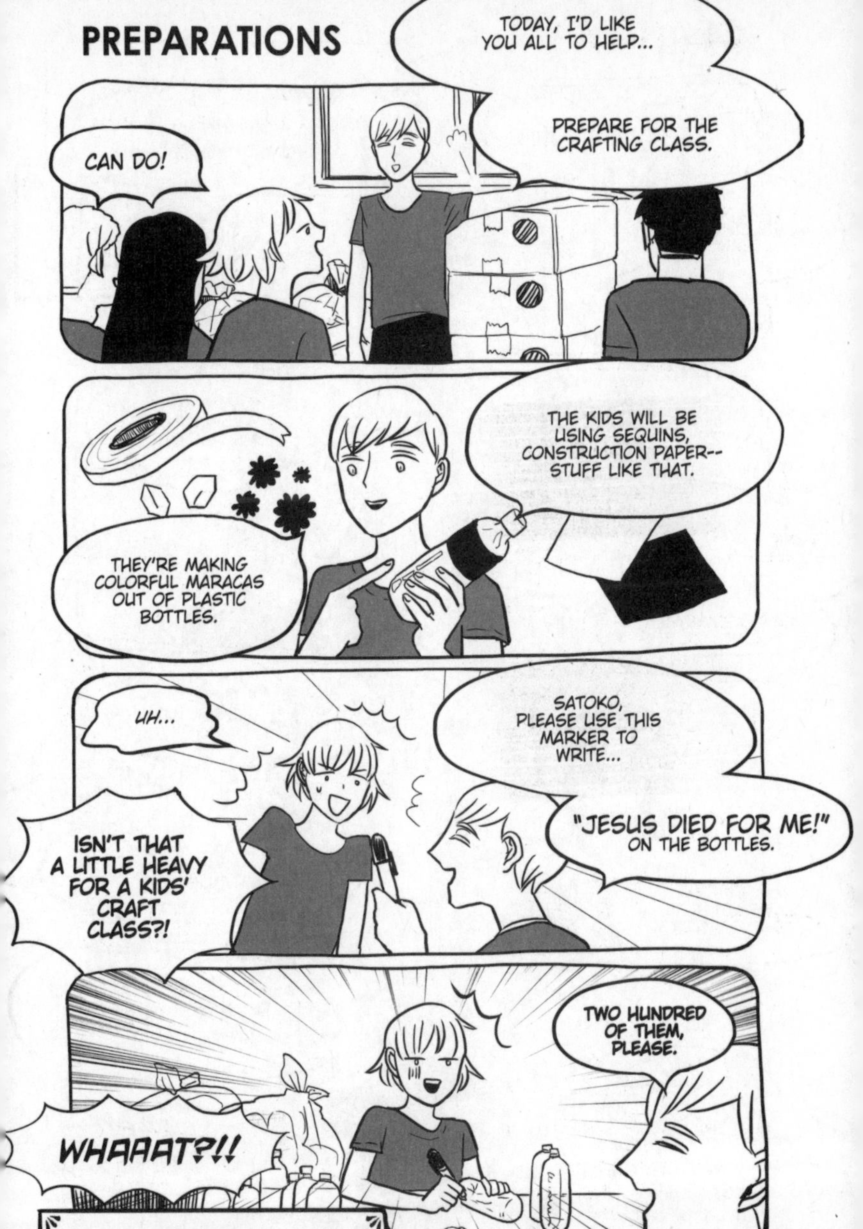
TODAY, I'D LIKE YOU ALL TO HELP...
PREPARE FOR THE CRAFTING CLASS.
CAN DO!
THE KIDS WILL BE USING SEQUINS, CONSTRUCTION PAPER--STUFF LIKE THAT.
THEY'RE MAKING COLORFUL MARACAS OUT OF PLASTIC BOTTLES.
SATOKO, PLEASE USE THIS MARKER TO WRITE...
"JESUS DIED FOR ME!" ON THE BOTTLES.
UH...
ISN'T THAT A LITTLE HEAVY FOR A KIDS' CRAFT CLASS?!
TWO HUNDRED OF THEM, PLEASE.
WHAAAT?!!
Satoko is dying for you!

GRANDMA

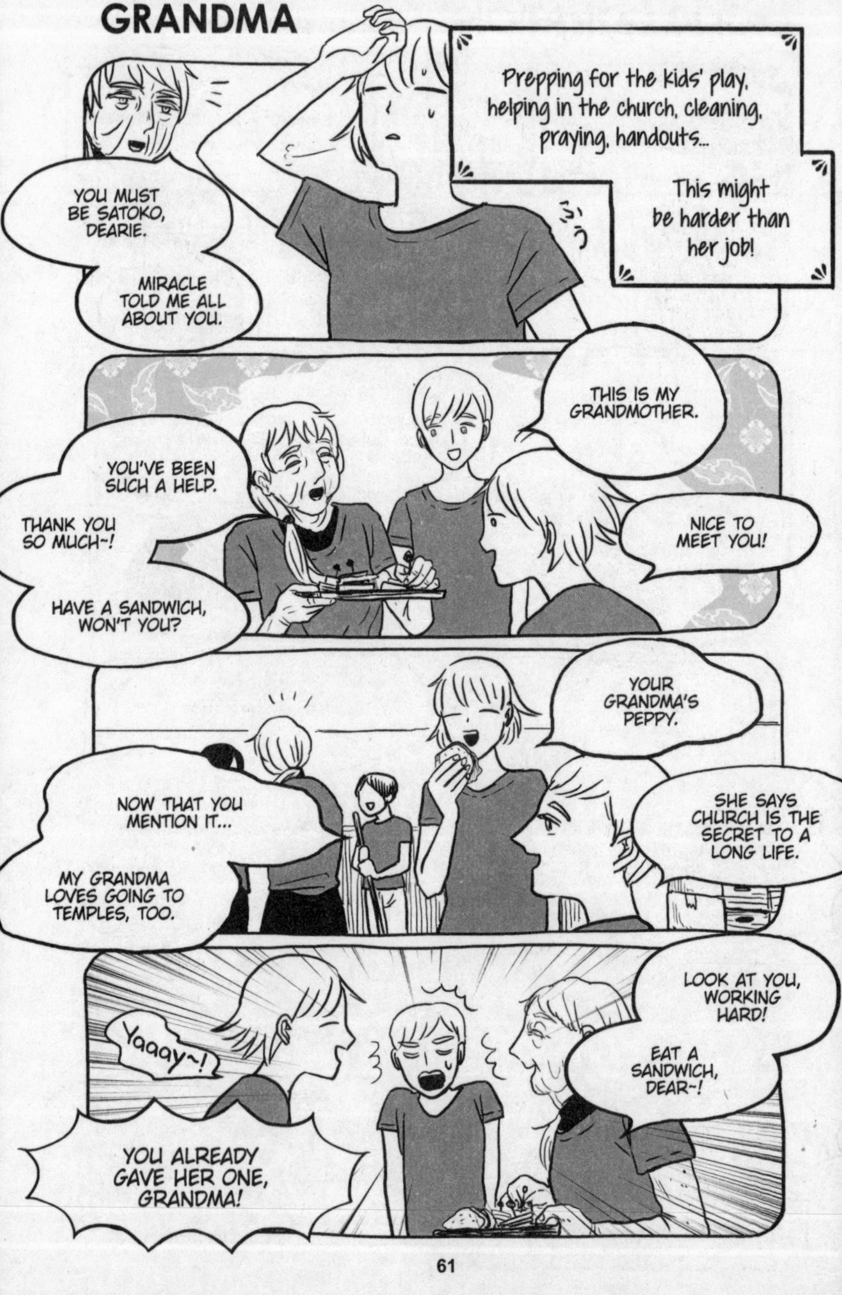
Prepping for the kids' play, helping in the church, cleaning, praying, handouts...
This might be harder than her job!
YOU MUST BE SATOKO, DEARIE.
MIRACLE TOLD ME ALL ABOUT YOU.
THIS IS MY GRANDMOTHER.
NICE TO MEET YOU!
YOU'VE BEEN SUCH A HELP.
THANK YOU SO MUCH~!
HAVE A SANDWICH, WON'T YOU?
YOUR GRANDMA'S PEPPY.
SHE SAYS CHURCH IS THE SECRET TO A LONG LIFE.
NOW THAT YOU MENTION IT...
MY GRANDMA LOVES GOING TO TEMPLES, TOO.
LOOK AT YOU, WORKING HARD!
EAT A SANDWICH, DEAR~!
Yaaay~!
YOU ALREADY GAVE HER ONE, GRANDMA!

FOOD DONATIONS

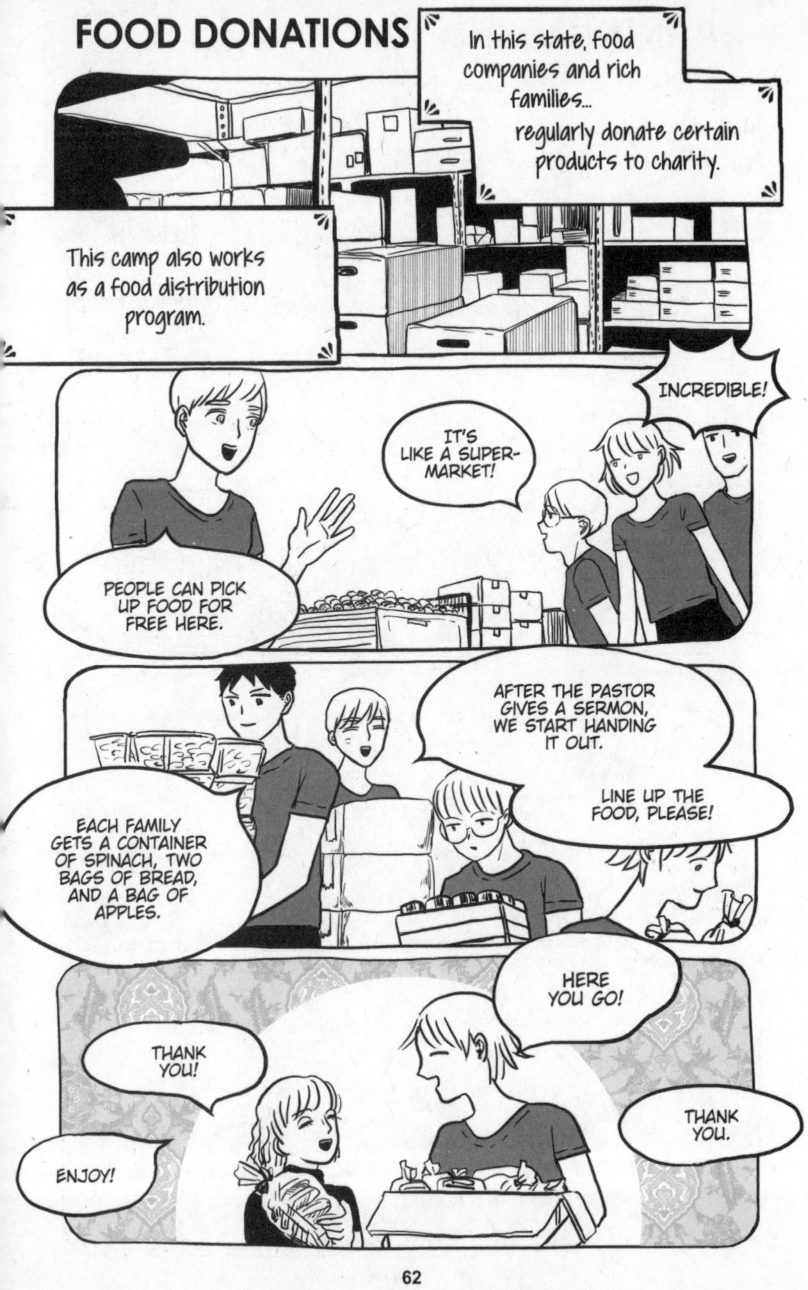
In this state, food companies and rich families...
regularly donate certain products to charity.
This camp also works as a food distribution program.
INCREDIBLE!
IT'S LIKE A SUPER-MARKET!
PEOPLE CAN PICK UP FOOD FOR FREE HERE.
AFTER THE PASTOR GIVES A SERMON, WE START HANDING IT OUT.
LINE UP THE FOOD, PLEASE!
EACH FAMILY GETS A CONTAINER OF SPINACH, TWO BAGS OF BREAD, AND A BAG OF APPLES.
HERE YOU GO!
THANK YOU.
THANK YOU!
ENJOY!

UNDERSTANDING

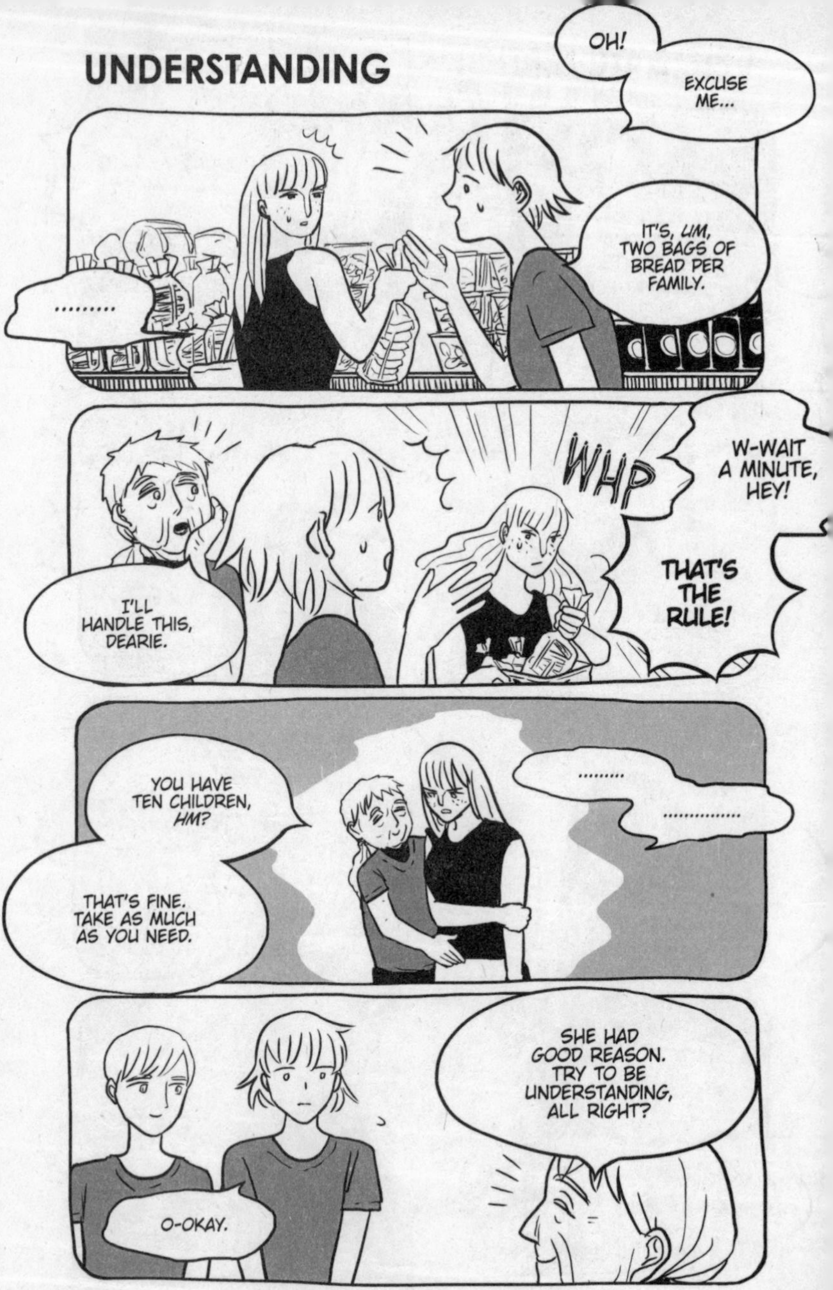
OH!
EXCUSE ME...
IT'S, *UM*, TWO BAGS OF BREAD PER FAMILY.
....
W-WAIT A MINUTE, HEY!
THAT'S THE RULE!
WHP
I'LL HANDLE THIS, DEARIE.
....
....
YOU HAVE TEN CHILDREN, *HM*?
THAT'S FINE. TAKE AS MUCH AS YOU NEED.
SHE HAD GOOD REASON. TRY TO BE UNDERSTANDING, ALL RIGHT?
O-OKAY.

VOCABULARY

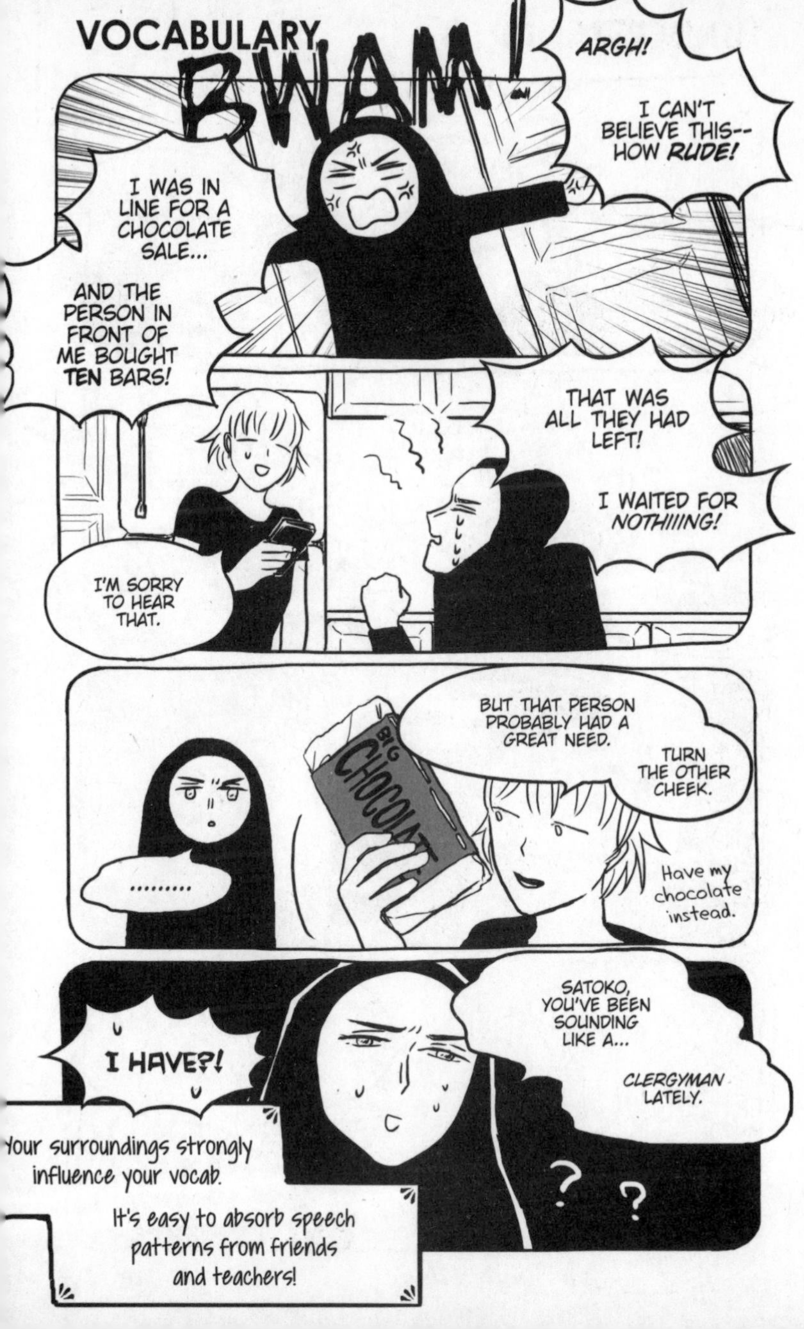
BWAM!
ARGH!
I CAN'T BELIEVE THIS-- HOW RUDE!
I WAS IN LINE FOR A CHOCOLATE SALE...
AND THE PERSON IN FRONT OF ME BOUGHT TEN BARS!
THAT WAS ALL THEY HAD LEFT!
I WAITED FOR NOTHIIIING!
I'M SORRY TO HEAR THAT.
BUT THAT PERSON PROBABLY HAD A GREAT NEED.
TURN THE OTHER CHEEK.
Have my chocolate instead.
BIG CHOCOLAT
....
SATOKO, YOU'VE BEEN SOUNDING LIKE A...
CLERGYMAN LATELY.
I HAVE?!
? ?
Your surroundings strongly influence your vocab.
It's easy to absorb speech patterns from friends and teachers!

FUR BOTTLE

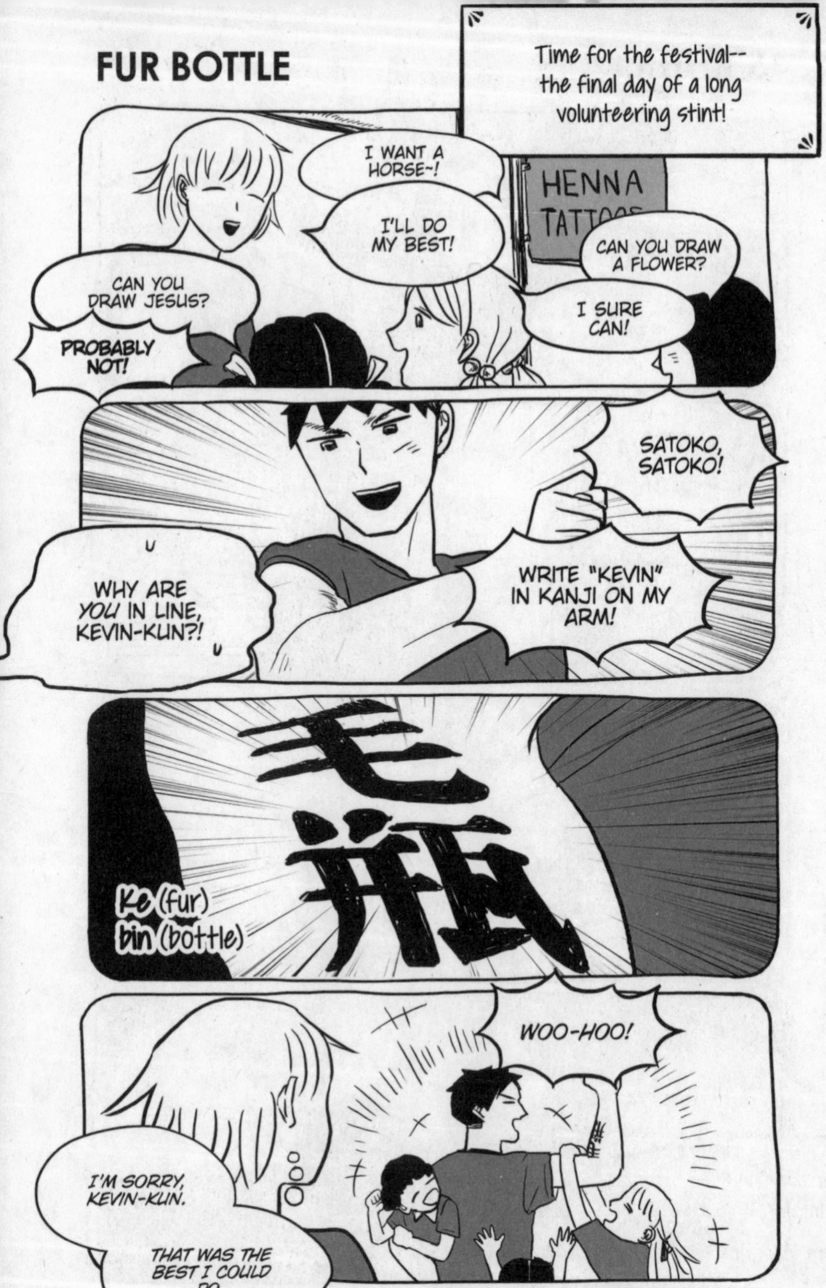

Time for the festival-- the final day of a long volunteering stint!
HENNA TATTOOS
CAN YOU DRAW A FLOWER?
I SURE CAN!
I WANT A HORSE~!
I'LL DO MY BEST!
CAN YOU DRAW JESUS?
PROBABLY NOT!
SATOKO, SATOKO!
WRITE "KEVIN" IN KANJI ON MY ARM!
WHY ARE *YOU* IN LINE, KEVIN-KUN?!
毛瓶
Ke (fur) bin (bottle)
WOO-HOO!
I'M SORRY, KEVIN-KUN.
THAT WAS THE BEST I COULD DO.

SHINING

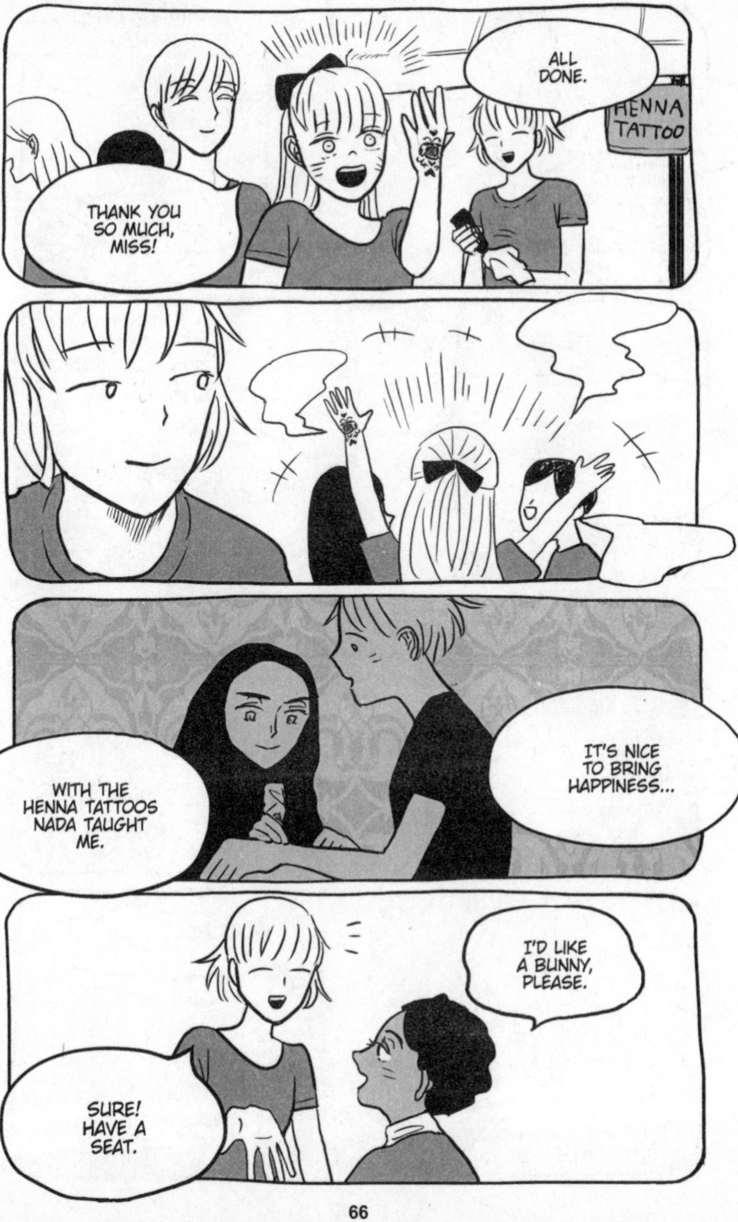
ALL DONE.
HENNA TATTOO
THANK YOU SO MUCH, MISS!
IT'S NICE TO BRING HAPPINESS...
WITH THE HENNA TATTOOS NADA TAUGHT ME.
I'D LIKE A BUNNY, PLEASE.
SURE! HAVE A SEAT.

WRAP PARTY

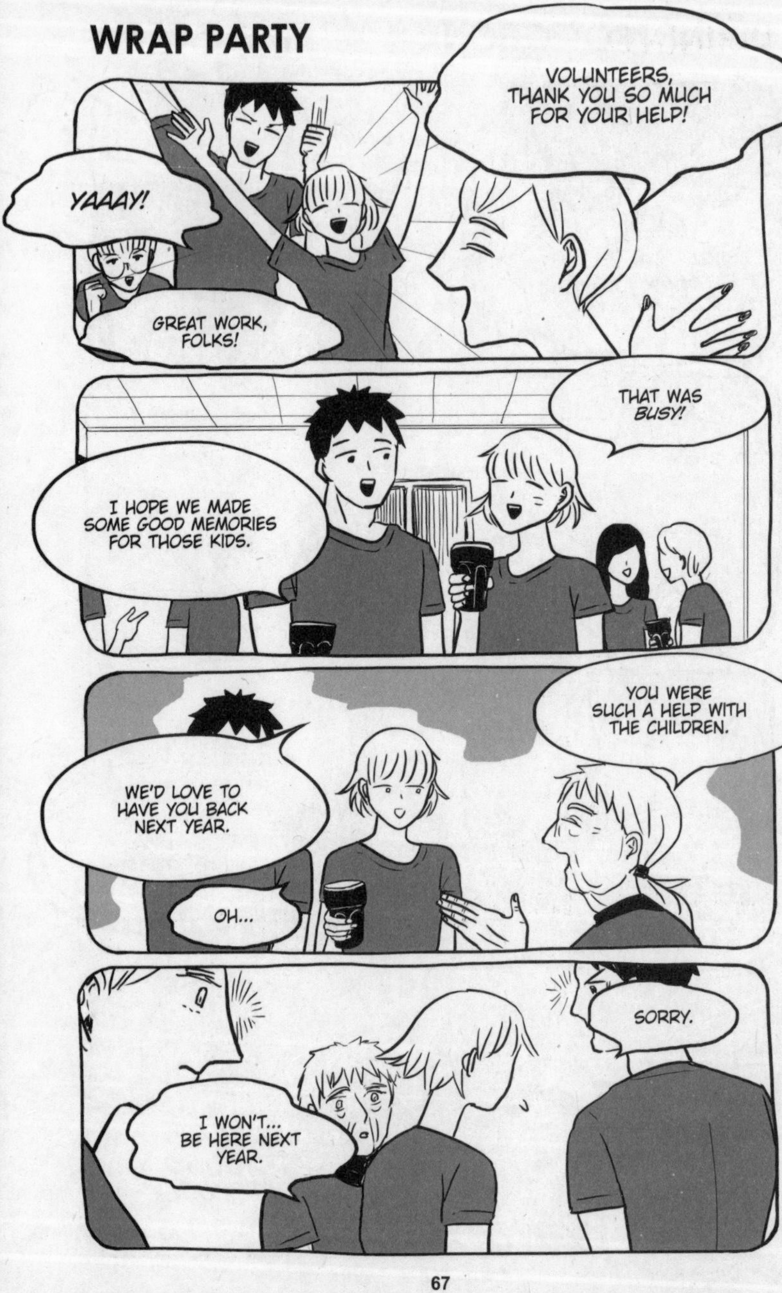
VOLUNTEERS, THANK YOU SO MUCH FOR YOUR HELP!
YAAAY!
GREAT WORK, FOLKS!
THAT WAS BUSY!
I HOPE WE MADE SOME GOOD MEMORIES FOR THOSE KIDS.
YOU WERE SUCH A HELP WITH THE CHILDREN.
WE'D LOVE TO HAVE YOU BACK NEXT YEAR.
OH...
SORRY.
I WON'T... BE HERE NEXT YEAR.

DIVINE PROTECTION

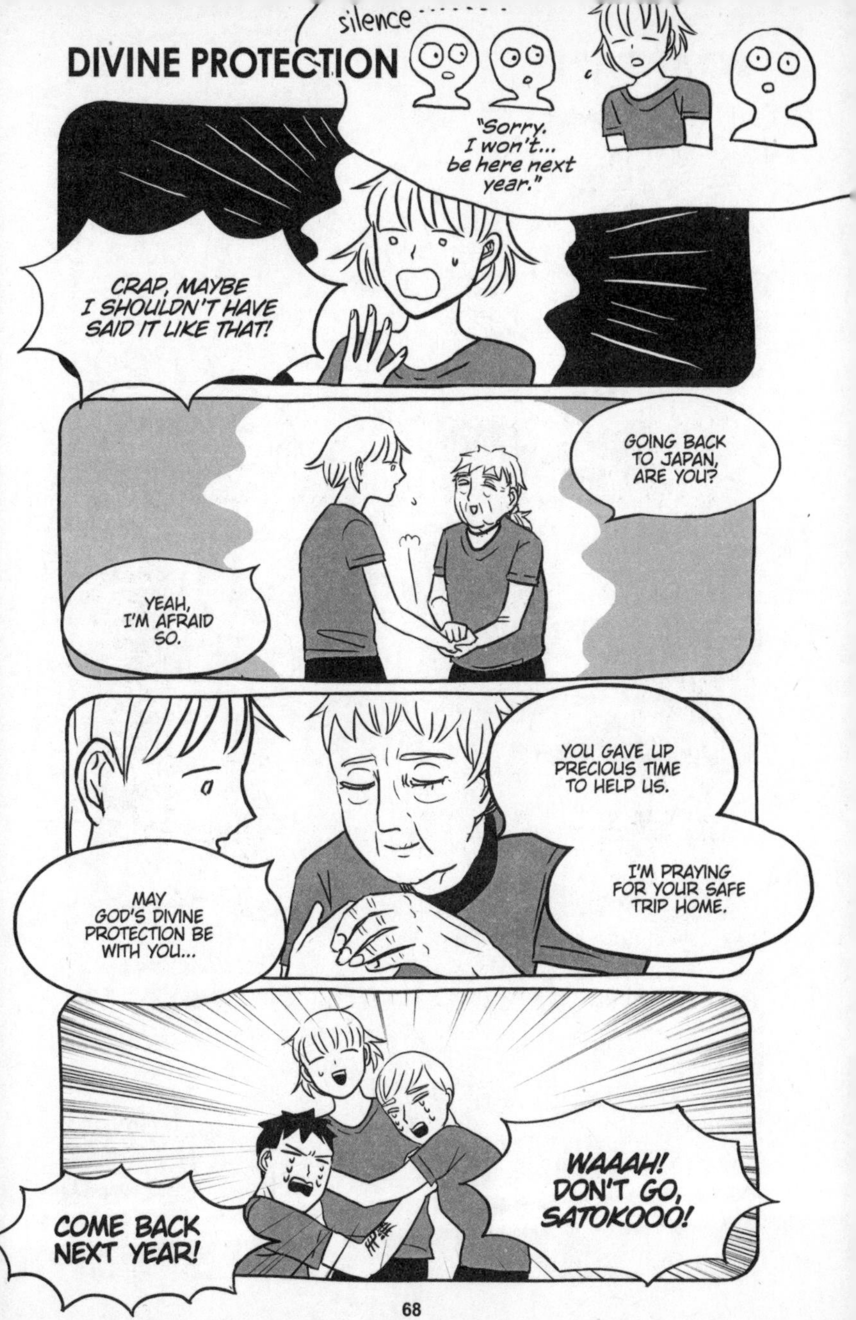
"Sorry. I won't... be here next year."
silence......
CRAP, MAYBE I SHOULDN'T HAVE SAID IT LIKE THAT!
GOING BACK TO JAPAN, ARE YOU?
YEAH, I'M AFRAID SO.
YOU GAVE UP PRECIOUS TIME TO HELP US.
I'M PRAYING FOR YOUR SAFE TRIP HOME.
MAY GOD'S DIVINE PROTECTION BE WITH YOU...
WAAAH! DON'T GO, SATOKOOO!
COME BACK NEXT YEAR!

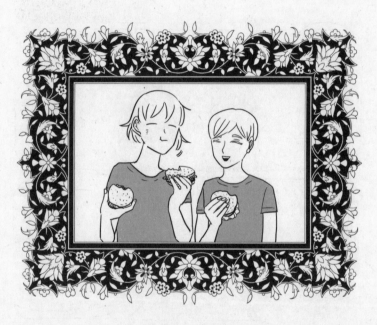

SATOKO AND NADA

Presented by Yupechika

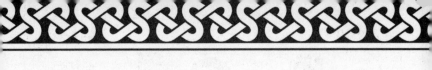

SATOKO AND NADA

Presented by Yupechika

SNOW

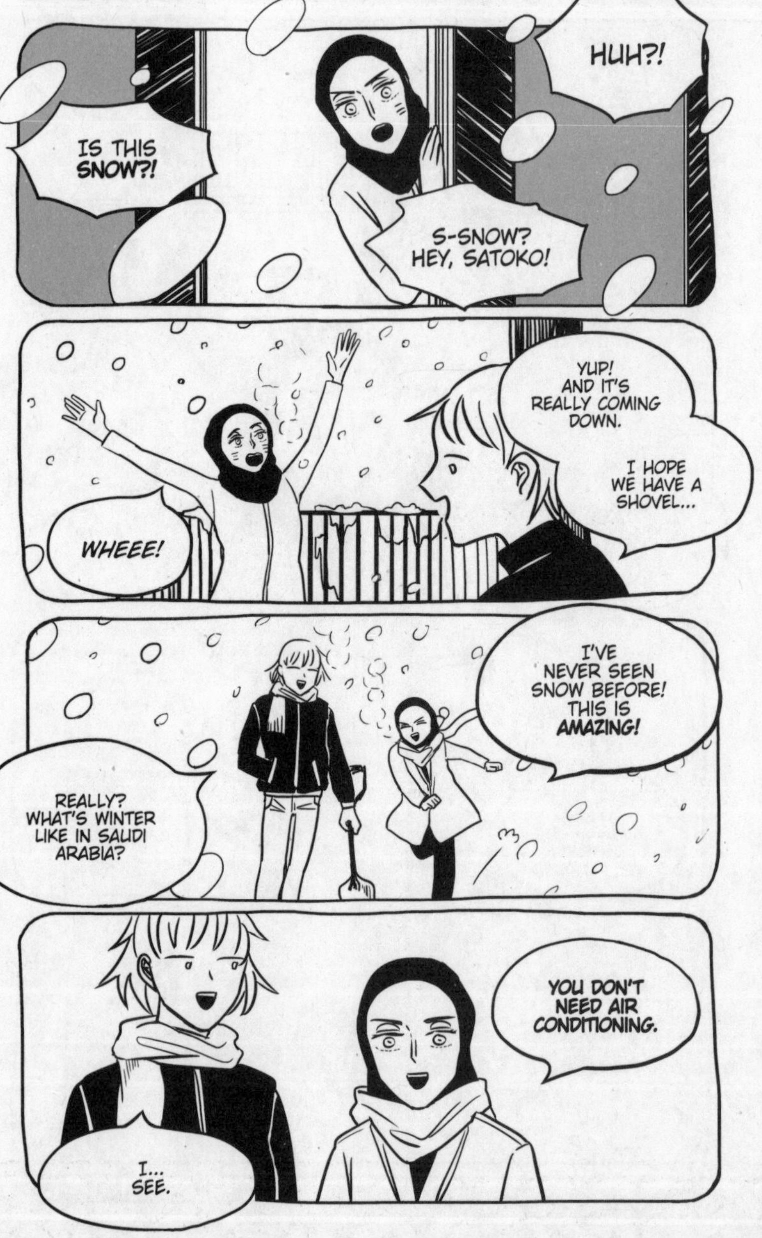
HUH?!
IS THIS SNOW?!
S-SNOW? HEY, SATOKO!
YUP! AND IT'S REALLY COMING DOWN.
I HOPE WE HAVE A SHOVEL...
WHEEE!
I'VE NEVER SEEN SNOW BEFORE! THIS IS AMAZING!
REALLY? WHAT'S WINTER LIKE IN SAUDI ARABIA?
YOU DON'T NEED AIR CONDITIONING.
I... SEE.

NADA AND THE SNOW

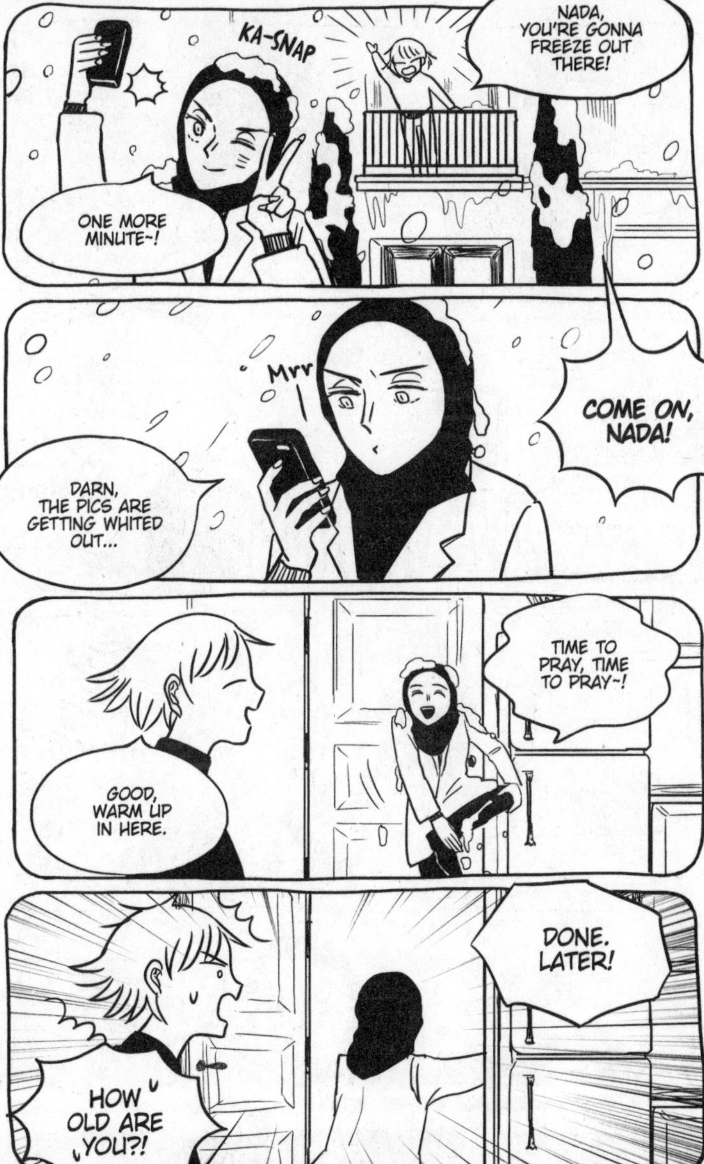
NADA, YOU'RE GONNA FREEZE OUT THERE!
KA-SNAP
ONE MORE MINUTE~!
COME ON, NADA!
Mrr
DARN, THE PICS ARE GETTING WHITED OUT...
TIME TO PRAY, TIME TO PRAY~!
GOOD, WARM UP IN HERE.
DONE. LATER!
HOW OLD ARE YOU?!

RESERVATION

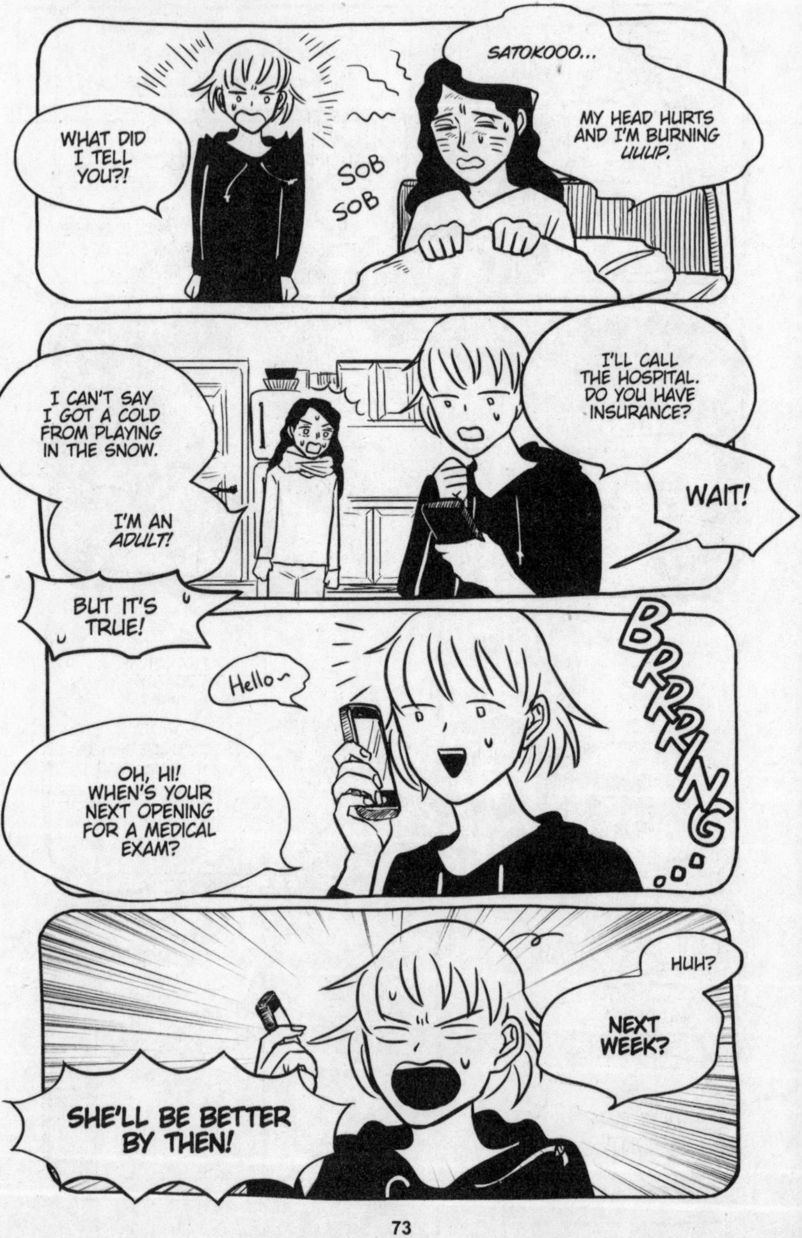
SATOKOOO...
MY HEAD HURTS AND I'M BURNING *UUUP.*
SOB SOB
WHAT DID I TELL YOU?!
I'LL CALL THE HOSPITAL. DO YOU HAVE INSURANCE?
WAIT!
I CAN'T SAY I GOT A COLD FROM PLAYING IN THE SNOW.
I'M AN *ADULT!*
BUT IT'S TRUE!
BRRRING
Hello~
OH, HI! WHEN'S YOUR NEXT OPENING FOR A MEDICAL EXAM?
HUH?
NEXT WEEK?
SHE'LL BE BETTER BY THEN!

EXAMINATION FEE

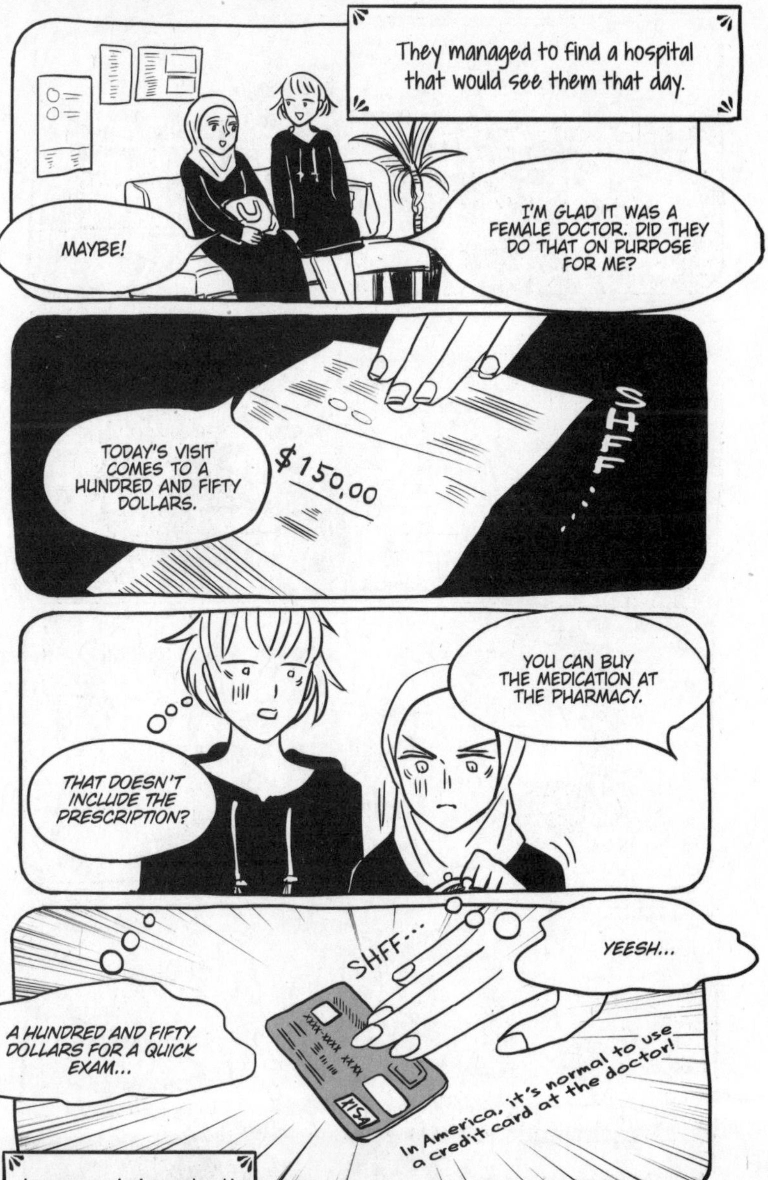

They managed to find a hospital that would see them that day.
I'M GLAD IT WAS A FEMALE DOCTOR. DID THEY DO THAT ON PURPOSE FOR ME?
MAYBE!
SHFF...
TODAY'S VISIT COMES TO A HUNDRED AND FIFTY DOLLARS.
$150.00
YOU CAN BUY THE MEDICATION AT THE PHARMACY.
THAT DOESN'T INCLUDE THE PRESCRIPTION?
YEESH...
SHFF...
A HUNDRED AND FIFTY DOLLARS FOR A QUICK EXAM...
In America, it's normal to use a credit card at the doctor!
Insurance is important!

SIZE

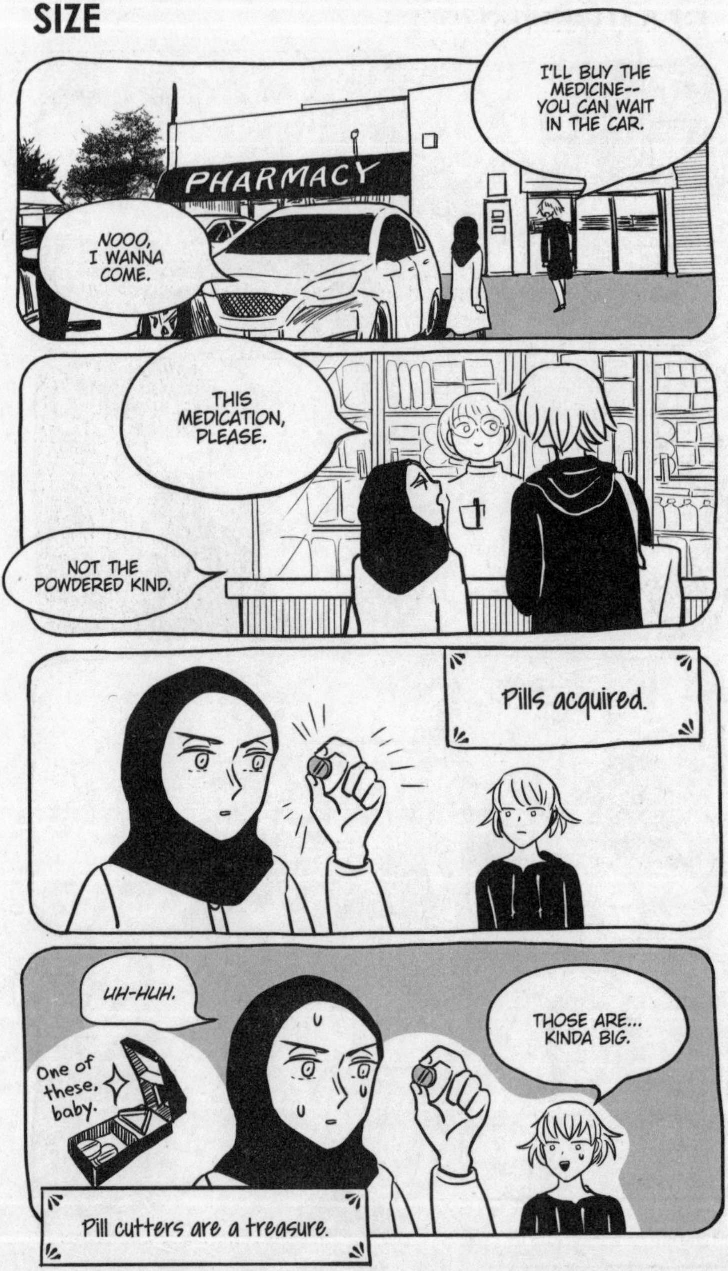
I'LL BUY THE MEDICINE-- YOU CAN WAIT IN THE CAR.
PHARMACY
NOOO, I WANNA COME.
THIS MEDICATION, PLEASE.
NOT THE POWDERED KIND.
Pills acquired.
THOSE ARE... KINDA BIG.
UH-HUH.
One of these, baby.
Pill cutters are a treasure.

DOCTOR EGO

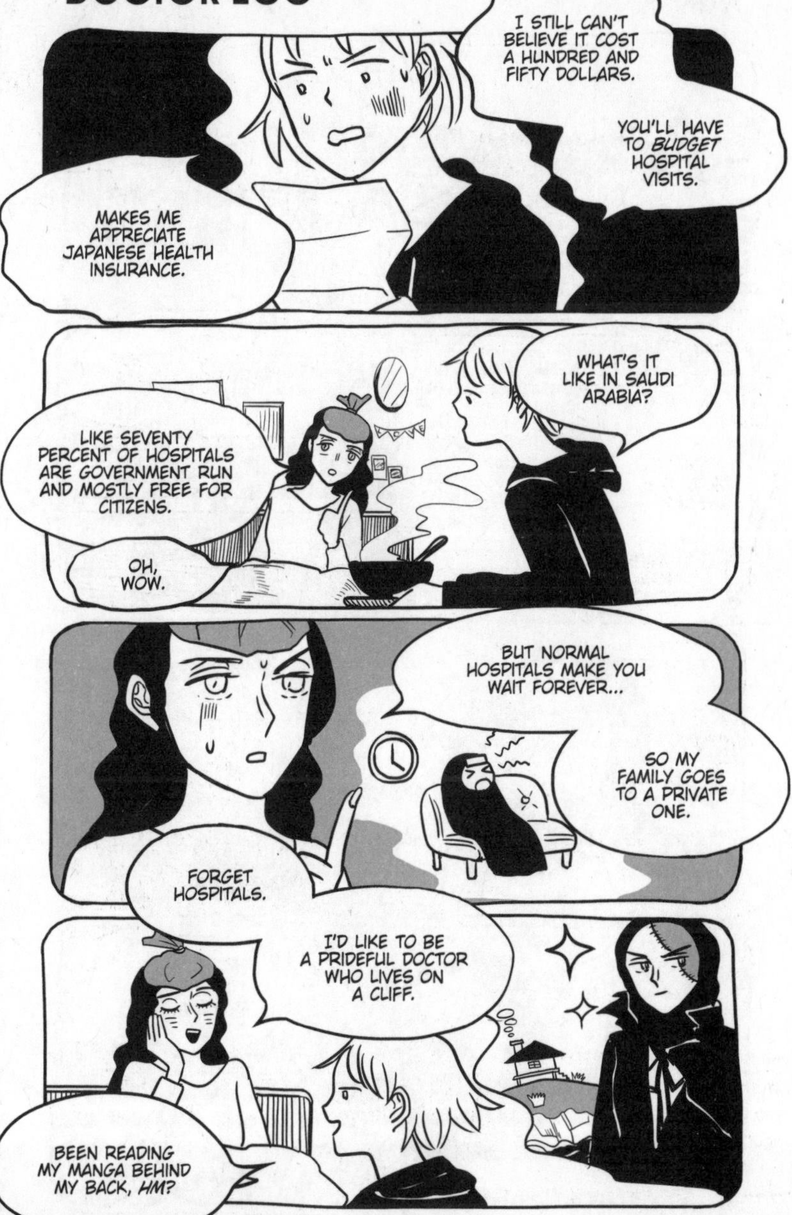
I STILL CAN'T BELIEVE IT COST A HUNDRED AND FIFTY DOLLARS.
YOU'LL HAVE TO *BUDGET* HOSPITAL VISITS.
MAKES ME APPRECIATE JAPANESE HEALTH INSURANCE.
WHAT'S IT LIKE IN SAUDI ARABIA?
LIKE SEVENTY PERCENT OF HOSPITALS ARE GOVERNMENT RUN AND MOSTLY FREE FOR CITIZENS.
OH, WOW.
BUT NORMAL HOSPITALS MAKE YOU WAIT FOREVER...
SO MY FAMILY GOES TO A PRIVATE ONE.
FORGET HOSPITALS.
I'D LIKE TO BE A PRIDEFUL DOCTOR WHO LIVES ON A CLIFF.
BEEN READING MY MANGA BEHIND MY BACK, *HM*?

MASK

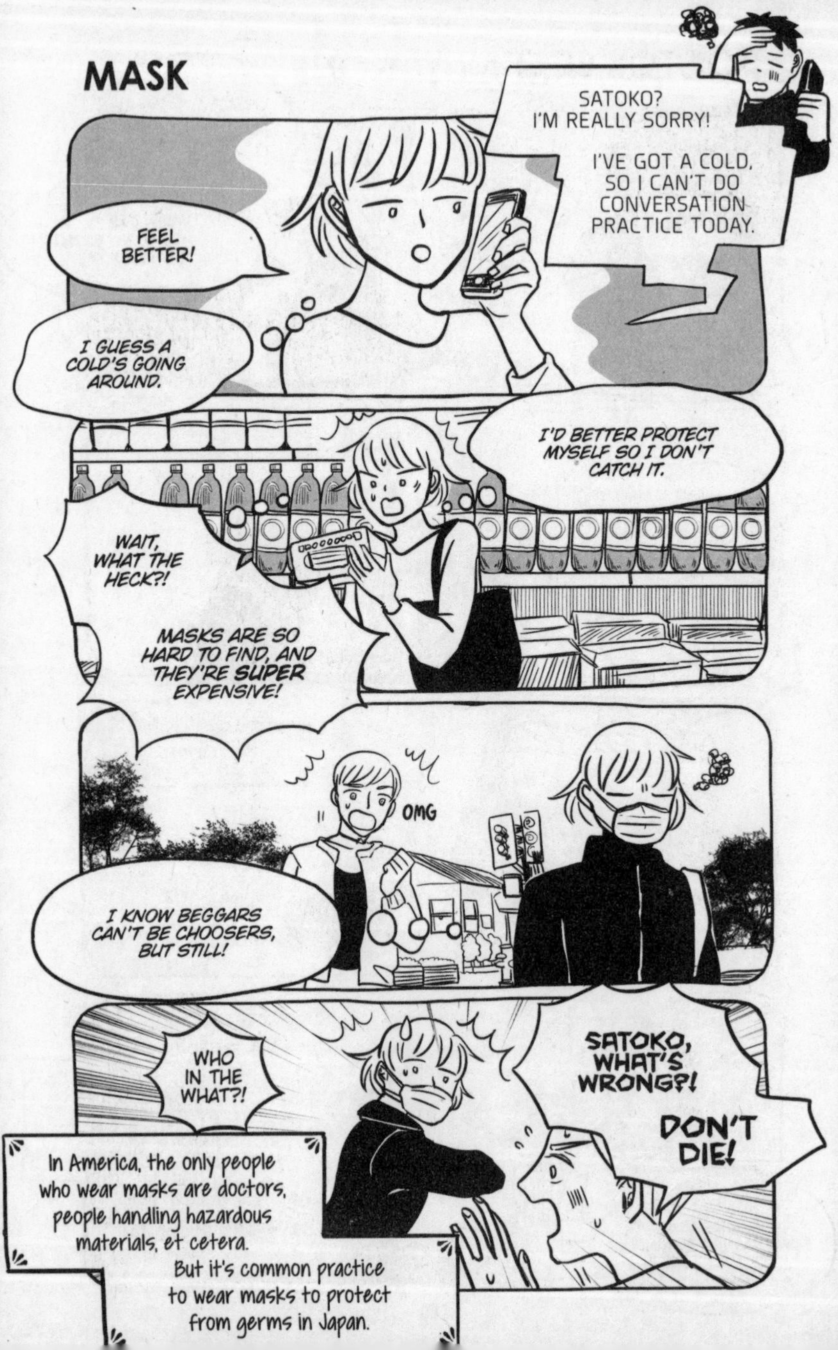
SATOKO? I'M REALLY SORRY!
I'VE GOT A COLD, SO I CAN'T DO CONVERSATION PRACTICE TODAY.
FEEL BETTER!
I GUESS A COLD'S GOING AROUND.
I'D BETTER PROTECT MYSELF SO I DON'T CATCH IT.
WAIT, WHAT THE HECK?!
MASKS ARE SO HARD TO FIND, AND THEY'RE SUPER EXPENSIVE!
OMG
I KNOW BEGGARS CAN'T BE CHOOSERS, BUT STILL!
SATOKO, WHAT'S WRONG?!
DON'T DIE!
WHO IN THE WHAT?!
In America, the only people who wear masks are doctors, people handling hazardous materials, et cetera.
But it's common practice to wear masks to protect from germs in Japan.

PRAYING WITH A LITTLE ONE

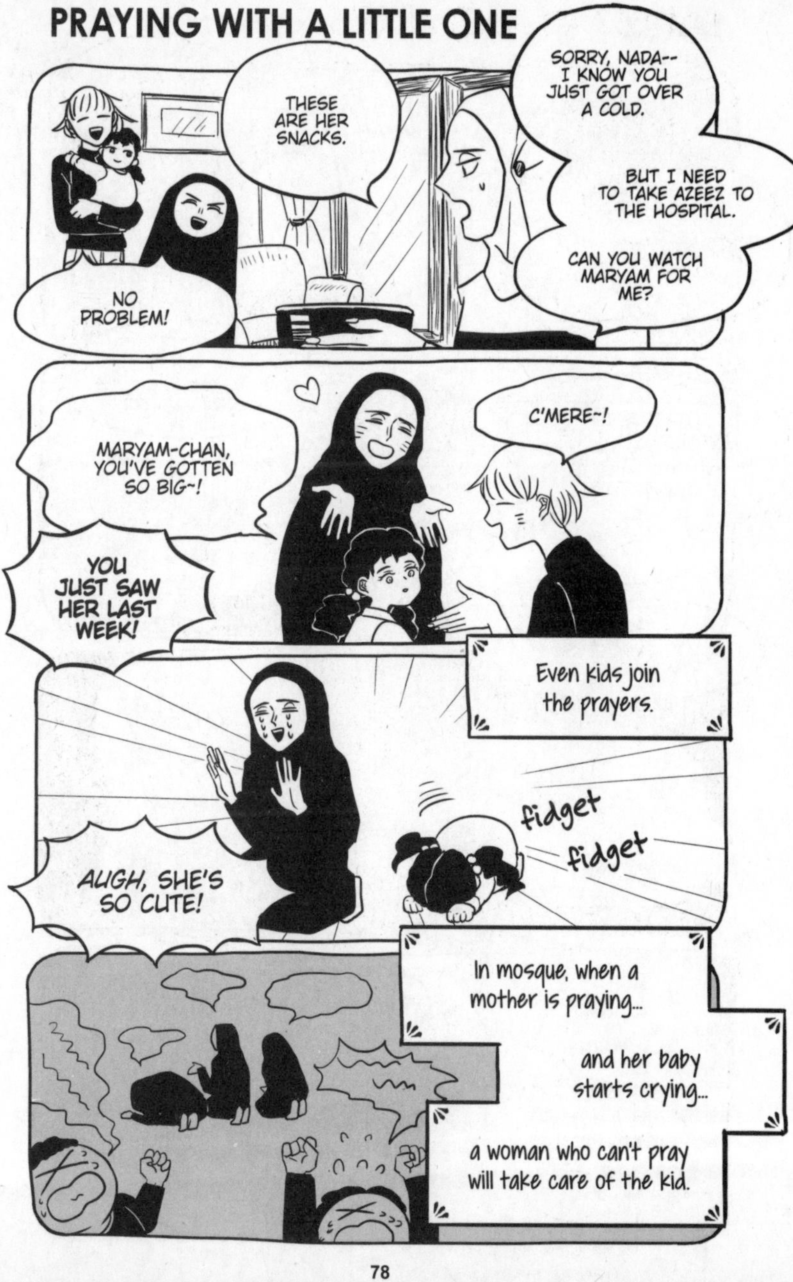
SORRY, NADA-- I KNOW YOU JUST GOT OVER A COLD.
BUT I NEED TO TAKE AZEEZ TO THE HOSPITAL.
CAN YOU WATCH MARYAM FOR ME?
THESE ARE HER SNACKS.
NO PROBLEM!
C'MERE~!
MARYAM-CHAN, YOU'VE GOTTEN SO BIG~!
YOU JUST SAW HER LAST WEEK!
Even kids join the prayers.
fidget
fidget
AUGH, SHE'S SO CUTE!
In mosque, when a mother is praying...
and her baby starts crying...
a woman who can't pray will take care of the kid.

PAKEEZAH AND AZEEZ

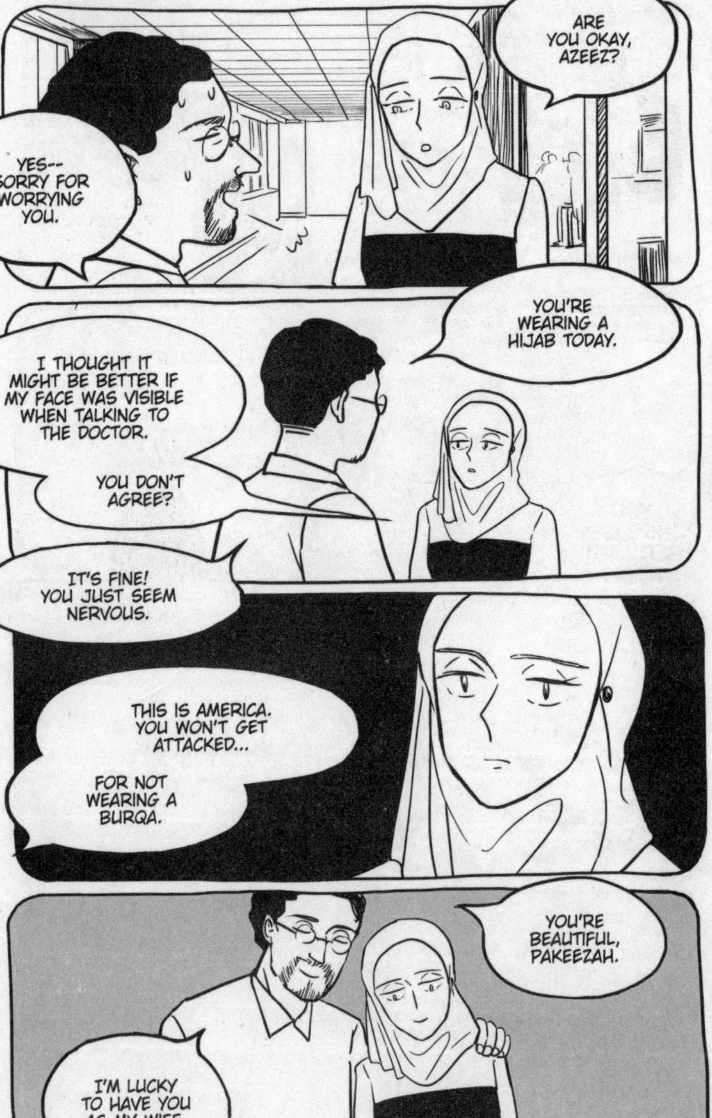
ARE YOU OKAY, AZEEZ?
YES-- SORRY FOR WORRYING YOU.
YOU'RE WEARING A HIJAB TODAY.
I THOUGHT IT MIGHT BE BETTER IF MY FACE WAS VISIBLE WHEN TALKING TO THE DOCTOR.
YOU DON'T AGREE?
IT'S FINE! YOU JUST SEEM NERVOUS.
THIS IS AMERICA. YOU WON'T GET ATTACKED...
FOR NOT WEARING A BURQA.
YOU'RE BEAUTIFUL, PAKEEZAH.
I'M LUCKY TO HAVE YOU AS MY WIFE.

DUAL CITIZENSHIP

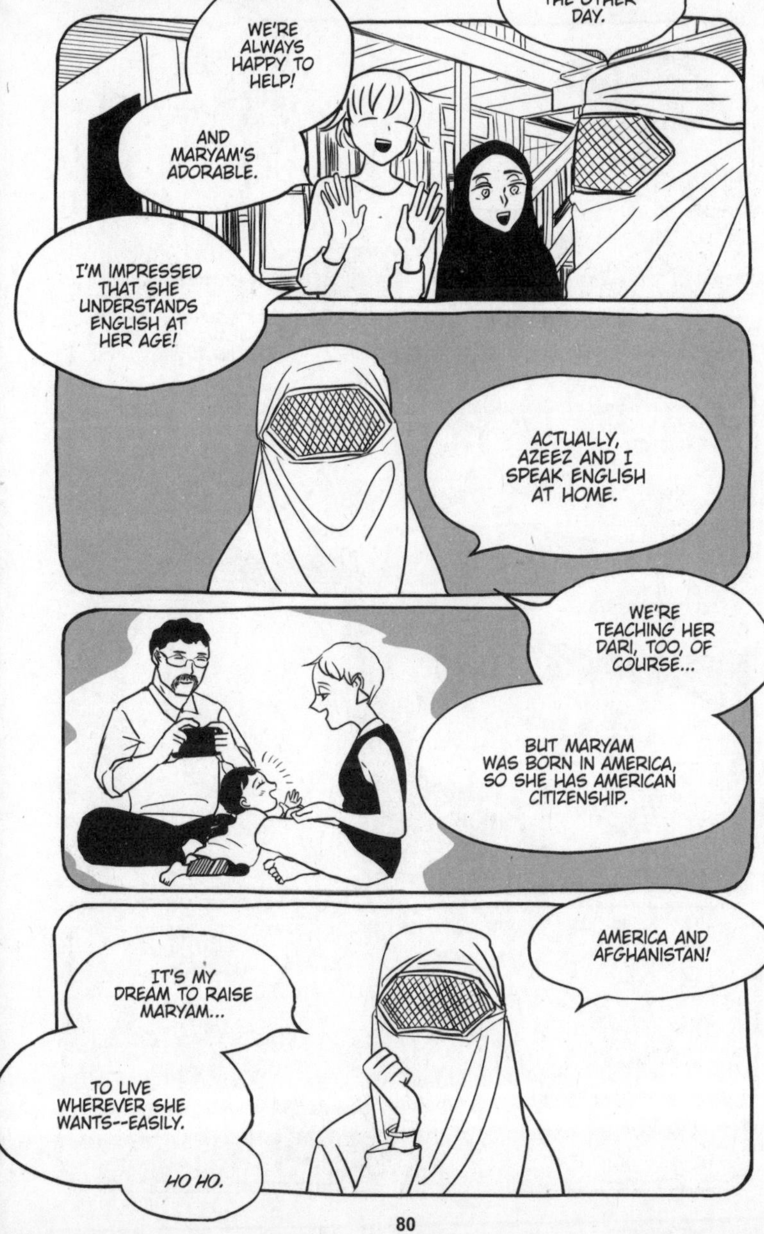
THANKS FOR THE OTHER DAY.
WE'RE ALWAYS HAPPY TO HELP!
AND MARYAM'S ADORABLE.
I'M IMPRESSED THAT SHE UNDERSTANDS ENGLISH AT HER AGE!
ACTUALLY, AZEEZ AND I SPEAK ENGLISH AT HOME.
WE'RE TEACHING HER DARI, TOO, OF COURSE...
BUT MARYAM WAS BORN IN AMERICA, SO SHE HAS AMERICAN CITIZENSHIP.
AMERICA AND AFGHANISTAN!
IT'S MY DREAM TO RAISE MARYAM...
TO LIVE WHEREVER SHE WANTS--EASILY.
HO HO.

HOMELAND

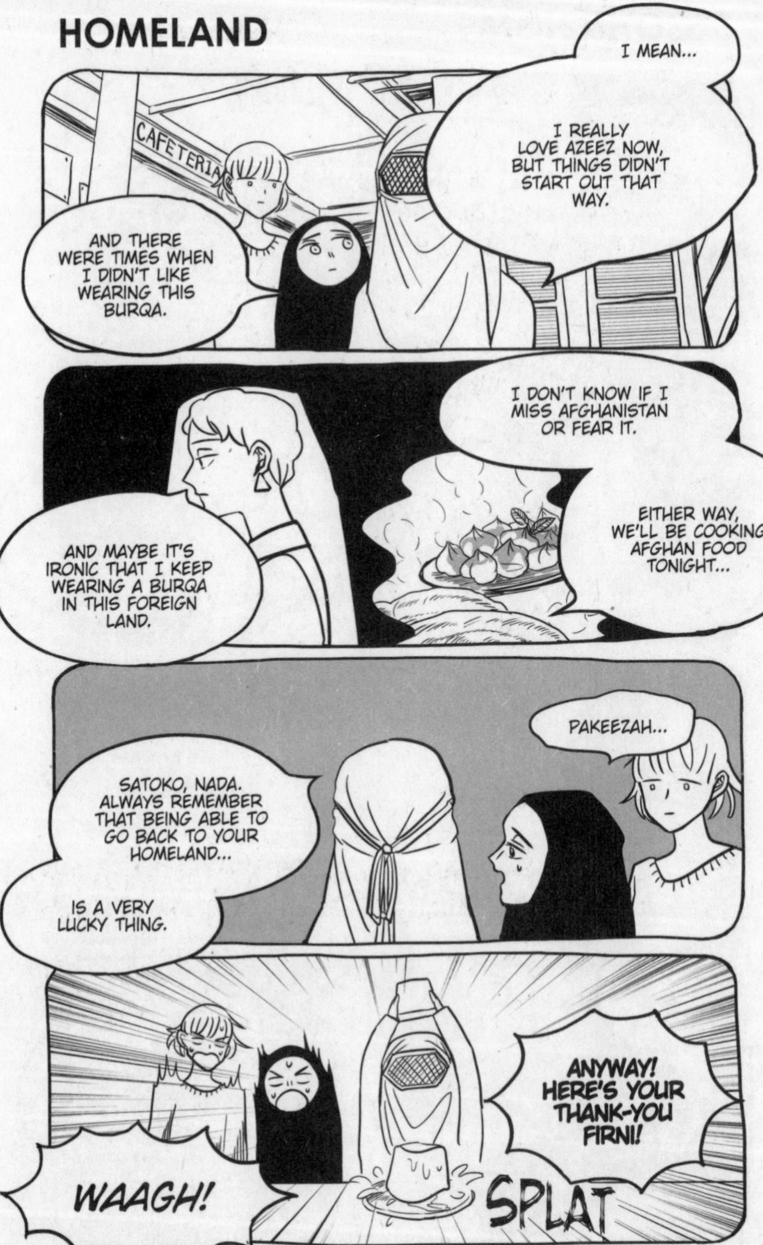
I MEAN...
I REALLY LOVE AZEEZ NOW, BUT THINGS DIDN'T START OUT THAT WAY.
AND THERE WERE TIMES WHEN I DIDN'T LIKE WEARING THIS BURQA.
I DON'T KNOW IF I MISS AFGHANISTAN OR FEAR IT.
EITHER WAY, WE'LL BE COOKING AFGHAN FOOD TONIGHT...
AND MAYBE IT'S IRONIC THAT I KEEP WEARING A BURQA IN THIS FOREIGN LAND.
PAKEEZAH...
SATOKO, NADA. ALWAYS REMEMBER THAT BEING ABLE TO GO BACK TO YOUR HOMELAND...
IS A VERY LUCKY THING.
ANYWAY! HERE'S YOUR THANK-YOU FIRNI!
SPLAT
WAAGH!

※ *A milk-based Afghan dessert--check out the recipe in Volume 1!*

SECOND HOME

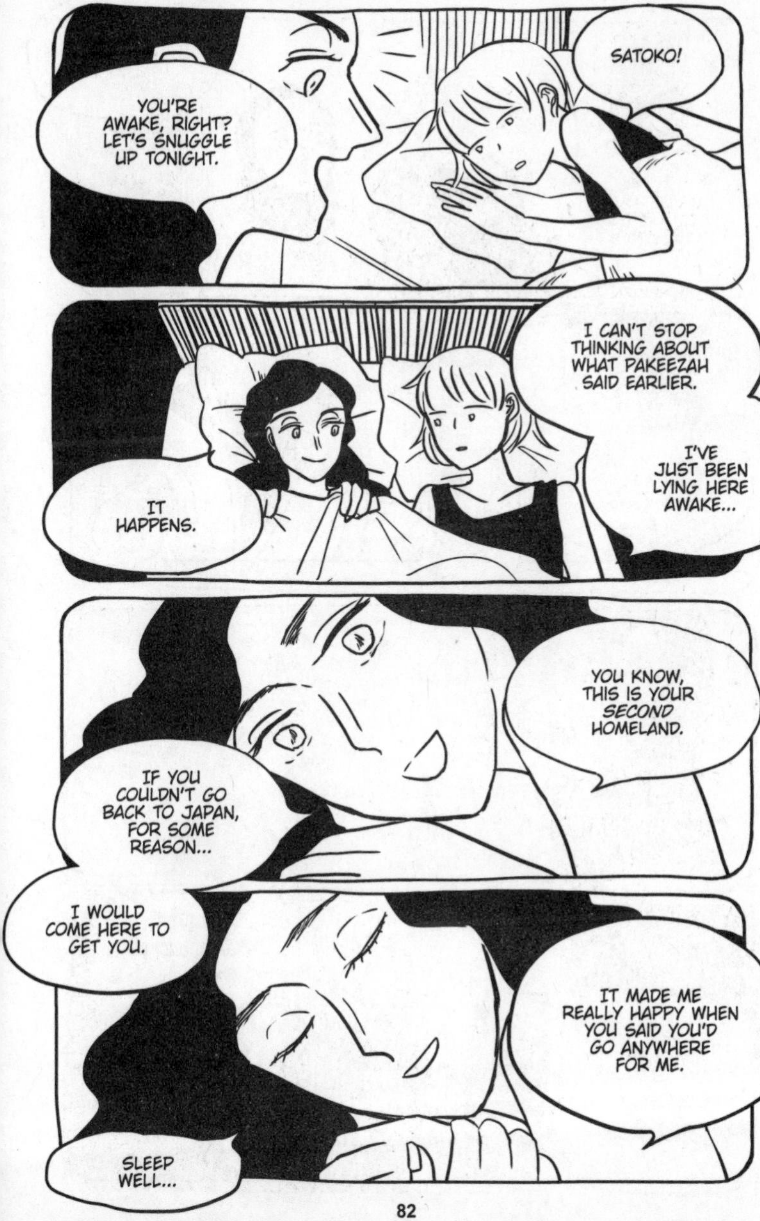
SATOKO!
YOU'RE AWAKE, RIGHT? LET'S SNUGGLE UP TONIGHT.
I CAN'T STOP THINKING ABOUT WHAT PAKEEZAH SAID EARLIER.
I'VE JUST BEEN LYING HERE AWAKE...
IT HAPPENS.
YOU KNOW, THIS IS YOUR *SECOND* HOMELAND.
IF YOU COULDN'T GO BACK TO JAPAN, FOR SOME REASON...
I WOULD COME HERE TO GET YOU.
IT MADE ME REALLY HAPPY WHEN YOU SAID YOU'D GO ANYWHERE FOR ME.
SLEEP WELL...

BACK WE GO

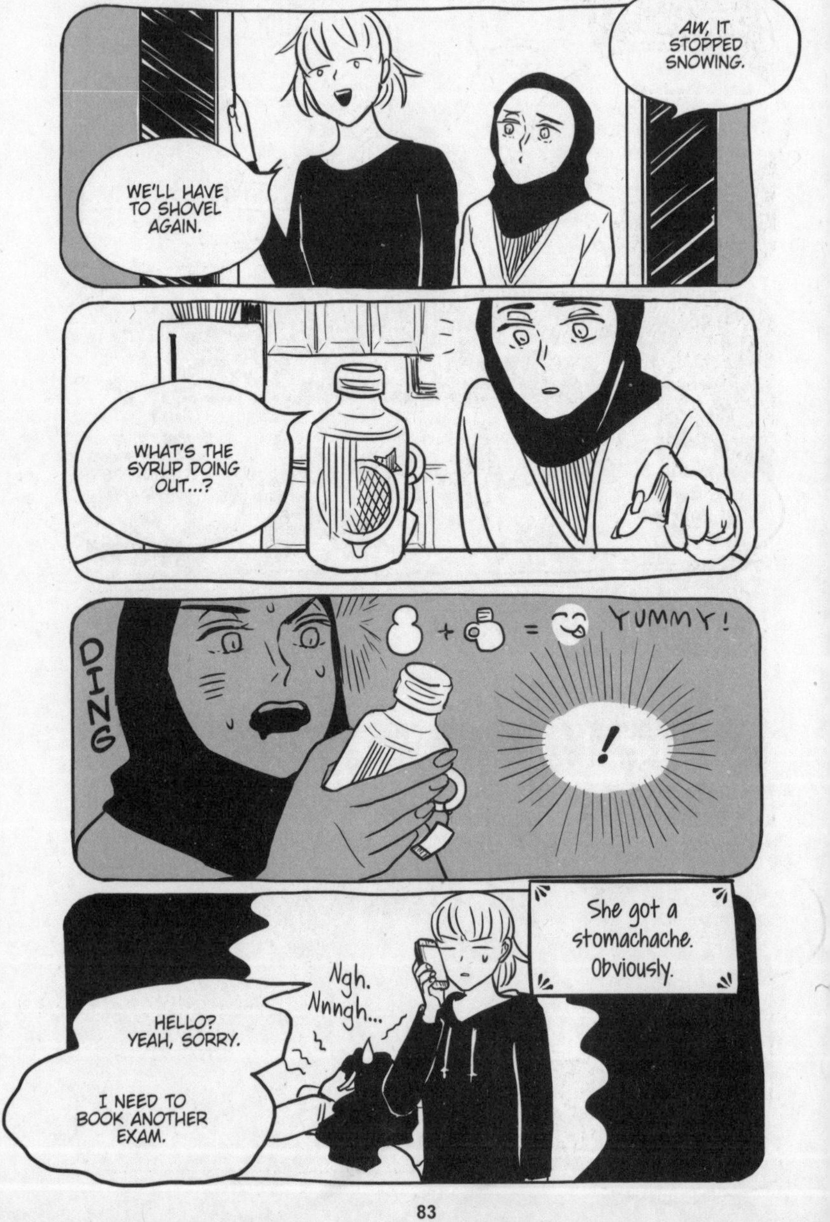

AW, IT STOPPED SNOWING.
WE'LL HAVE TO SHOVEL AGAIN.
WHAT'S THE SYRUP DOING OUT...?
YUMMY!
DING
!
She got a stomachache. Obviously.
Ngh. Nnngh...
HELLO? YEAH, SORRY.
I NEED TO BOOK ANOTHER EXAM.

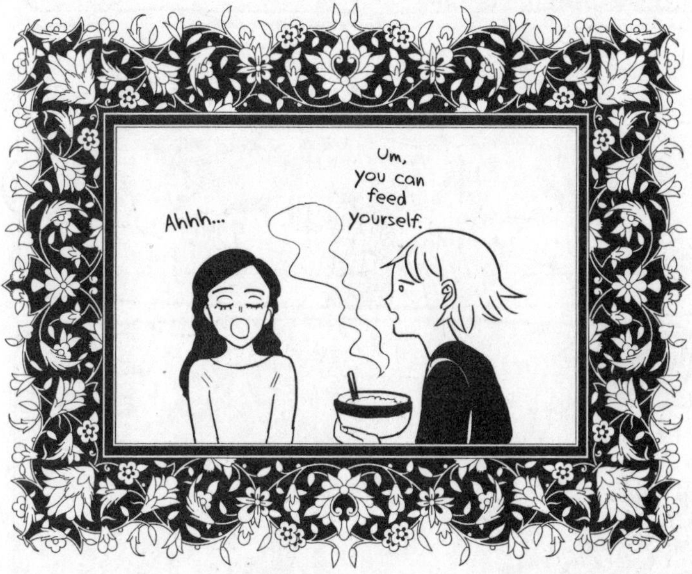

Um, you can feed yourself.
Ahhh...

SATOKO AND NADA

Presented by Yupechika

LUCK

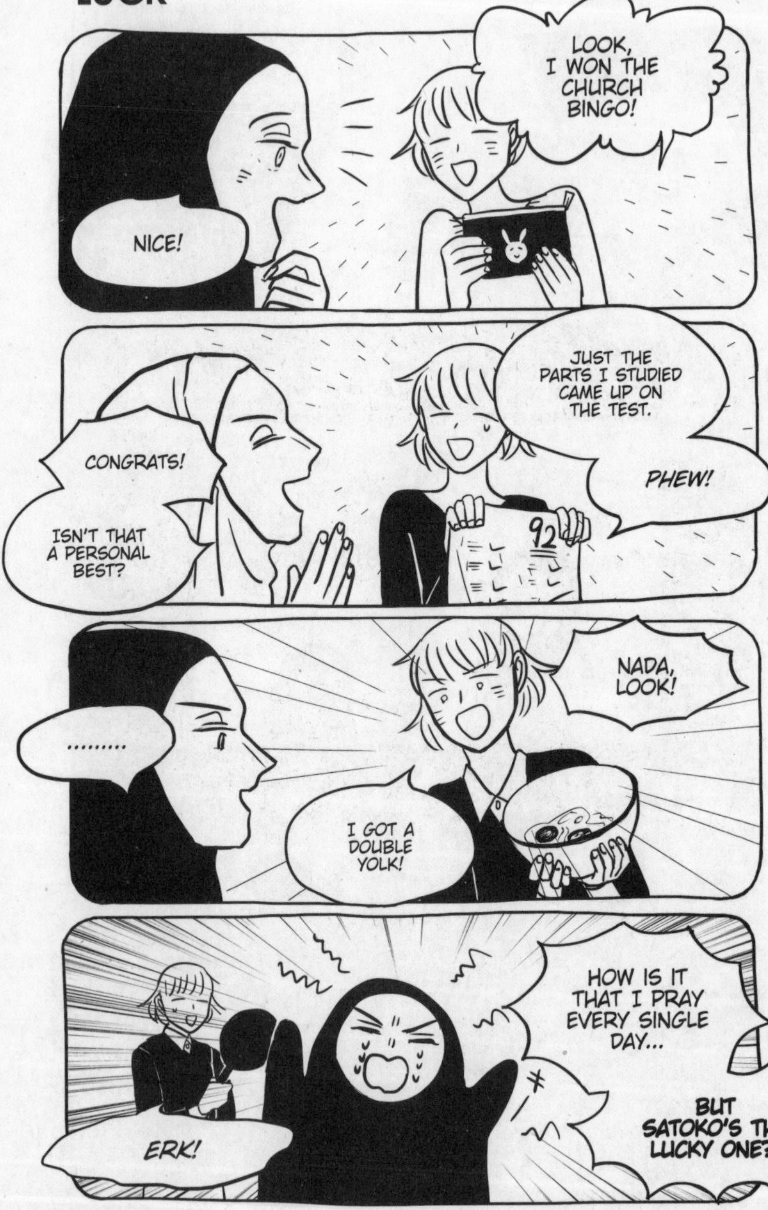
LOOK, I WON THE CHURCH BINGO!
NICE!
JUST THE PARTS I STUDIED CAME UP ON THE TEST.
PHEW!
92
CONGRATS!
ISN'T THAT A PERSONAL BEST?
NADA, LOOK!
I GOT A DOUBLE YOLK!
....
HOW IS IT THAT I PRAY EVERY SINGLE DAY...
BUT SATOKO'S THE LUCKY ONE?!
ERK!

TESTS

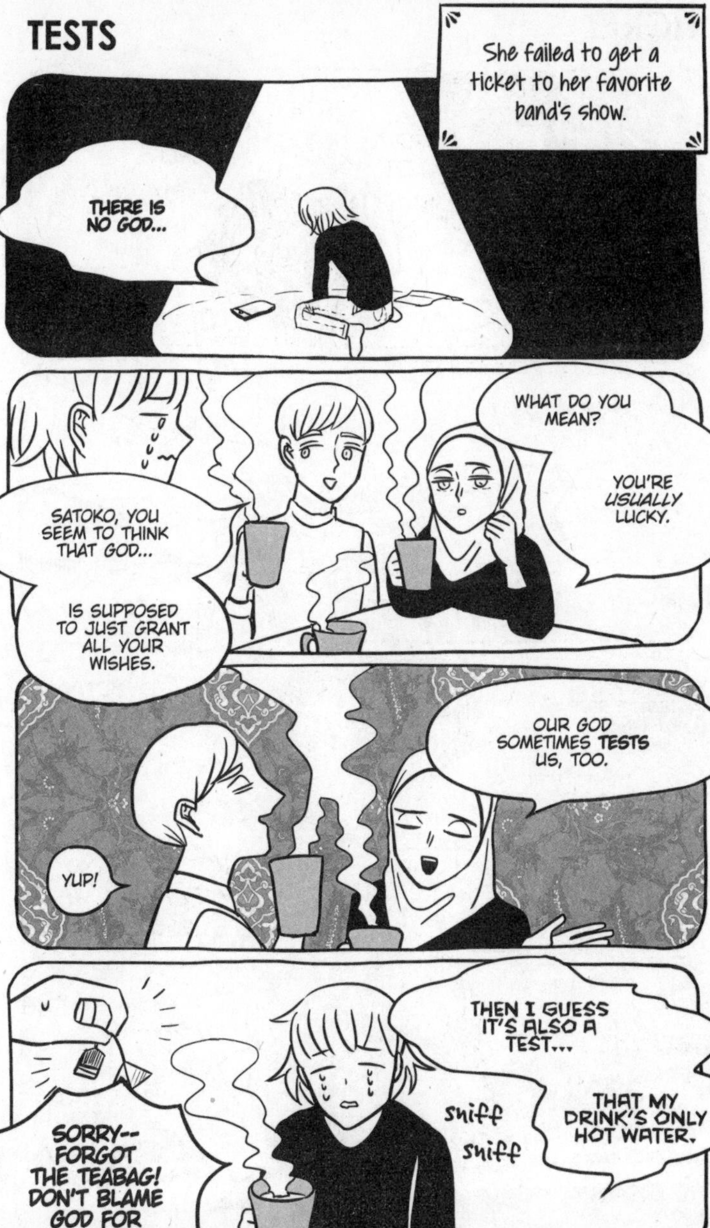
She failed to get a ticket to her favorite band's show.
THERE IS NO GOD...
WHAT DO YOU MEAN?
YOU'RE *USUALLY* LUCKY.
SATOKO, YOU SEEM TO THINK THAT GOD...
IS SUPPOSED TO JUST GRANT ALL YOUR WISHES.
OUR GOD SOMETIMES **TESTS** US, TOO.
YUP!
THEN I GUESS IT'S ALSO A TEST...
THAT MY DRINK'S ONLY HOT WATER.
sniff
sniff
SORRY-- FORGOT THE TEABAG! DON'T BLAME GOD FOR THAT ONE!

TICKET

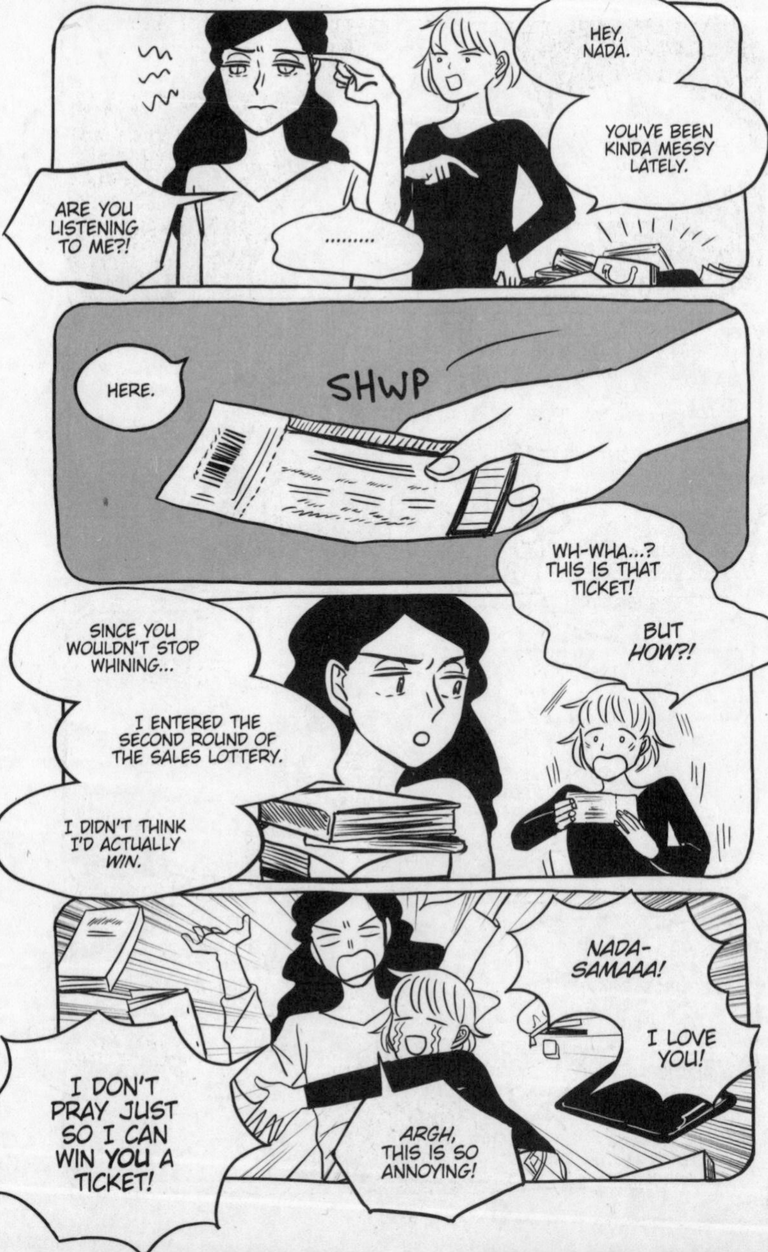
HEY, NADA.
YOU'VE BEEN KINDA MESSY LATELY.
ARE YOU LISTENING TO ME?!
....
SHWP
HERE.
WH-WHA...? THIS IS THAT TICKET!
BUT HOW?!
SINCE YOU WOULDN'T STOP WHINING...
I ENTERED THE SECOND ROUND OF THE SALES LOTTERY.
I DIDN'T THINK I'D ACTUALLY WIN.
NADA-SAMAAA!
I LOVE YOU!
I DON'T PRAY JUST SO I CAN WIN YOU A TICKET!
ARGH, THIS IS SO ANNOYING!

SIMPLE PLEASURES

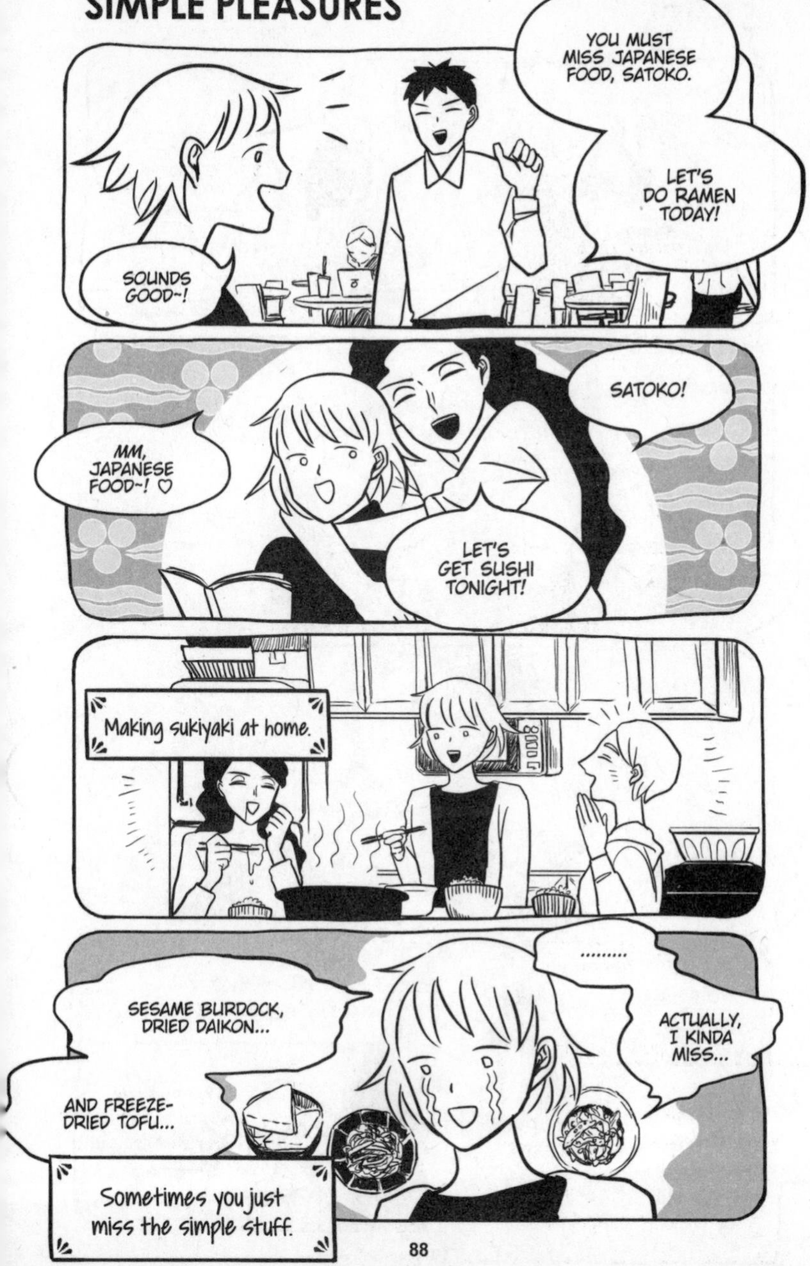
YOU MUST MISS JAPANESE FOOD, SATOKO.
LET'S DO RAMEN TODAY!
SOUNDS GOOD~!
SATOKO!
LET'S GET SUSHI TONIGHT!
MM, JAPANESE FOOD~! ♡
Making sukiyaki at home.
....
ACTUALLY, I KINDA MISS...
SESAME BURDOCK, DRIED DAIKON...
AND FREEZE-DRIED TOFU...
Sometimes you just miss the simple stuff.

SAND

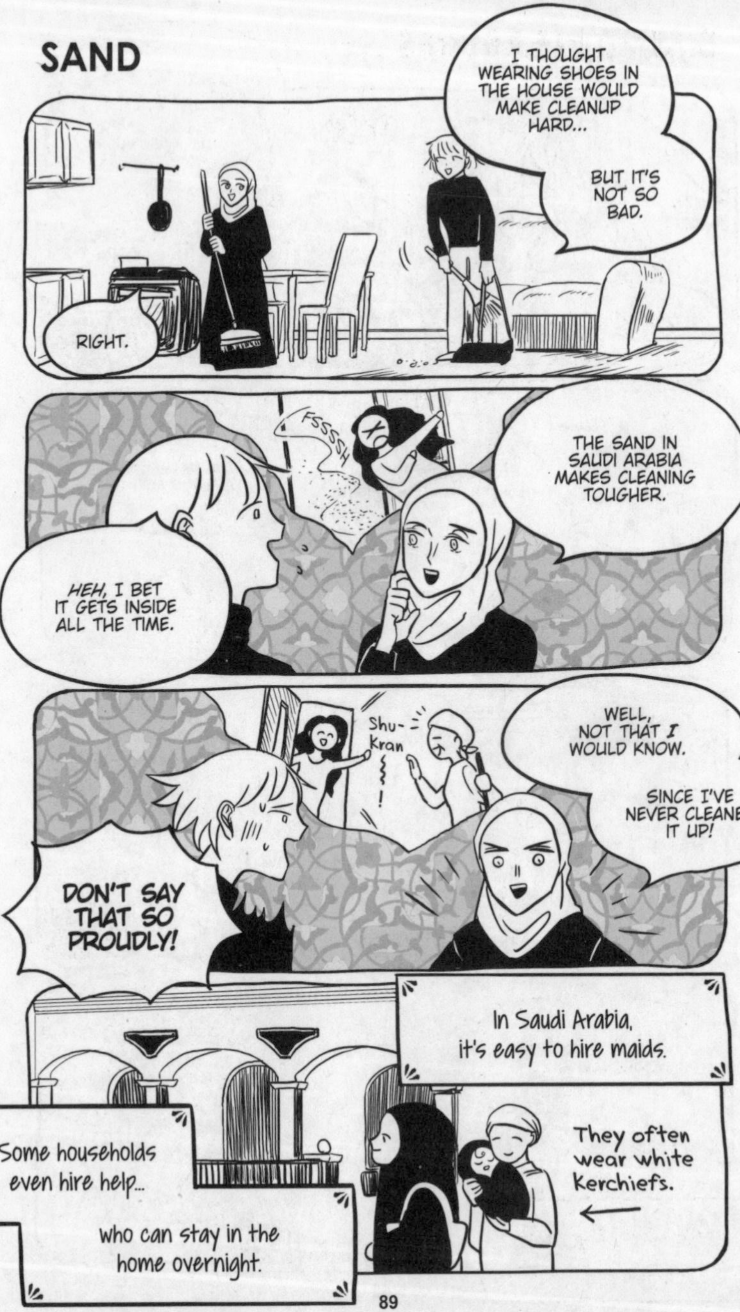
I THOUGHT WEARING SHOES IN THE HOUSE WOULD MAKE CLEANUP HARD...
BUT IT'S NOT SO BAD.
RIGHT.
THE SAND IN SAUDI ARABIA MAKES CLEANING TOUGHER.
FSSSSH
HEH, I BET IT GETS INSIDE ALL THE TIME.
WELL, NOT THAT *I* WOULD KNOW.
Shu-kran
SINCE I'VE NEVER CLEANED IT UP!
DON'T SAY THAT SO PROUDLY!
In Saudi Arabia, it's easy to hire maids.
They often wear white Kerchiefs.
Some households even hire help...
who can stay in the home overnight.

HANGING OUT TO DRY

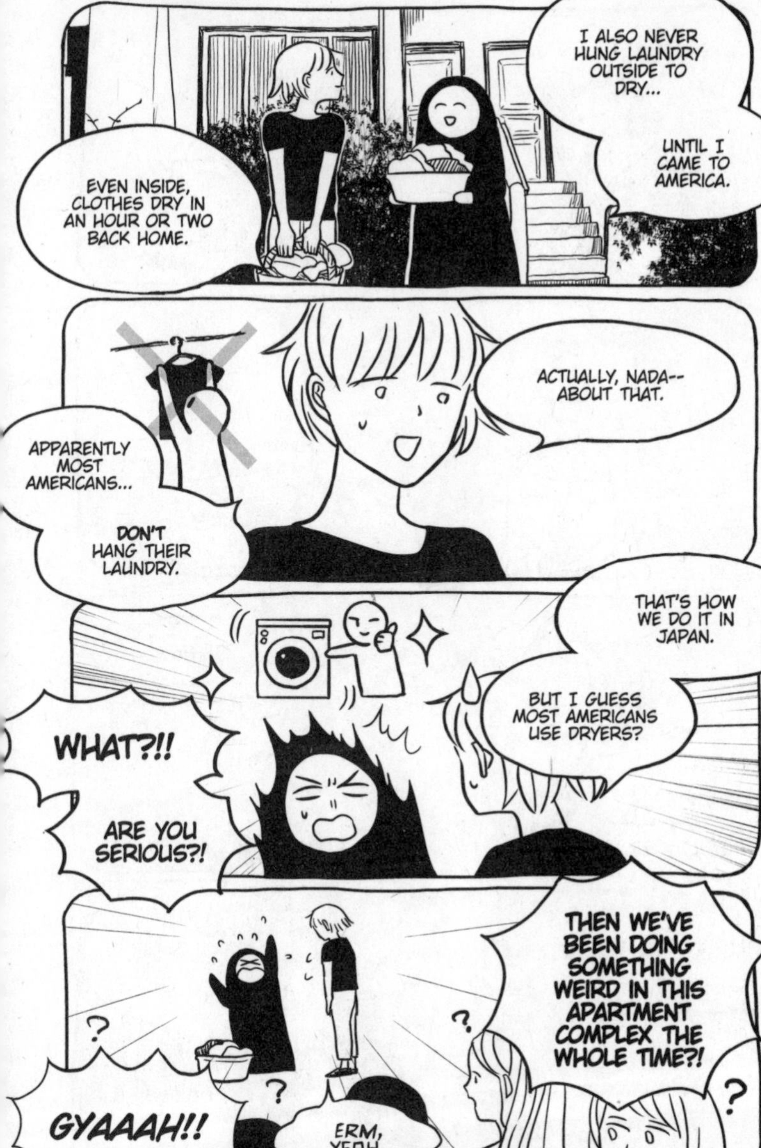
I ALSO NEVER HUNG LAUNDRY OUTSIDE TO DRY...
UNTIL I CAME TO AMERICA.
EVEN INSIDE, CLOTHES DRY IN AN HOUR OR TWO BACK HOME.
ACTUALLY, NADA-- ABOUT THAT.
APPARENTLY MOST AMERICANS...
DON'T HANG THEIR LAUNDRY.
THAT'S HOW WE DO IT IN JAPAN.
BUT I GUESS MOST AMERICANS USE DRYERS?
WHAT?!!
ARE YOU SERIOUS?!
THEN WE'VE BEEN DOING SOMETHING WEIRD IN THIS APARTMENT COMPLEX THE WHOLE TIME?!
ERM, YEAH.
GYAAAH!!

COLOR

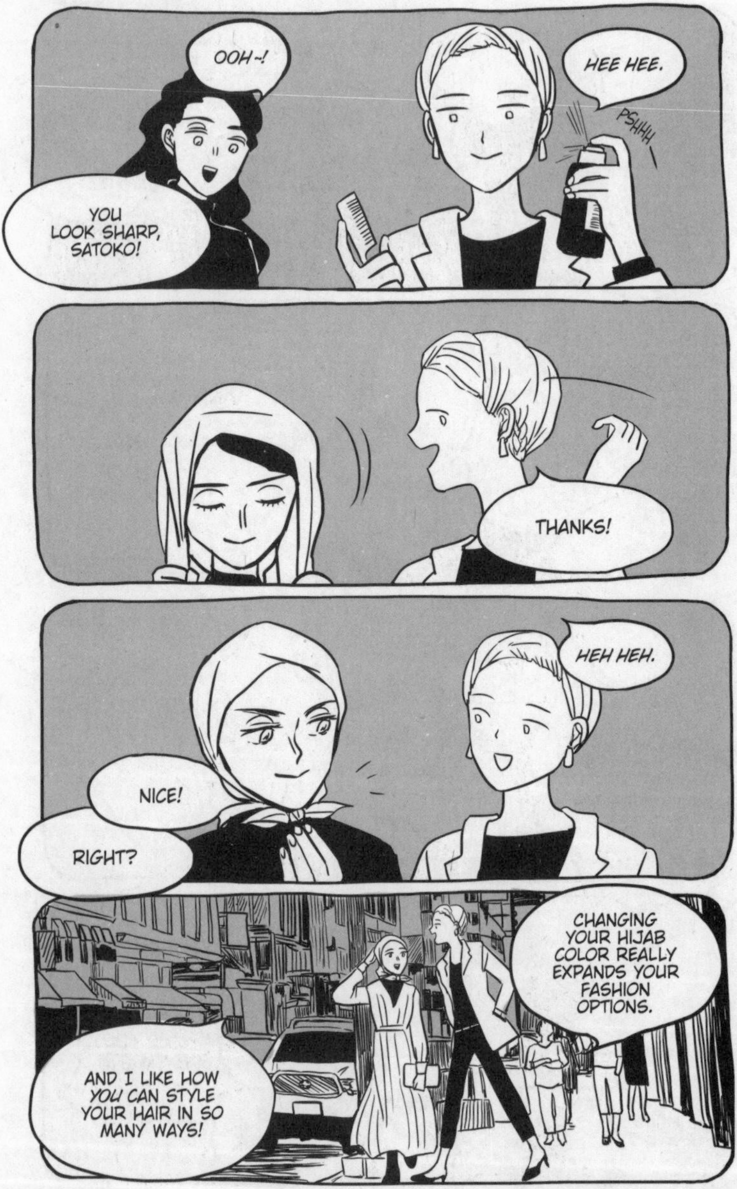
HEE HEE.
PSHHH
OOH~!
YOU LOOK SHARP, SATOKO!
THANKS!
HEH HEH.
NICE!
RIGHT?
CHANGING YOUR HIJAB COLOR REALLY EXPANDS YOUR FASHION OPTIONS.
AND I LIKE HOW YOU CAN STYLE YOUR HAIR IN SO MANY WAYS!

ENCOUNTER

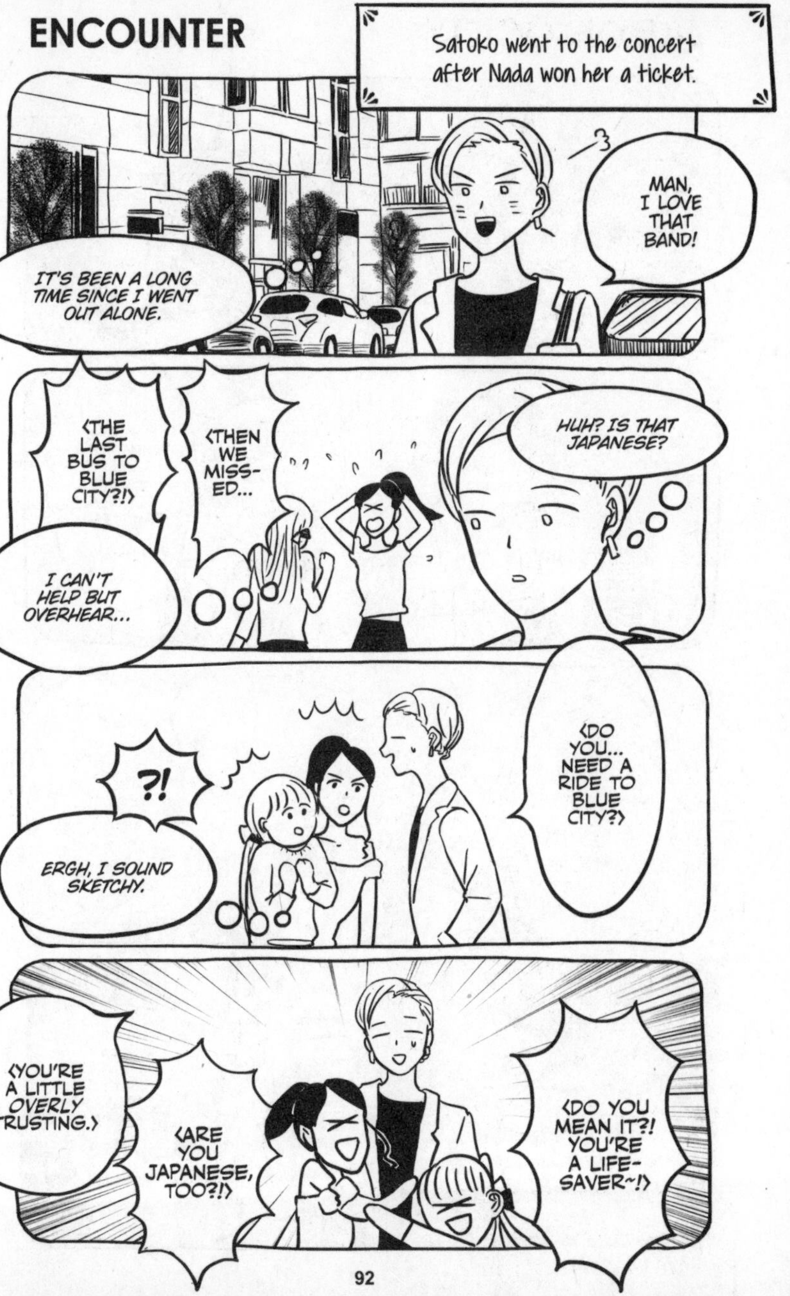

Satoko went to the concert after Nada won her a ticket.
MAN, I LOVE THAT BAND!
IT'S BEEN A LONG TIME SINCE I WENT OUT ALONE.
HUH? IS THAT JAPANESE?
‹THEN WE MISSED...
‹THE LAST BUS TO BLUE CITY?!›
I CAN'T HELP BUT OVERHEAR...
‹DO YOU... NEED A RIDE TO BLUE CITY?›
?!
ERGH, I SOUND SKETCHY.
‹DO YOU MEAN IT?! YOU'RE A LIFE-SAVER~!›
‹ARE YOU JAPANESE, TOO?!›
‹YOU'RE A LITTLE *OVERLY* TRUSTING.›

JAPAN SOCIETY

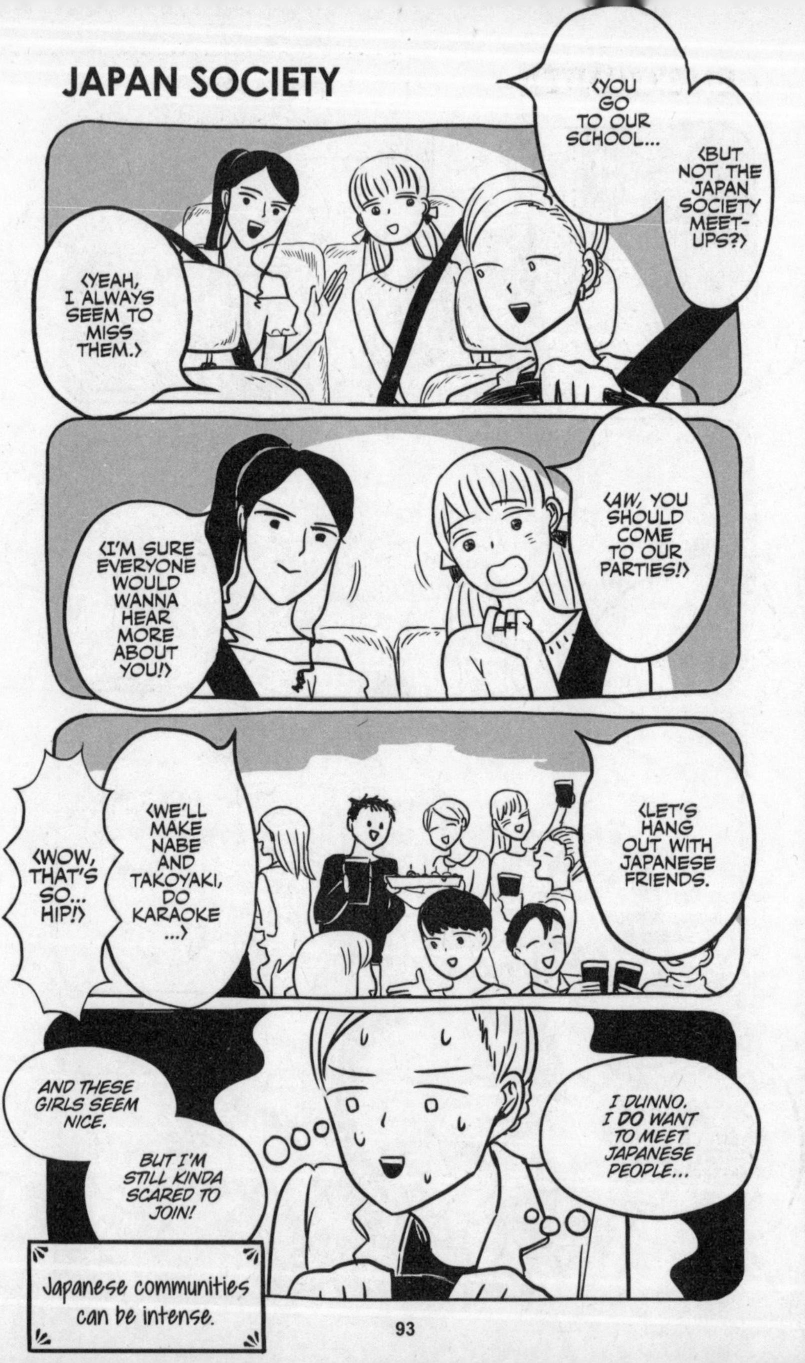

‹YOU GO TO OUR SCHOOL...
‹BUT NOT THE JAPAN SOCIETY MEET-UPS?›
‹YEAH, I ALWAYS SEEM TO MISS THEM.›
‹AW, YOU SHOULD COME TO OUR PARTIES!›
‹I'M SURE EVERYONE WOULD WANNA HEAR MORE ABOUT YOU!›
‹LET'S HANG OUT WITH JAPANESE FRIENDS.
‹WE'LL MAKE NABE AND TAKOYAKI, DO KARAOKE ...›
‹WOW, THAT'S SO... HIP!›
I DUNNO. I DO WANT TO MEET JAPANESE PEOPLE...
AND THESE GIRLS SEEM NICE.
BUT I'M STILL KINDA SCARED TO JOIN!
Japanese communities can be intense.

EVERY DAY

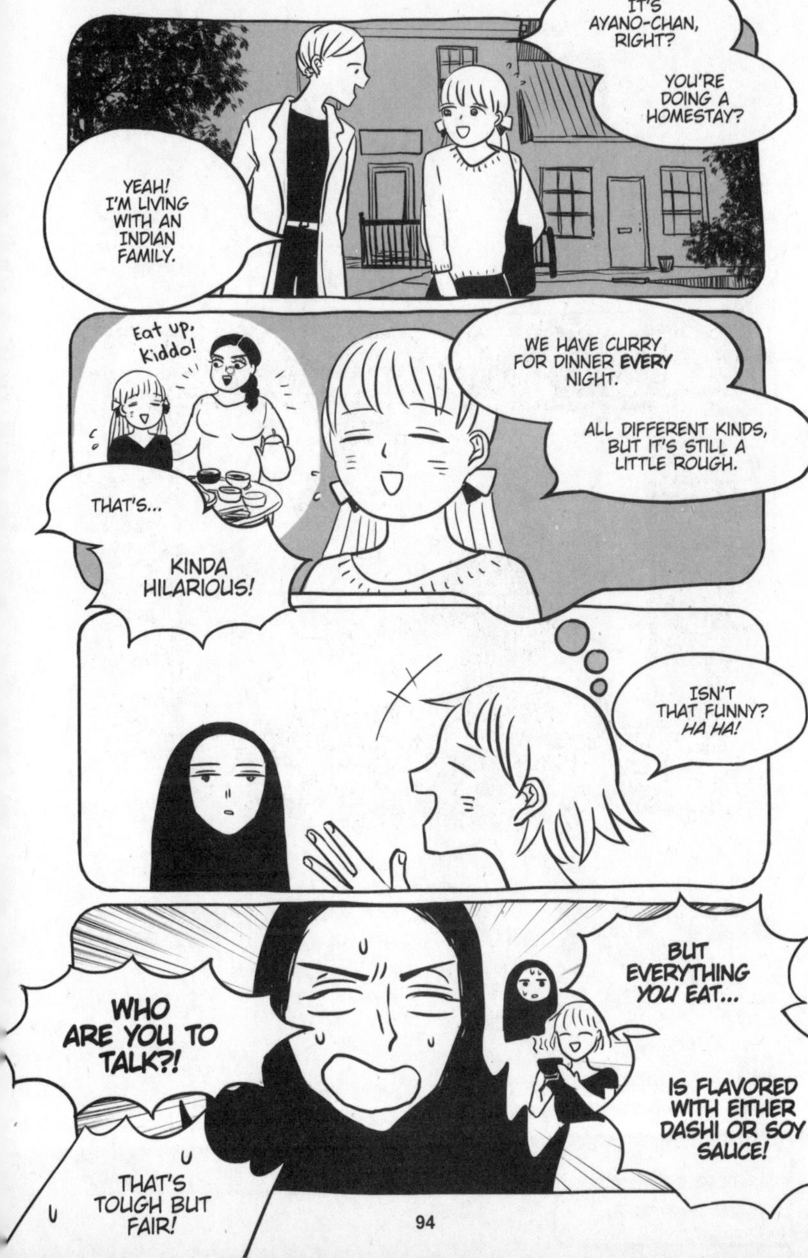
IT'S AYANO-CHAN, RIGHT?
YOU'RE DOING A HOMESTAY?
YEAH! I'M LIVING WITH AN INDIAN FAMILY.
WE HAVE CURRY FOR DINNER **EVERY** NIGHT.
ALL DIFFERENT KINDS, BUT IT'S STILL A LITTLE ROUGH.
Eat up, Kiddo!
THAT'S...
KINDA HILARIOUS!
ISN'T THAT FUNNY? *HA HA!*
BUT EVERYTHING *YOU* EAT...
IS FLAVORED WITH EITHER DASHI OR SOY SAUCE!
WHO ARE YOU TO TALK?!
THAT'S TOUGH BUT FAIR!

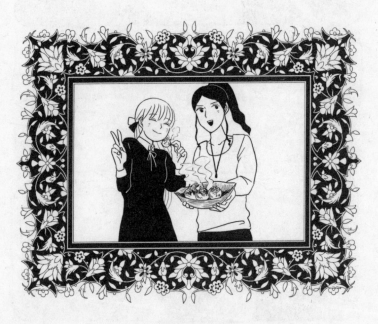

SATOKO AND NADA

Presented by Yupechika

INVITATION

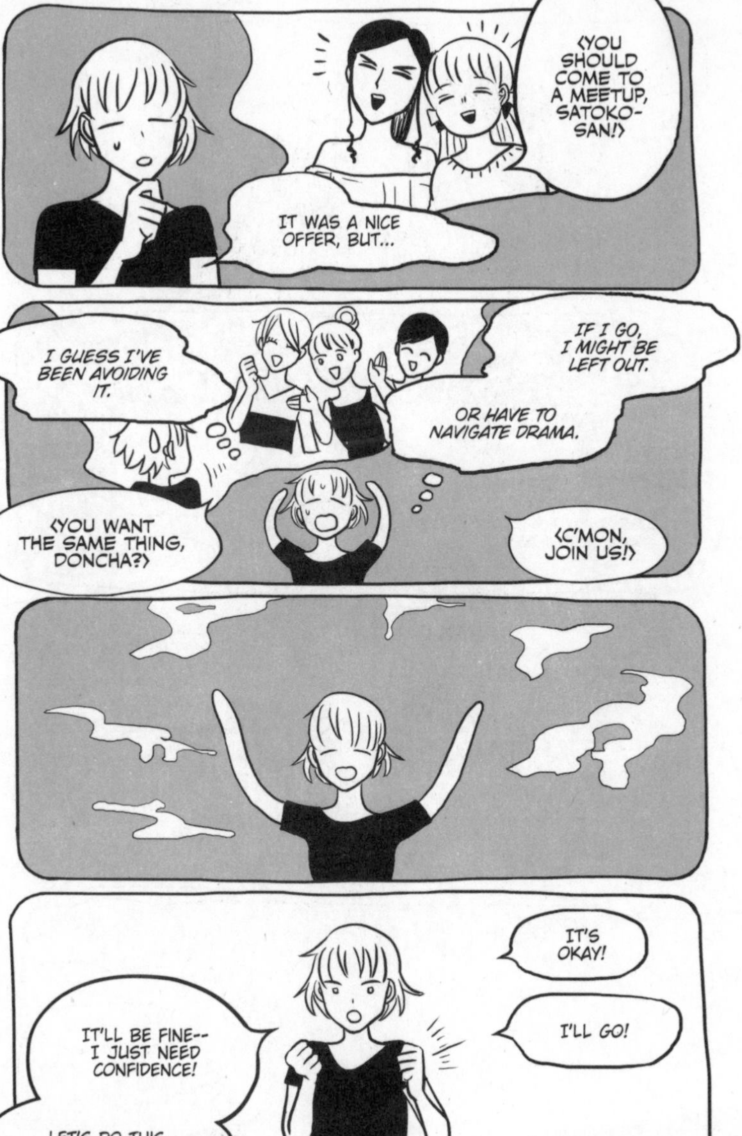
‹YOU SHOULD COME TO A MEETUP, SATOKO-SAN!›
IT WAS A NICE OFFER, BUT...
IF I GO, I MIGHT BE LEFT OUT.
OR HAVE TO NAVIGATE DRAMA.
I GUESS I'VE BEEN AVOIDING IT.
‹C'MON, JOIN US!›
‹YOU WANT THE SAME THING, DONCHA?›
IT'S OKAY!
I'LL GO!
IT'LL BE FINE-- I JUST NEED CONFIDENCE!
LET'S DO THIS JAPAN SOCIETY THING, *WOO!*

OKONOMIYAKI

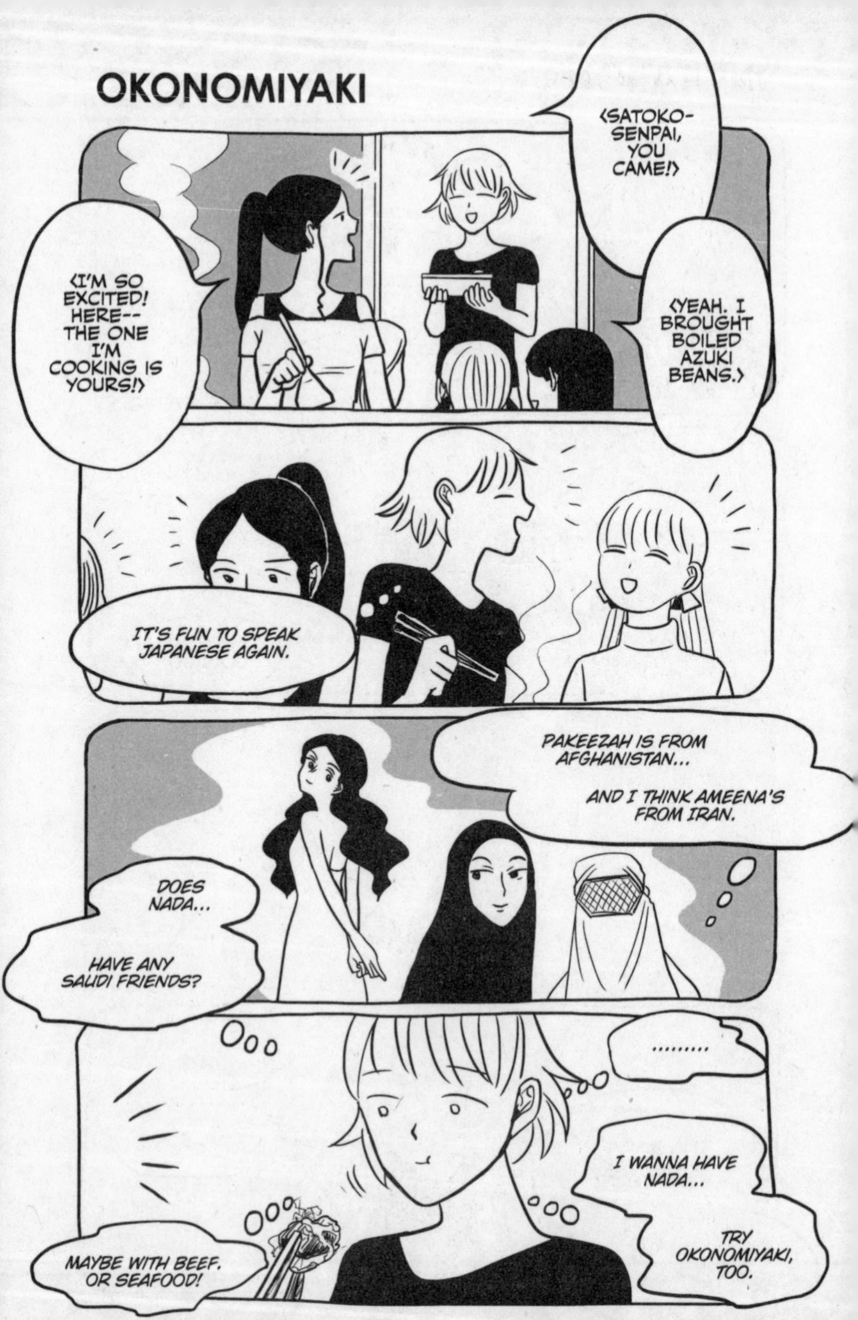
‹SATOKO-SENPAI, YOU CAME!›
‹YEAH. I BROUGHT BOILED AZUKI BEANS.›
‹I'M SO EXCITED! HERE-- THE ONE I'M COOKING IS YOURS!›
IT'S FUN TO SPEAK JAPANESE AGAIN.
PAKEEZAH IS FROM AFGHANISTAN...
AND I THINK AMEENA'S FROM IRAN.
DOES NADA...
HAVE ANY SAUDI FRIENDS?
....
I WANNA HAVE NADA...
TRY OKONOMIYAKI, TOO.
MAYBE WITH BEEF. OR SEAFOOD!

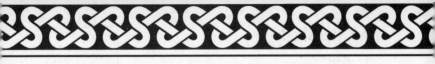

SATOKO AND NADA

Presented by Yupechika

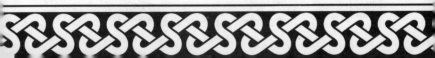

IMPRESSION

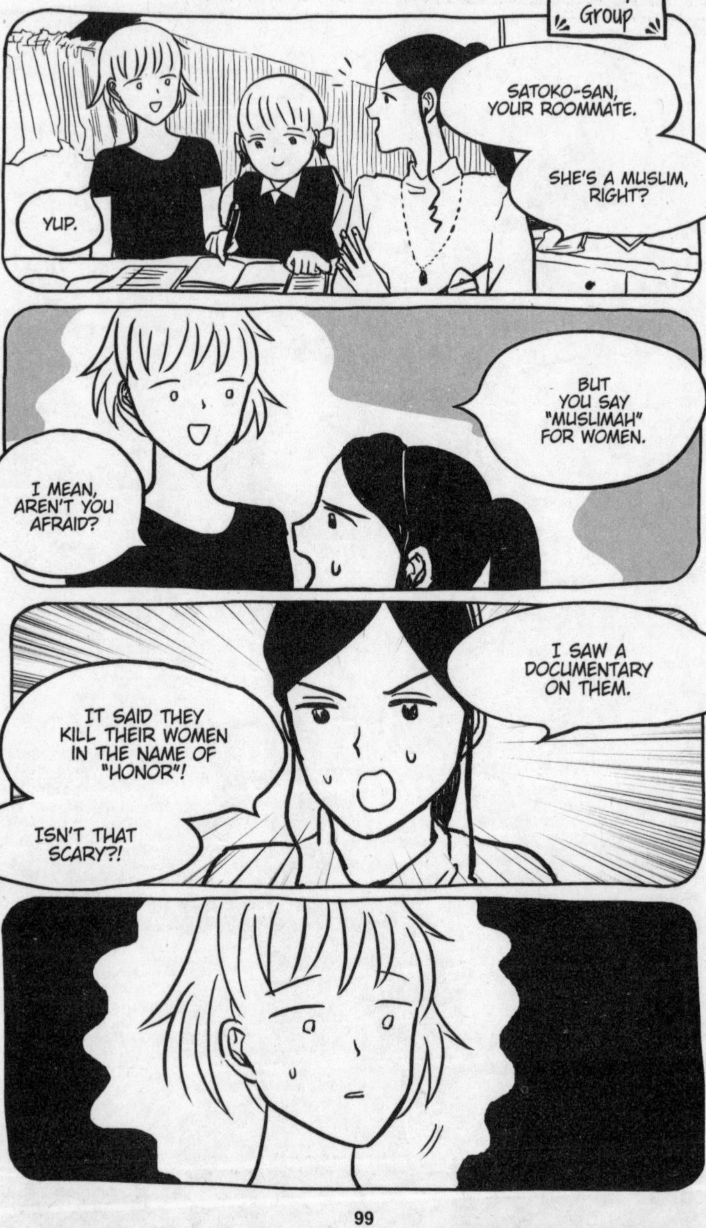

Study Group
SATOKO-SAN, YOUR ROOMMATE.
SHE'S A MUSLIM, RIGHT?
YUP.
BUT YOU SAY "MUSLIMAH" FOR WOMEN.
I MEAN, AREN'T YOU AFRAID?
I SAW A DOCUMENTARY ON THEM.
IT SAID THEY KILL THEIR WOMEN IN THE NAME OF "HONOR"!
ISN'T THAT SCARY?!

MISINTERPRETATION

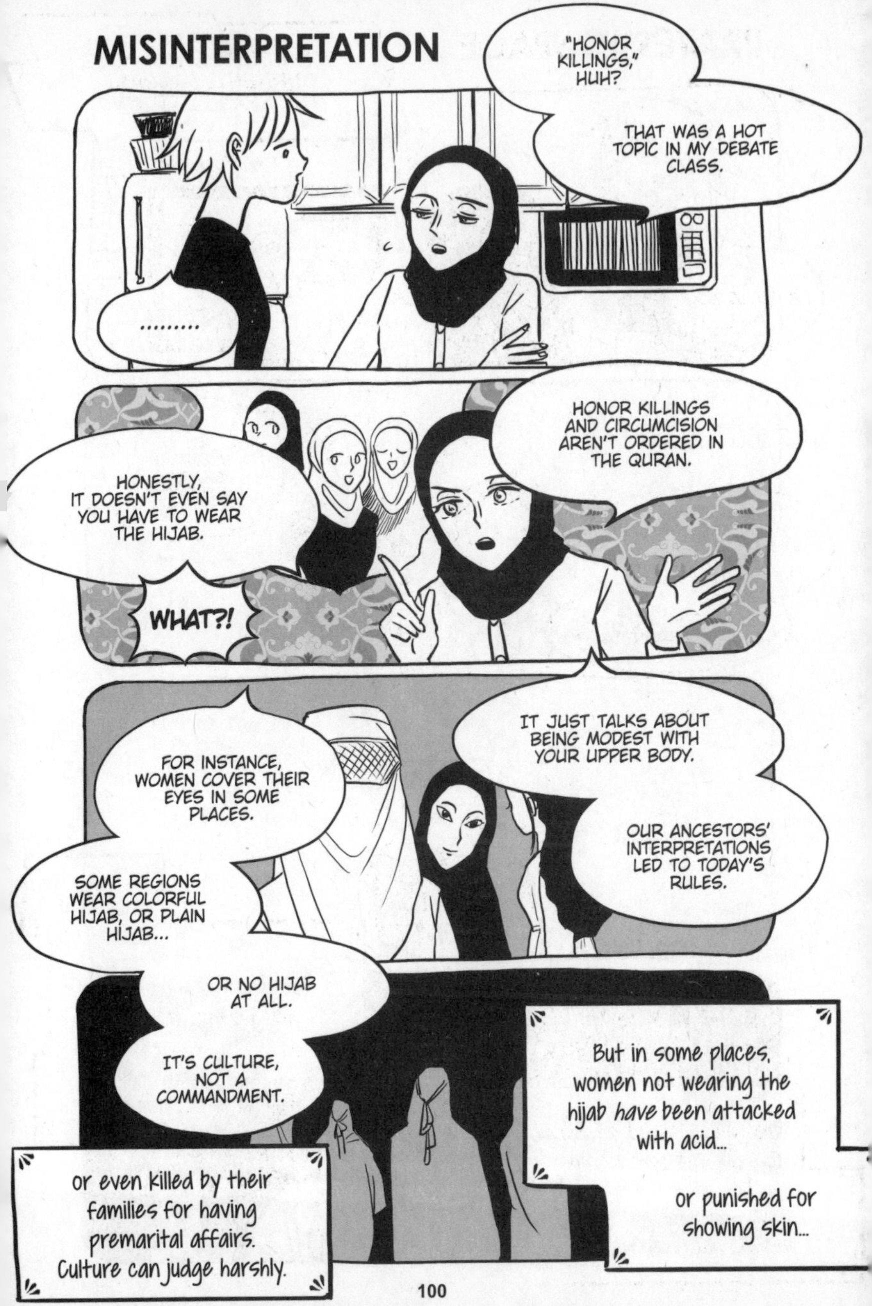
"HONOR KILLINGS," HUH?
THAT WAS A HOT TOPIC IN MY DEBATE CLASS.
....
HONOR KILLINGS AND CIRCUMCISION AREN'T ORDERED IN THE QURAN.
HONESTLY, IT DOESN'T EVEN SAY YOU HAVE TO WEAR THE HIJAB.
WHAT?!
IT JUST TALKS ABOUT BEING MODEST WITH YOUR UPPER BODY.
OUR ANCESTORS' INTERPRETATIONS LED TO TODAY'S RULES.
FOR INSTANCE, WOMEN COVER THEIR EYES IN SOME PLACES.
SOME REGIONS WEAR COLORFUL HIJAB, OR PLAIN HIJAB...
OR NO HIJAB AT ALL.
IT'S CULTURE, NOT A COMMANDMENT.
But in some places, women not wearing the hijab have been attacked with acid...
or punished for showing skin...
or even killed by their families for having premarital affairs. Culture can judge harshly.

PRAYER IN SPACE

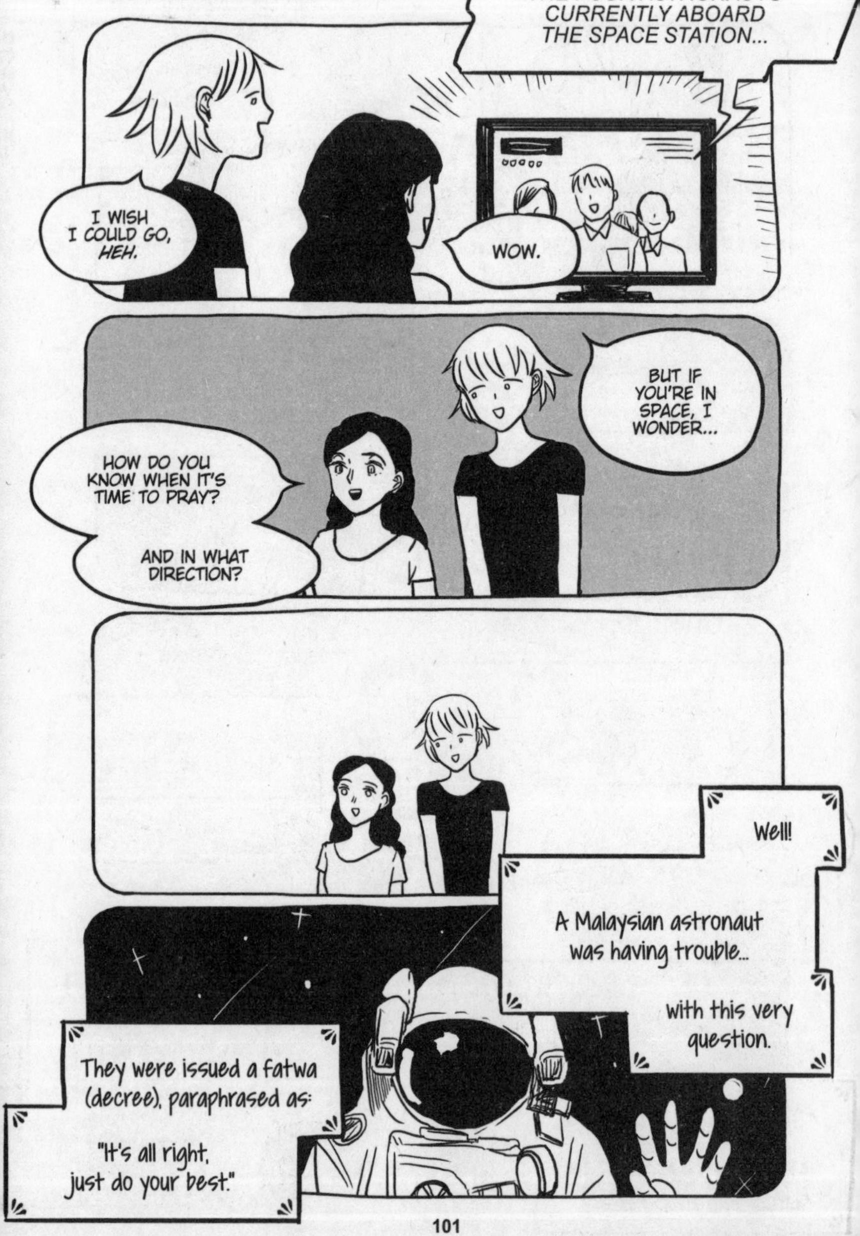
THE FOUR ASTRONAUTS CURRENTLY ABOARD THE SPACE STATION...
WOW.
I WISH I COULD GO, HEH.
BUT IF YOU'RE IN SPACE, I WONDER...
HOW DO YOU KNOW WHEN IT'S TIME TO PRAY?
AND IN WHAT DIRECTION?
Well!
A Malaysian astronaut was having trouble...
with this very question.
They were issued a fatwa (decree), paraphrased as:
"It's all right, just do your best."

FATWA (PART 1)

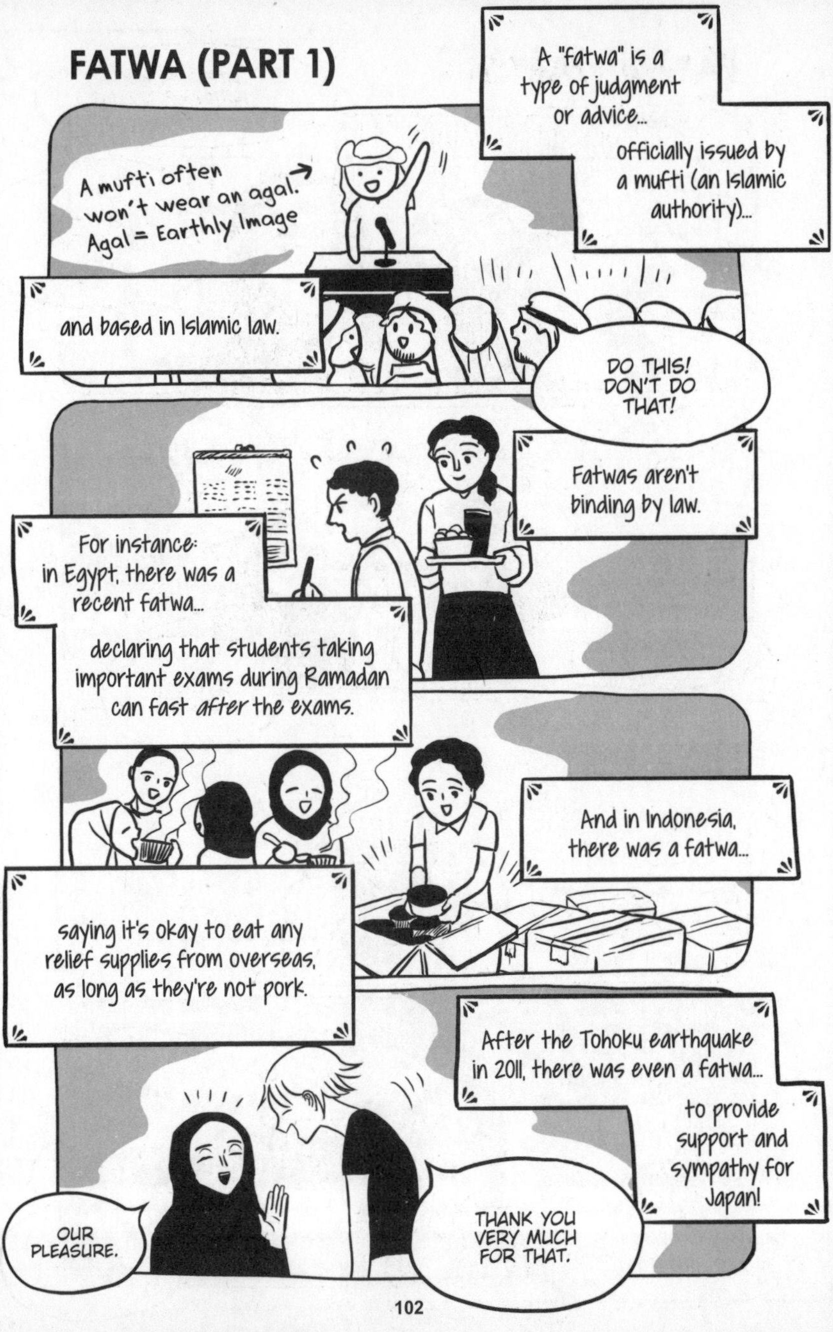

A "fatwa" is a type of judgment or advice...
officially issued by a mufti (an Islamic authority)...
A mufti often won't wear an agal. Agal = Earthly Image
and based in Islamic law.
DO THIS! DON'T DO THAT!
Fatwas aren't binding by law.
For instance: in Egypt, there was a recent fatwa...
declaring that students taking important exams during Ramadan can fast after the exams.
And in Indonesia, there was a fatwa...
saying it's okay to eat any relief supplies from overseas, as long as they're not pork.
After the Tohoku earthquake in 2011, there was even a fatwa...
to provide support and sympathy for Japan!
THANK YOU VERY MUCH FOR THAT.
OUR PLEASURE.

FATWA (PART 2)

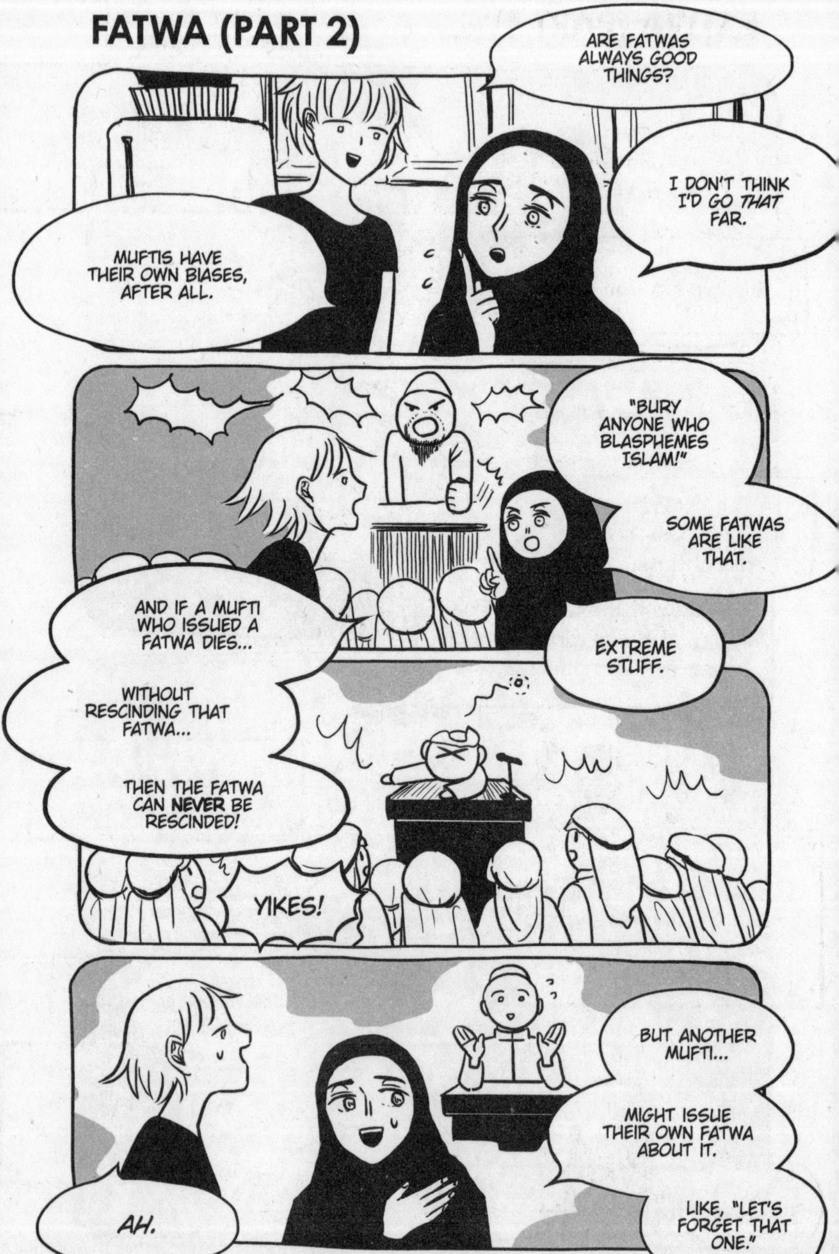
ARE FATWAS ALWAYS GOOD THINGS?
I DON'T THINK I'D GO *THAT* FAR.
MUFTIS HAVE THEIR OWN BIASES, AFTER ALL.
"BURY ANYONE WHO BLASPHEMES ISLAM!"
SOME FATWAS ARE LIKE THAT.
EXTREME STUFF.
AND IF A MUFTI WHO ISSUED A FATWA DIES...
WITHOUT RESCINDING THAT FATWA...
THEN THE FATWA CAN **NEVER** BE RESCINDED!
YIKES!
BUT ANOTHER MUFTI...
MIGHT ISSUE THEIR OWN FATWA ABOUT IT.
LIKE, "LET'S FORGET THAT ONE."
AH.

※*If the mufti who issued a fatwa is dead, an organization or mufti with higher authority can rescind it.*

BAN LIFTED

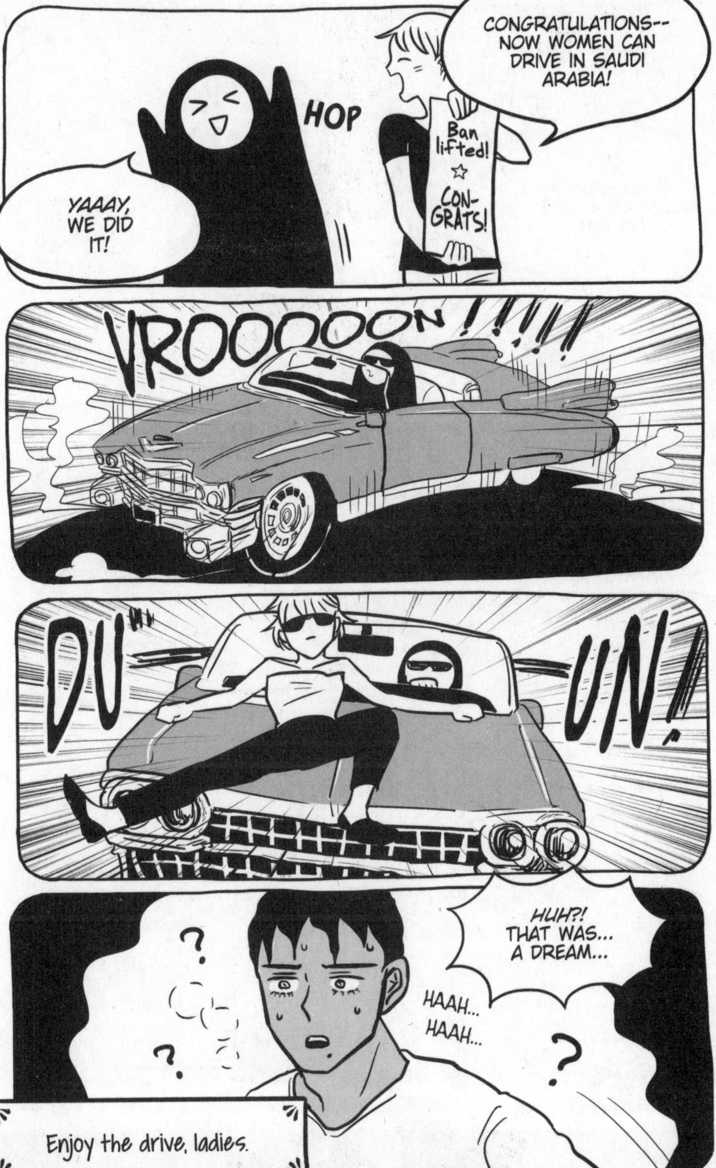
CONGRATULATIONS-- NOW WOMEN CAN DRIVE IN SAUDI ARABIA!
Ban lifted! ☆ CON-GRATS!
HOP
YAAAY, WE DID IT!
VROOOOOON!!!!!
DU
UN!
HUH?! THAT WAS... A DREAM...
HAAH... HAAH...
Enjoy the drive, ladies.

FEAT OF STRENGTH

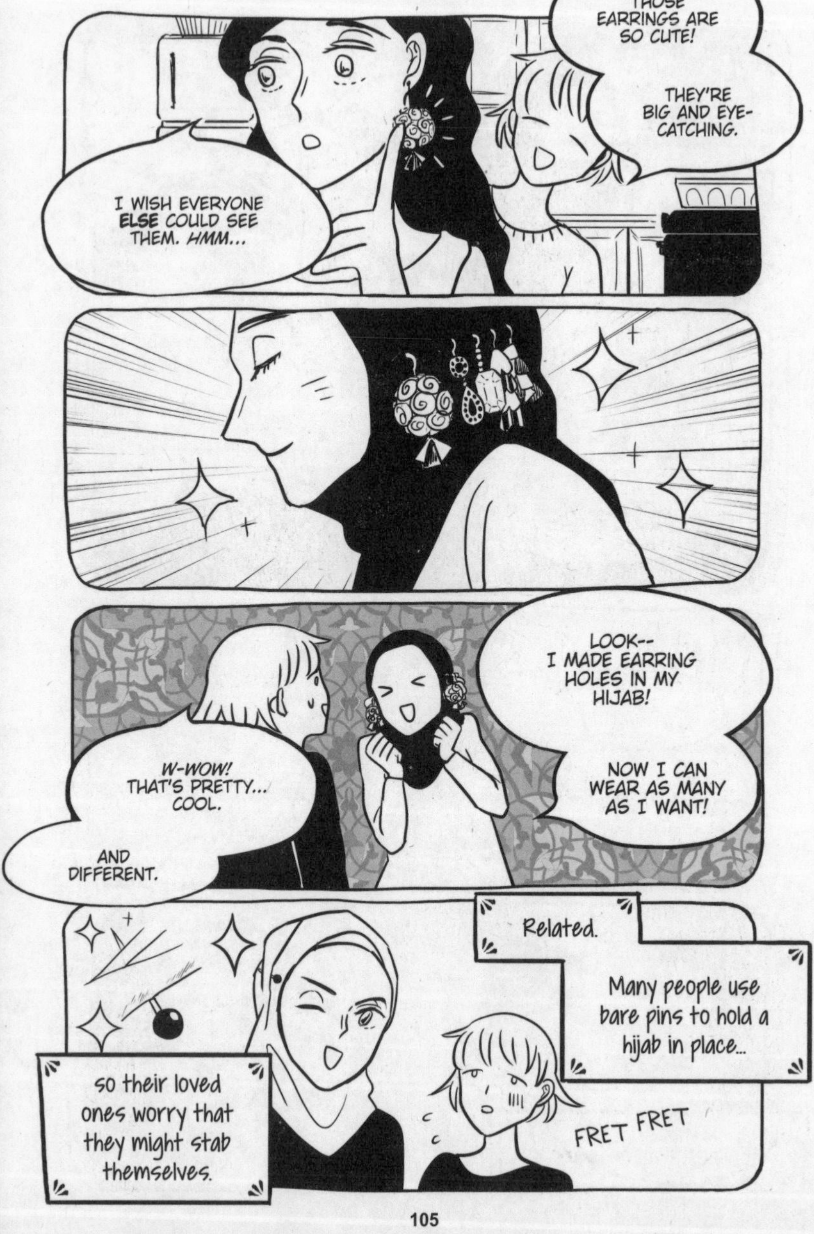

THOSE EARRINGS ARE SO CUTE!
THEY'RE BIG AND EYE-CATCHING.
I WISH EVERYONE **ELSE** COULD SEE THEM. *HMM...*
LOOK-- I MADE EARRING HOLES IN MY HIJAB!
NOW I CAN WEAR AS MANY AS I WANT!
W-WOW! THAT'S PRETTY... COOL.
AND DIFFERENT.
Related.
Many people use bare pins to hold a hijab in place...
FRET FRET
so their loved ones worry that they might stab themselves.

HABIBI

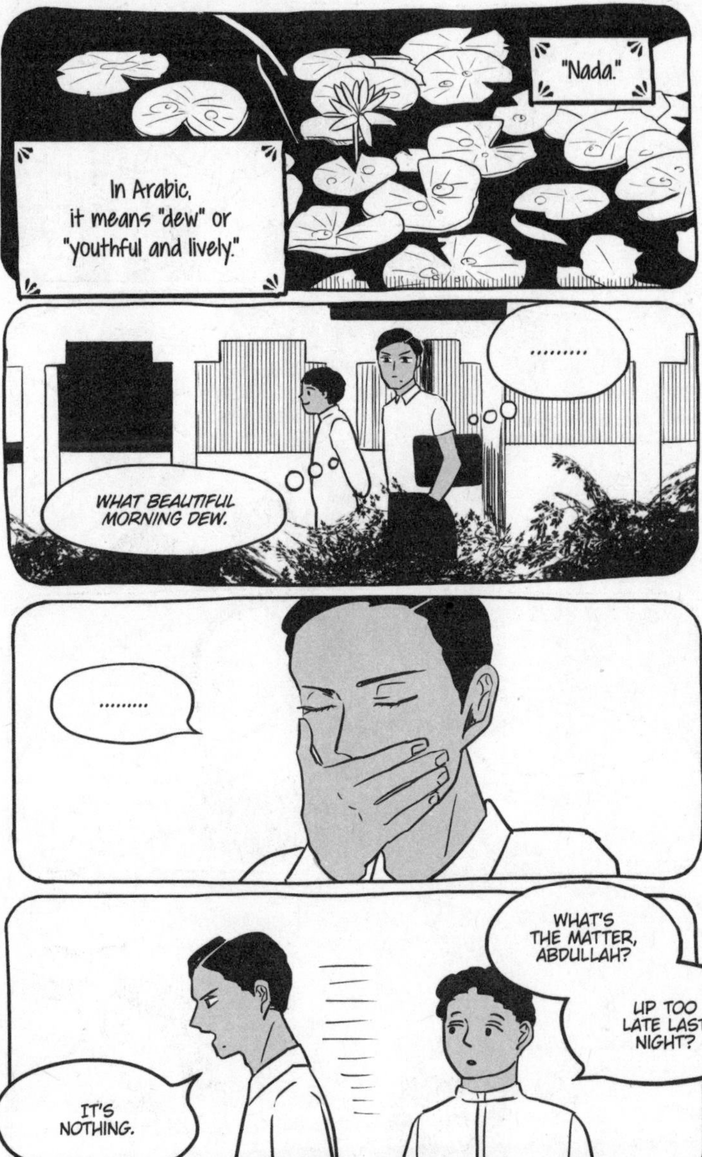

"Nada."
In Arabic, it means "dew" or "youthful and lively."
....
WHAT BEAUTIFUL MORNING DEW.
....
WHAT'S THE MATTER, ABDULLAH?
UP TOO LATE LAST NIGHT?
IT'S NOTHING.

EYE COLOR

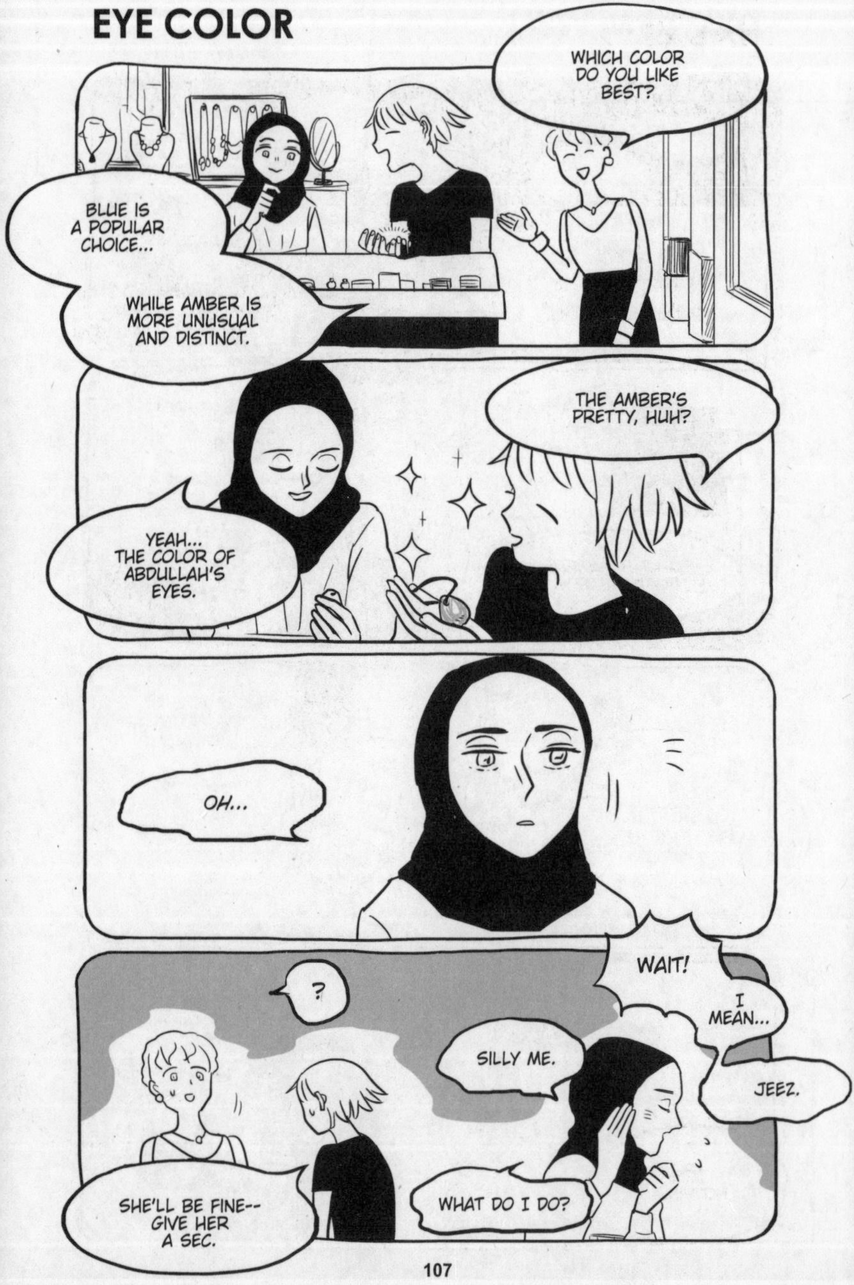
WHICH COLOR DO YOU LIKE BEST?
BLUE IS A POPULAR CHOICE...
WHILE AMBER IS MORE UNUSUAL AND DISTINCT.
THE AMBER'S PRETTY, HUH?
YEAH... THE COLOR OF ABDULLAH'S EYES.
OH...
WAIT!
I MEAN...
JEEZ.
?
SILLY ME.
WHAT DO I DO?
SHE'LL BE FINE--GIVE HER A SEC.

ZAMZAM WELL

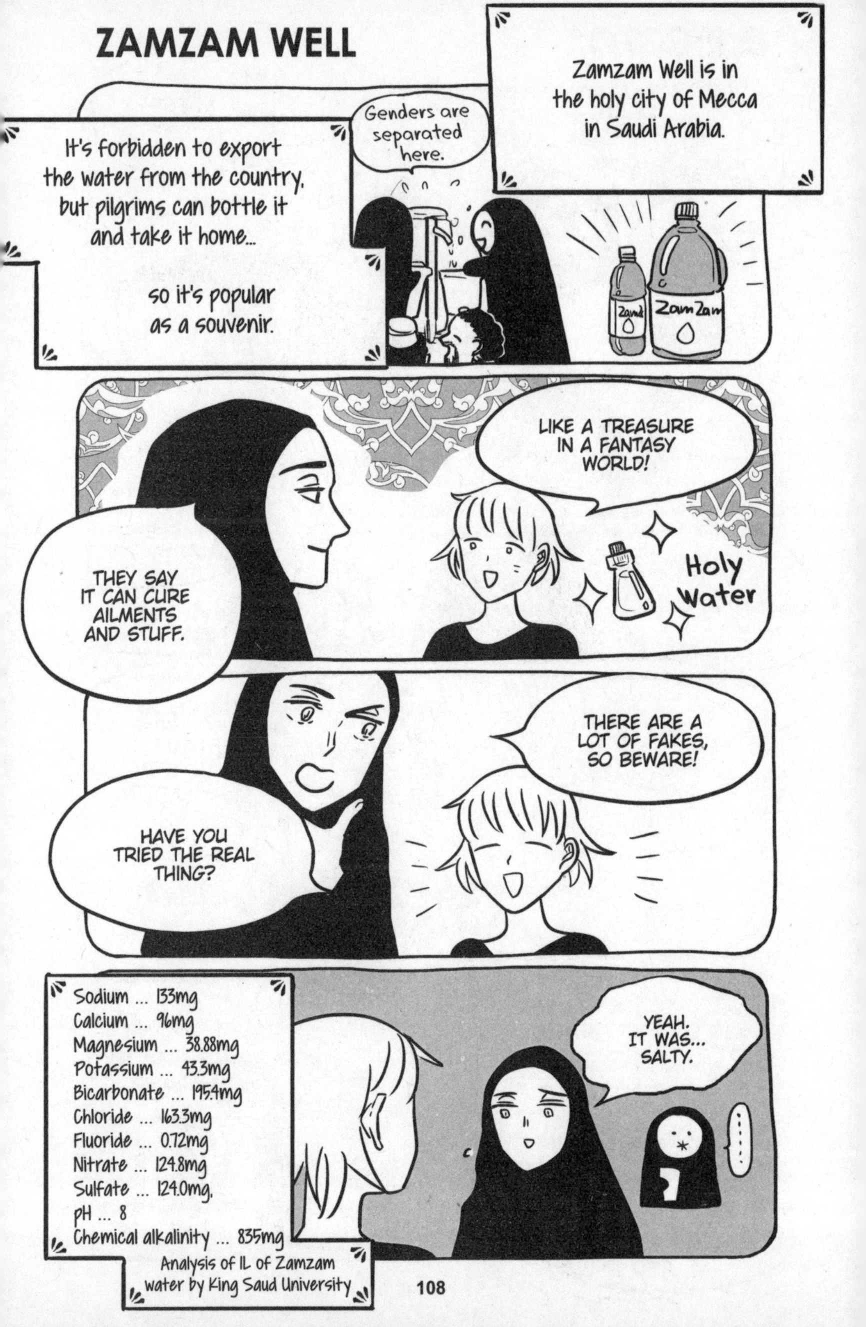
Zamzam Well is in the holy city of Mecca in Saudi Arabia.
Genders are separated here.
ZamZam
It's forbidden to export the water from the country, but pilgrims can bottle it and take it home...
so it's popular as a souvenir.
LIKE A TREASURE IN A FANTASY WORLD!
Holy Water
THEY SAY IT CAN CURE AILMENTS AND STUFF.
THERE ARE A LOT OF FAKES, SO BEWARE!
HAVE YOU TRIED THE REAL THING?
YEAH. IT WAS... SALTY.
......
Sodium ... 133mg
Calcium ... 96mg
Magnesium ... 38.88mg
Potassium ... 43.3mg
Bicarbonate ... 195.4mg
Chloride ... 163.3mg
Fluoride ... 0.72mg
Nitrate ... 124.8mg
Sulfate ... 124.0mg,
pH ... 8
Chemical alkalinity ... 835mg
Analysis of 1L of Zamzam water by King Saud University

AJWA

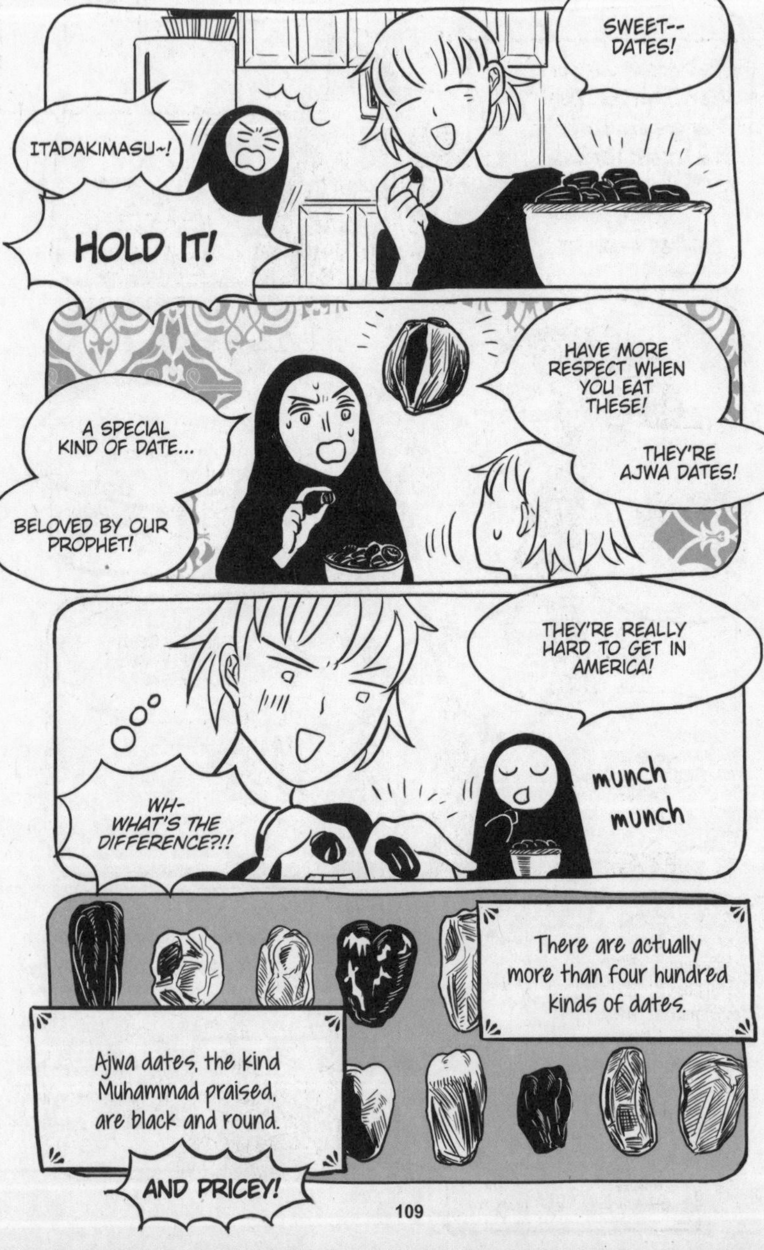
SWEET-- DATES!
ITADAKIMASU~!
HOLD IT!
HAVE MORE RESPECT WHEN YOU EAT THESE!
THEY'RE AJWA DATES!
A SPECIAL KIND OF DATE...
BELOVED BY OUR PROPHET!
THEY'RE REALLY HARD TO GET IN AMERICA!
munch munch
WH- WHAT'S THE DIFFERENCE?!!
There are actually more than four hundred kinds of dates.
Ajwa dates, the kind Muhammad praised, are black and round.
AND PRICEY!

BUSINESS LIFE

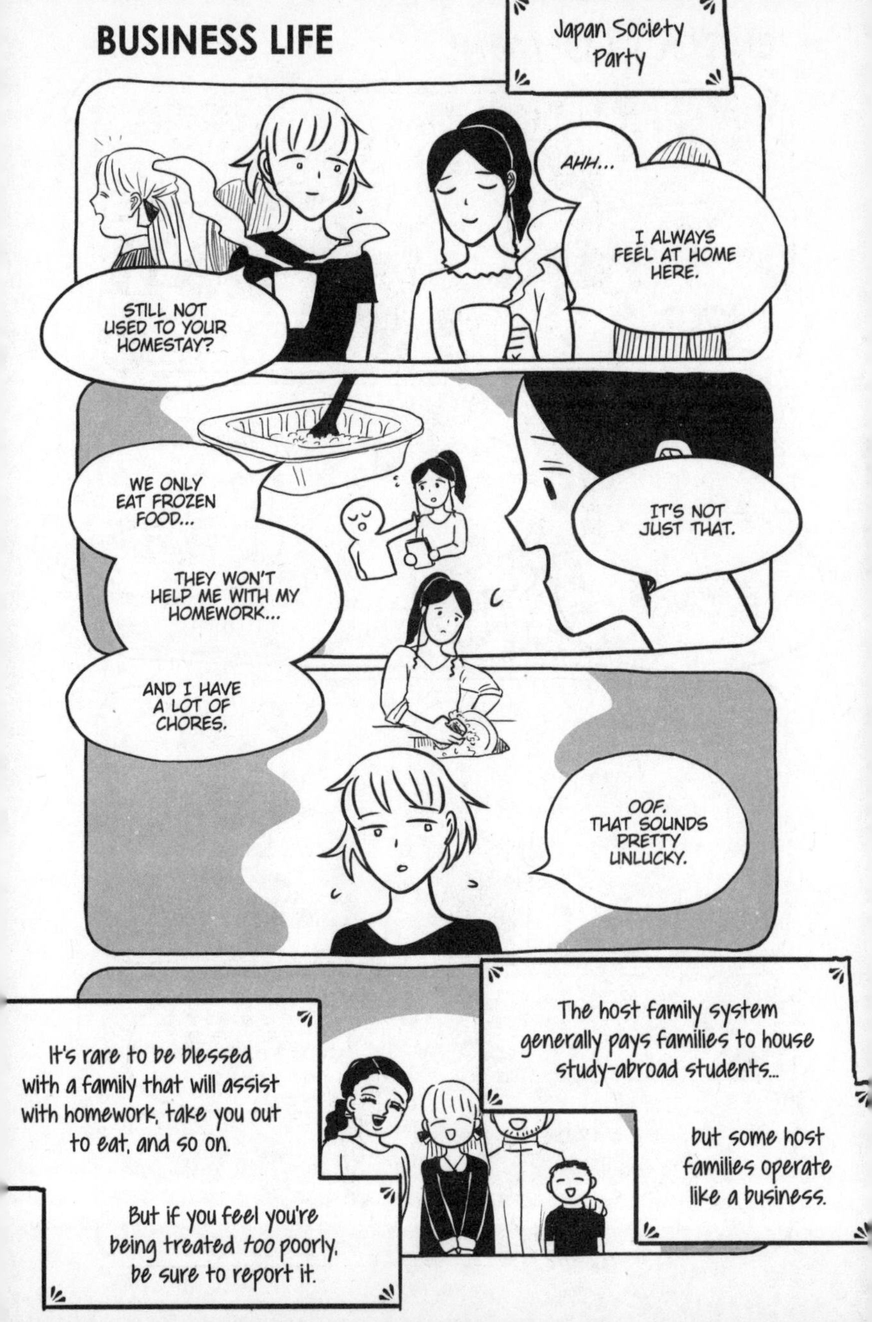
Japan Society Party
AHH...
I ALWAYS FEEL AT HOME HERE.
STILL NOT USED TO YOUR HOMESTAY?
IT'S NOT JUST THAT.
WE ONLY EAT FROZEN FOOD...
THEY WON'T HELP ME WITH MY HOMEWORK...
AND I HAVE A LOT OF CHORES.
OOF. THAT SOUNDS PRETTY UNLUCKY.
The host family system generally pays families to house study-abroad students...
but some host families operate like a business.
It's rare to be blessed with a family that will assist with homework, take you out to eat, and so on.
But if you feel you're being treated *too* poorly, be sure to report it.

ENCOURAGEMENT

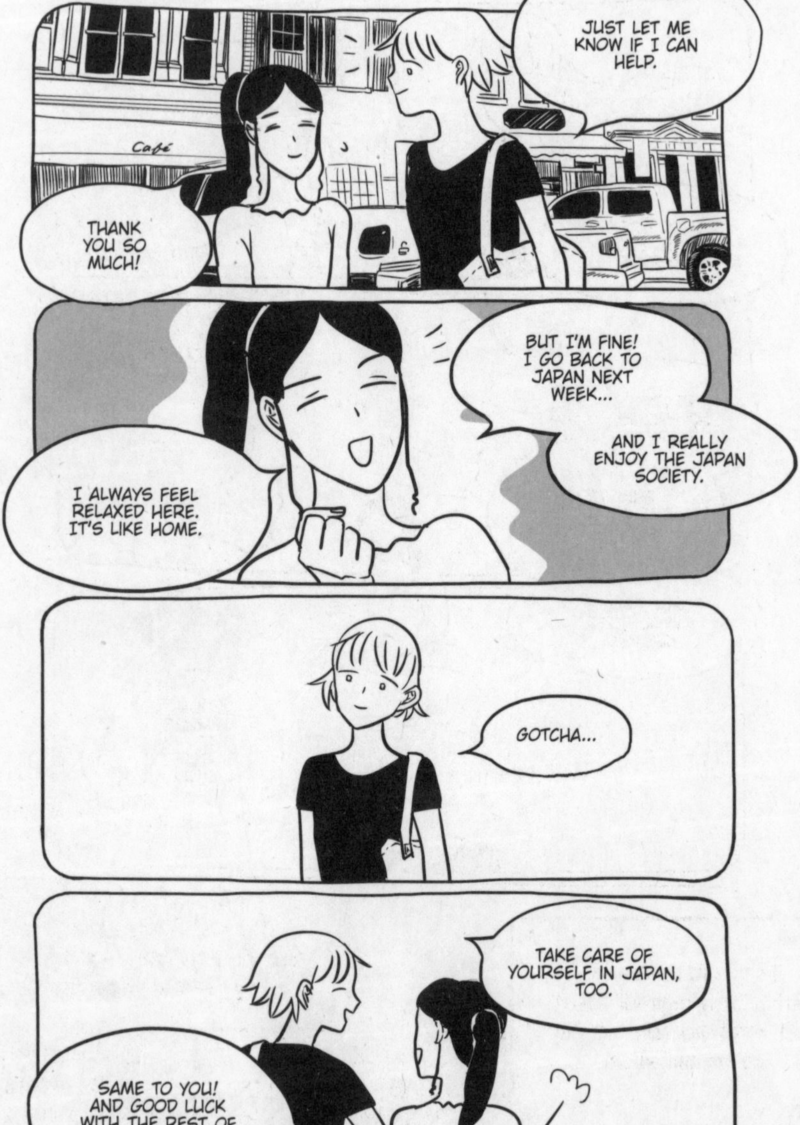
JUST LET ME KNOW IF I CAN HELP.
Café
THANK YOU SO MUCH!
BUT I'M FINE! I GO BACK TO JAPAN NEXT WEEK...
AND I REALLY ENJOY THE JAPAN SOCIETY.
I ALWAYS FEEL RELAXED HERE. IT'S LIKE HOME.
GOTCHA...
TAKE CARE OF YOURSELF IN JAPAN, TOO.
SAME TO YOU! AND GOOD LUCK WITH THE REST OF YOUR TIME HERE.

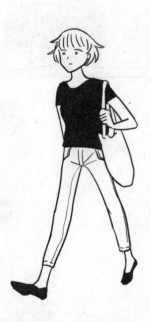

SATOKO AND **NADA**

Presented by Yupechika

HOME

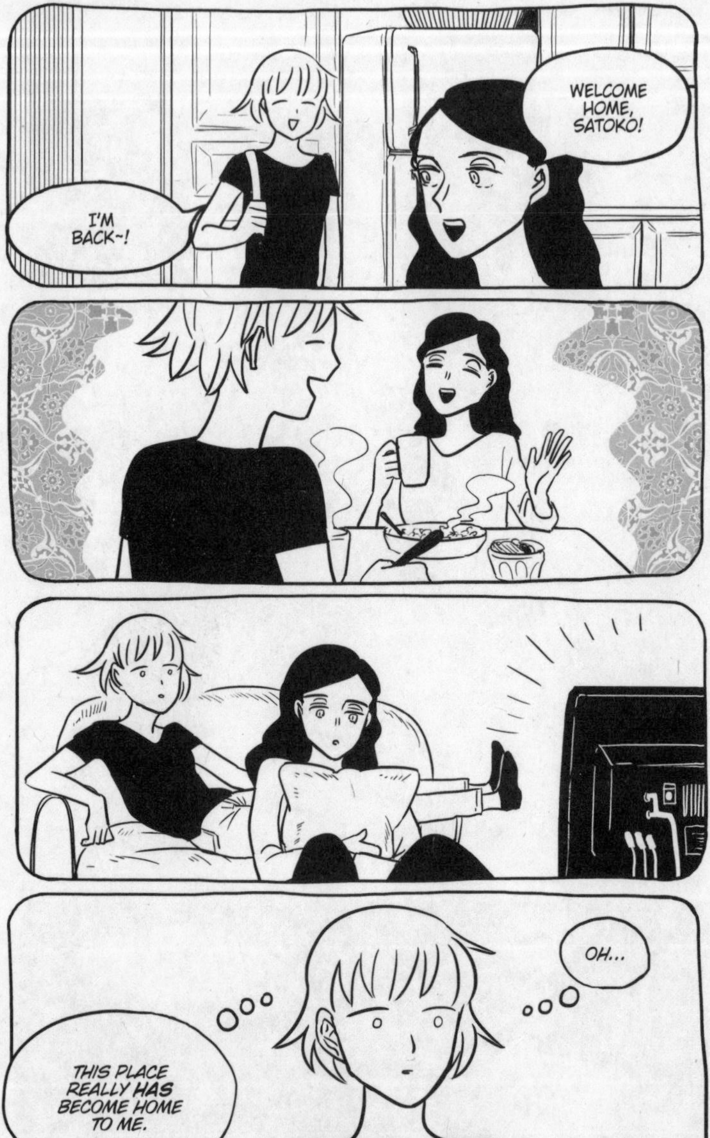
WELCOME HOME, SATOKO!
I'M BACK~!
OH...
THIS PLACE REALLY HAS BECOME HOME TO ME.

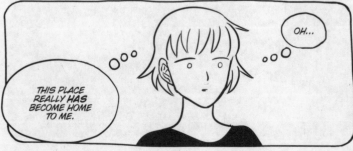

RELAXED

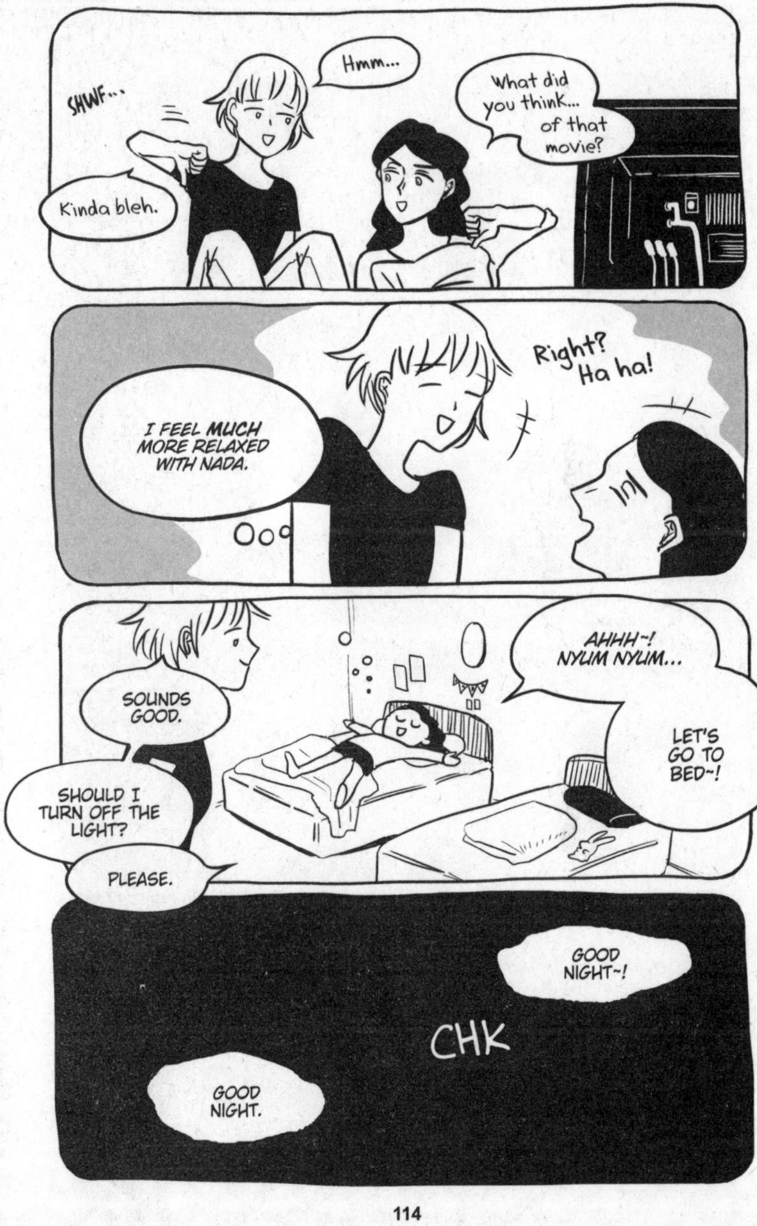
What did you think... of that movie?
Hmm...
SHWF...
Kinda bleh.
Right? Ha ha!
I FEEL MUCH MORE RELAXED WITH NADA.
AHHH~! NYUM NYUM...
LET'S GO TO BED~!
SOUNDS GOOD.
SHOULD I TURN OFF THE LIGHT?
PLEASE.
GOOD NIGHT~!
CHK
GOOD NIGHT.

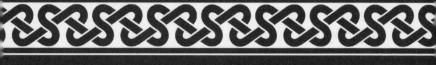

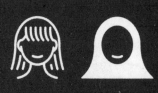

SATOKO AND NADA

Presented by Yupechika

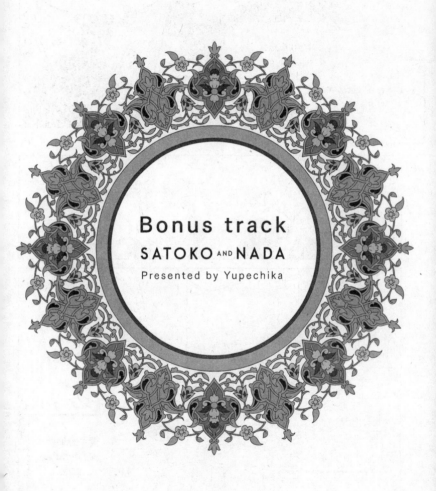

Bonus track

SATOKO AND NADA

Presented by Yupechika

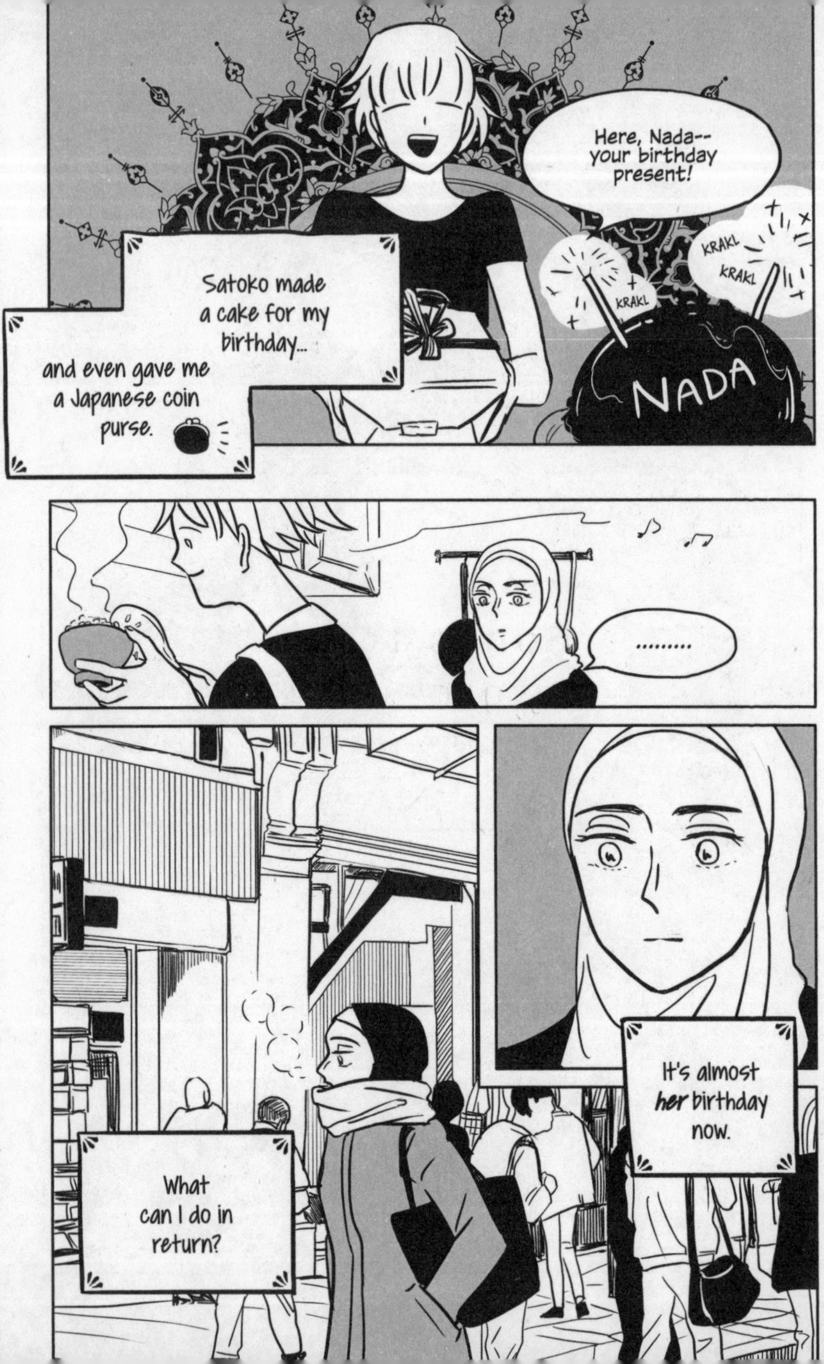
Here, Nada-- your birthday present!
KRAKL
KRAKL
KRAKL
NADA
Satoko made a cake for my birthday...
and even gave me a Japanese coin purse.
....
It's almost *her* birthday now.
What can I do in return?

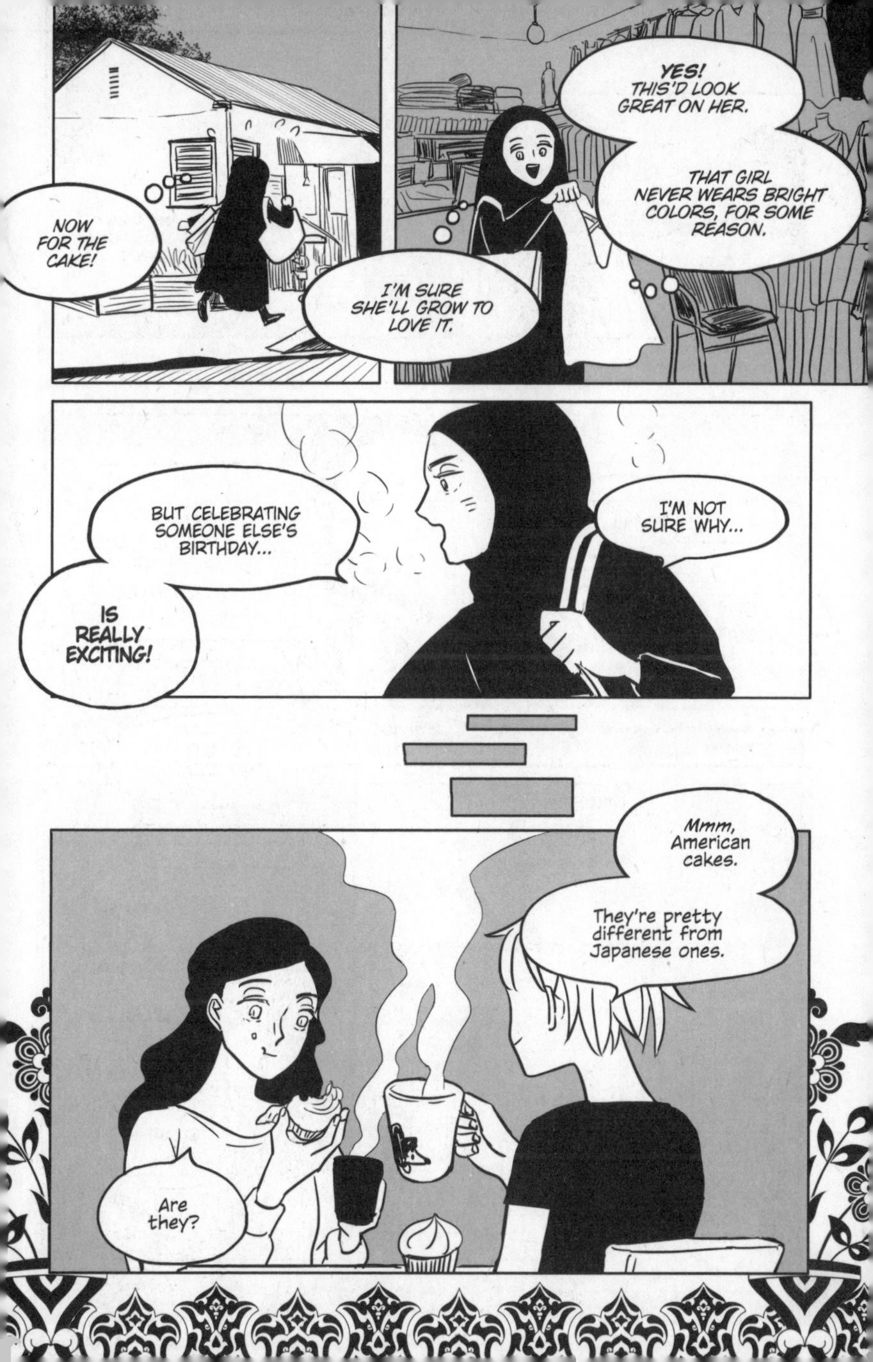
YES! THIS'D LOOK GREAT ON HER.
THAT GIRL NEVER WEARS BRIGHT COLORS, FOR SOME REASON.
I'M SURE SHE'LL GROW TO LOVE IT.
NOW FOR THE CAKE!
I'M NOT SURE WHY...
BUT CELEBRATING SOMEONE ELSE'S BIRTHDAY...
IS REALLY EXCITING!
Mmm, American cakes.
They're pretty different from Japanese ones.
Are they?

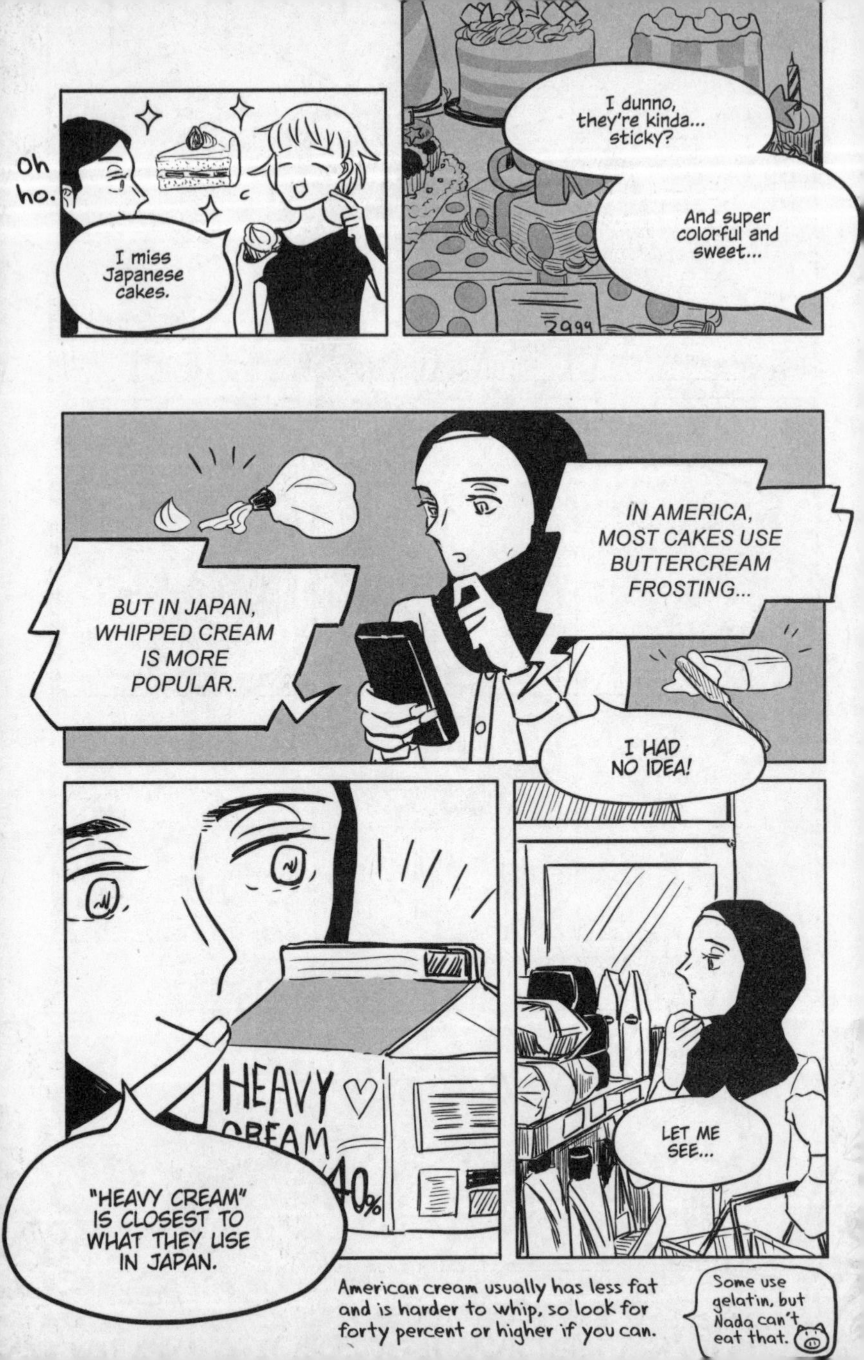
I dunno, they're kinda... sticky?
And super colorful and sweet...
3999
Oh ho.
I miss Japanese cakes.
IN AMERICA, MOST CAKES USE BUTTERCREAM FROSTING...
BUT IN JAPAN, WHIPPED CREAM IS MORE POPULAR.
I HAD NO IDEA!
LET ME SEE...
HEAVY ♡ CREAM 40%
"HEAVY CREAM" IS CLOSEST TO WHAT THEY USE IN JAPAN.
Some use gelatin, but Nada can't eat that.
American cream usually has less fat and is harder to whip, so look for forty percent or higher if you can.

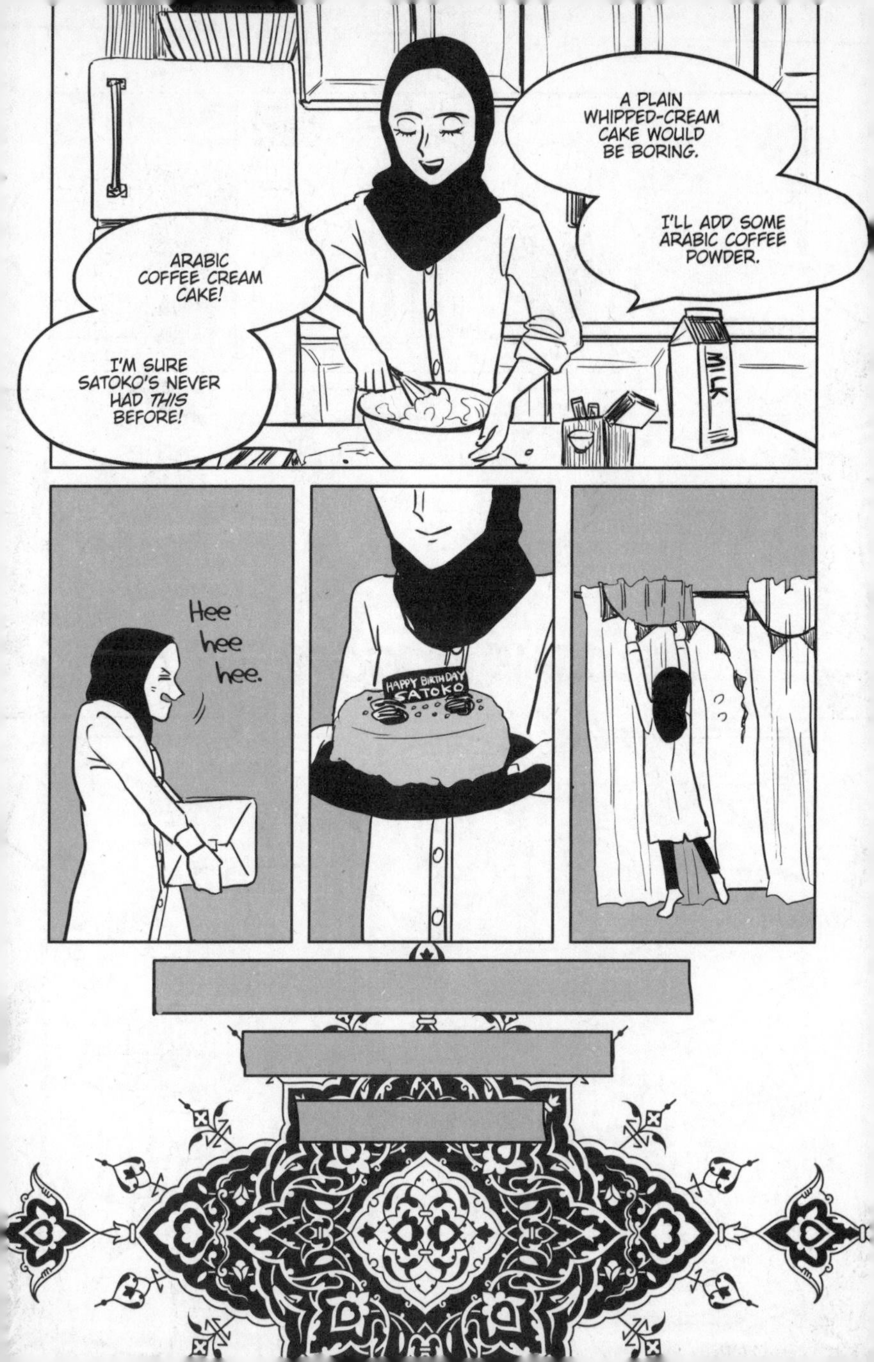
A PLAIN WHIPPED-CREAM CAKE WOULD BE BORING.
I'LL ADD SOME ARABIC COFFEE POWDER.
MILK
ARABIC COFFEE CREAM CAKE!
I'M SURE SATOKO'S NEVER HAD *THIS* BEFORE!
HAPPY BIRTHDAY SATOKO
Hee hee hee.

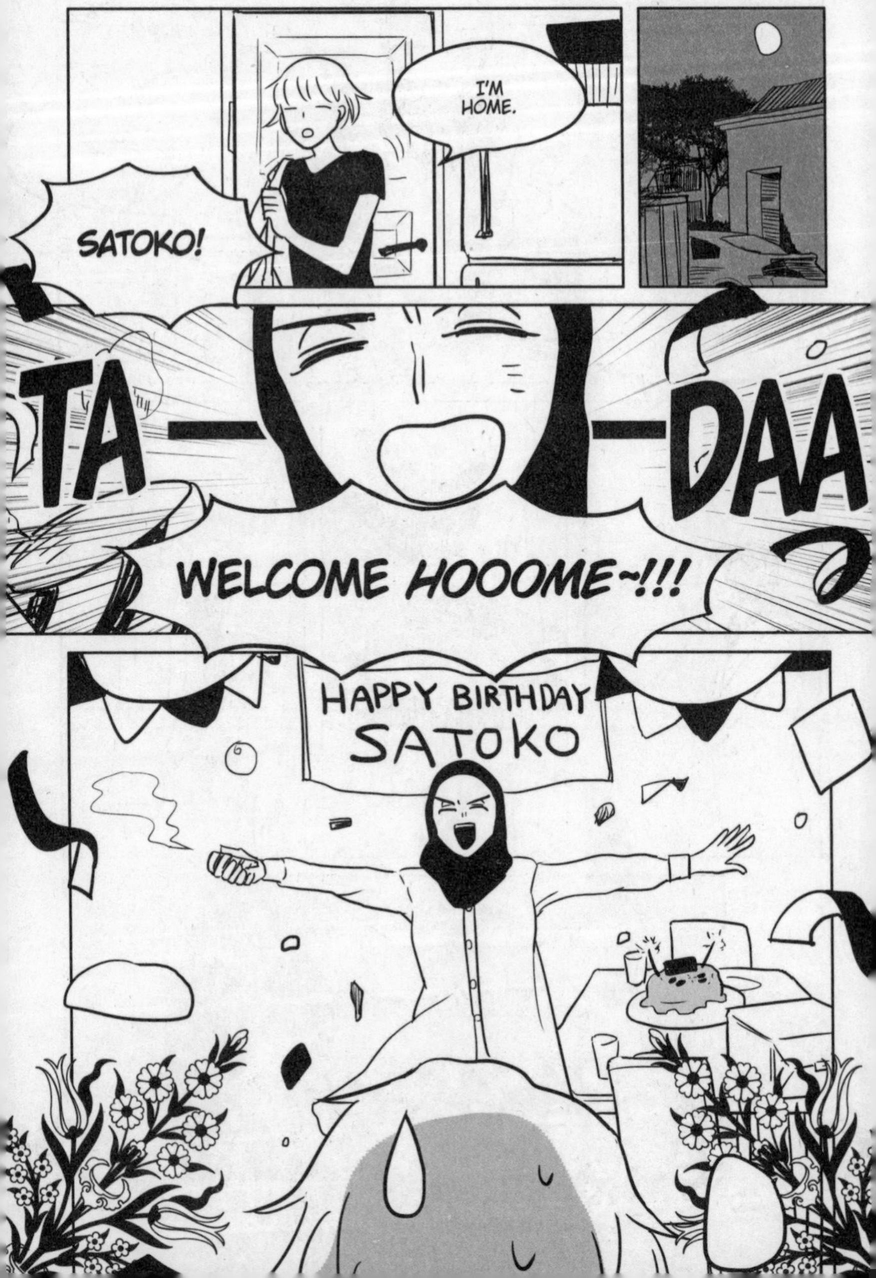
I'M HOME.
SATOKO!
TA— —DAA
WELCOME HOOOME~!!!
HAPPY BIRTHDAY SATOKO

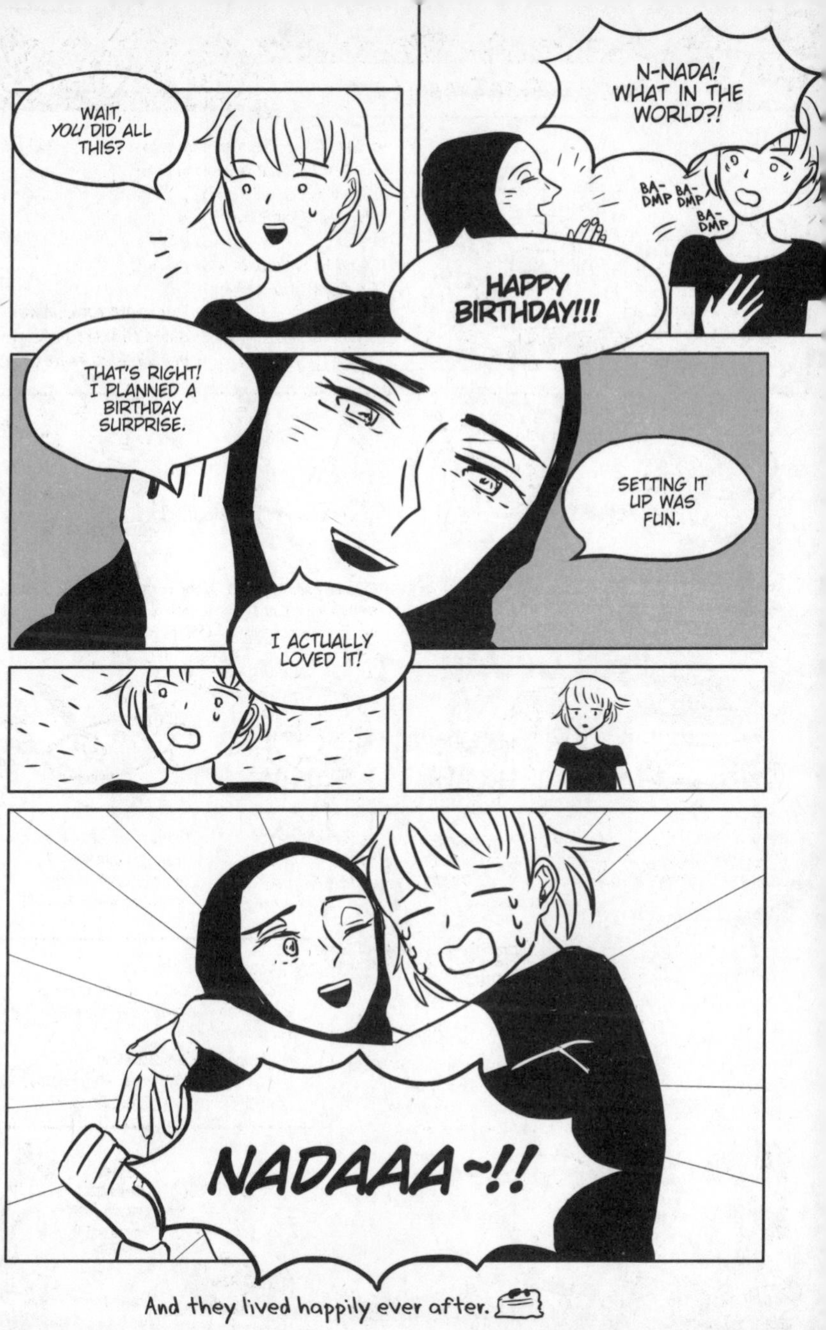
N-NADA! WHAT IN THE WORLD?!
BA-DMP BA-DMP BA-DMP
HAPPY BIRTHDAY!!!
WAIT, *YOU* DID ALL THIS?
THAT'S RIGHT! I PLANNED A BIRTHDAY SURPRISE.
SETTING IT UP WAS FUN.
I ACTUALLY LOVED IT!
NADAAA~!!

And they lived happily ever after.

NADA'S

Arabic Coffee Cream Cake

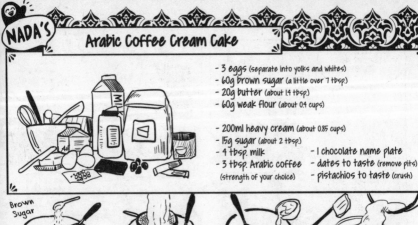

- 3 eggs (separate into yolks and whites)
- 60g brown sugar (a little over 7 tbsp.)
- 20g butter (about 1.4 tbsp.)
- 60g weak flour (about 0.4 cups)

- 200ml heavy cream (about 0.85 cups)
- 15g sugar (about 2 tbsp.)
- 4 tbsp. milk
- 3 tbsp. Arabic coffee (strength of your choice)
- 1 chocolate name plate
- dates to taste (remove pits)
- pistachios to taste (crush)

1 : 1

Brown Sugar

Gradually add sugar to egg whites, beating into a meringue.

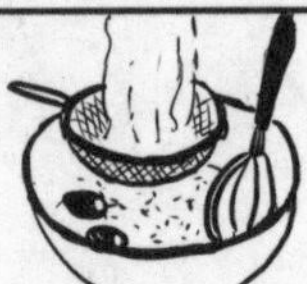

٢ : 2

Add the egg yolks, then sift the flour into the mix, mixing briskly to avoid clumps.

٣ : 3

Gradually add the melted butter and mix it in thoroughly.

Smells good!

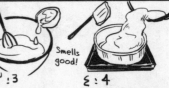

٤ : 4

Pour the batter into a cake pan (6-inch diameter), then bake at 170° C (338° F) for about 30 minutes.

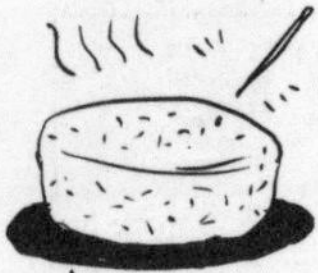

٥ : 5

Use a toothpick to test whether the cake is cooked through, then cool.

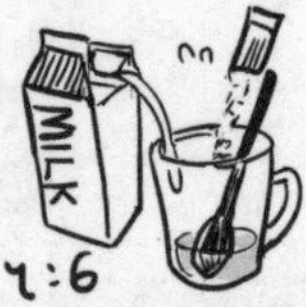

٦ : 6

Pour the milk in a cup, mix in the Arabic coffee, and microwave for 1 minute; leave to cool.

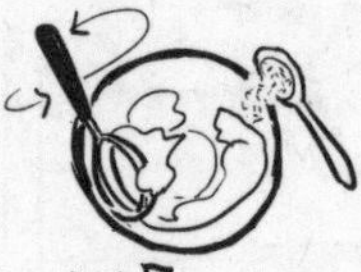

٧ : 7

Add the brown sugar to the heavy cream and whisk.

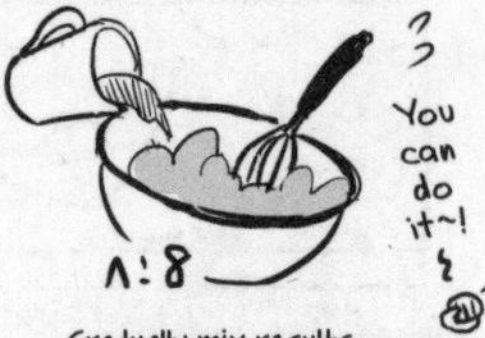

٨ : 8

You can do it~!

Gradually mix results of step 6 into step 7, whisking until desired consistency is achieved.

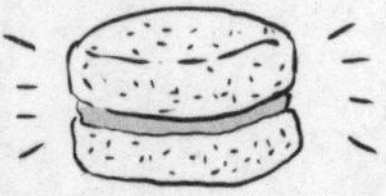

٩ : 9

Cut the cooled cake sponge in two and spread whipped cream in the middle.

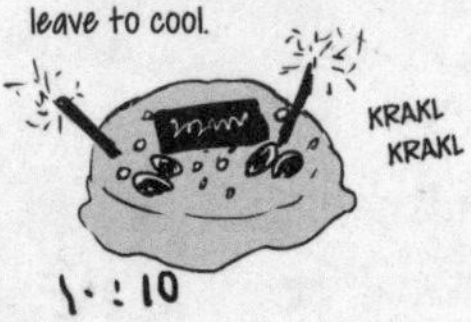

١٠ : 10

KRAKL KRAKL

Frost the cake with the remaining cream, add the name plate and dates, sprinkle on some pistachios, and you're done!

> ★ **About Weak Flour**
> Refers to the level of gluten content. In America, you should use "cake flour" for this recipe!
>
> Strong Flour = Bread Flour
> Medium-Strength Flour = All-Purpose Flour
> Weak Flour = Cake Flour! Be careful!

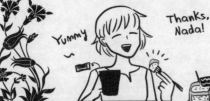

Yummy

Thanks, Nada!

Feel free to adjust the recipe to taste.

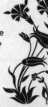

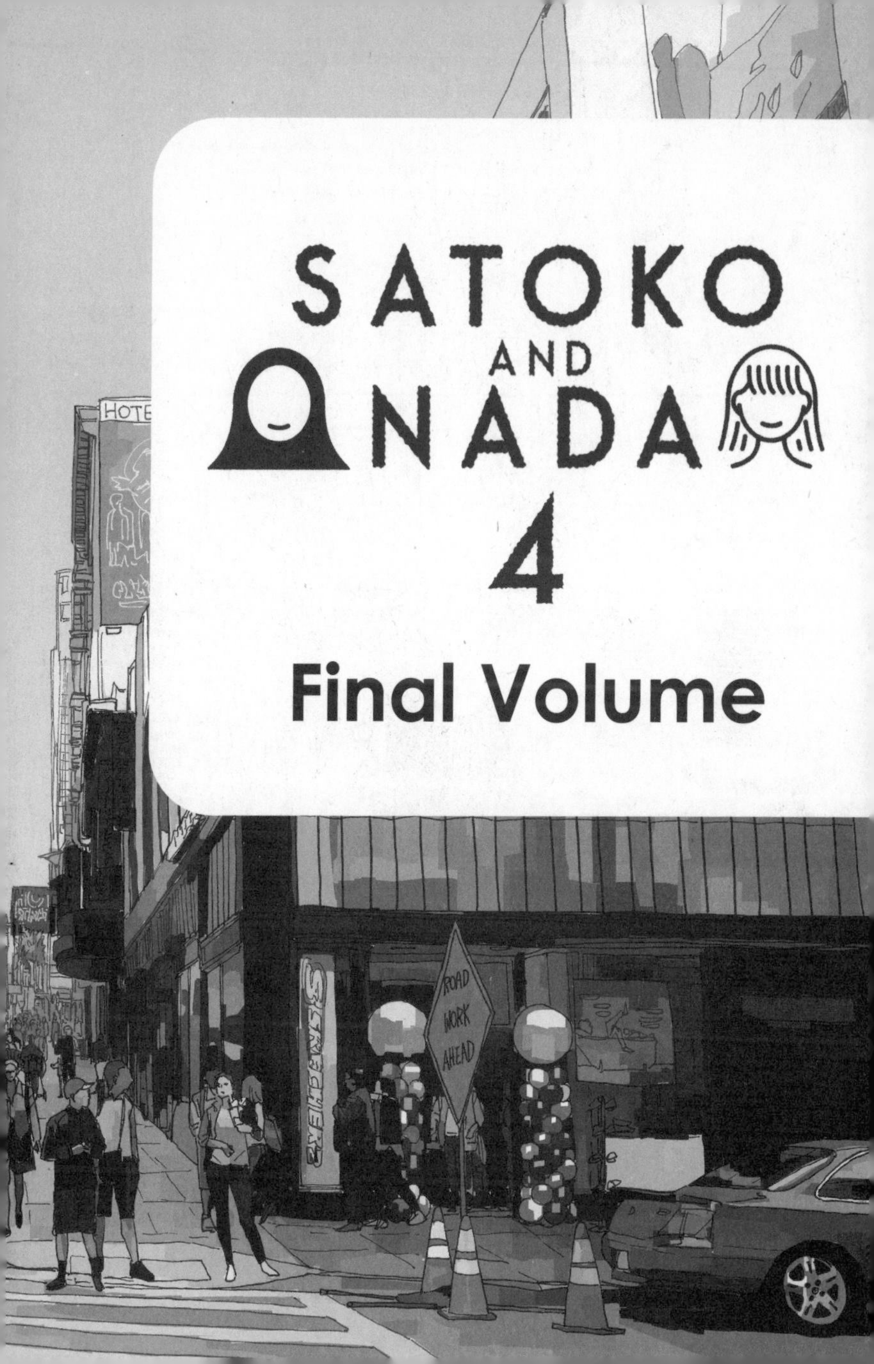
ROAD
WORK
AHEAD

SATOKO AND NADA 4

Final Volume

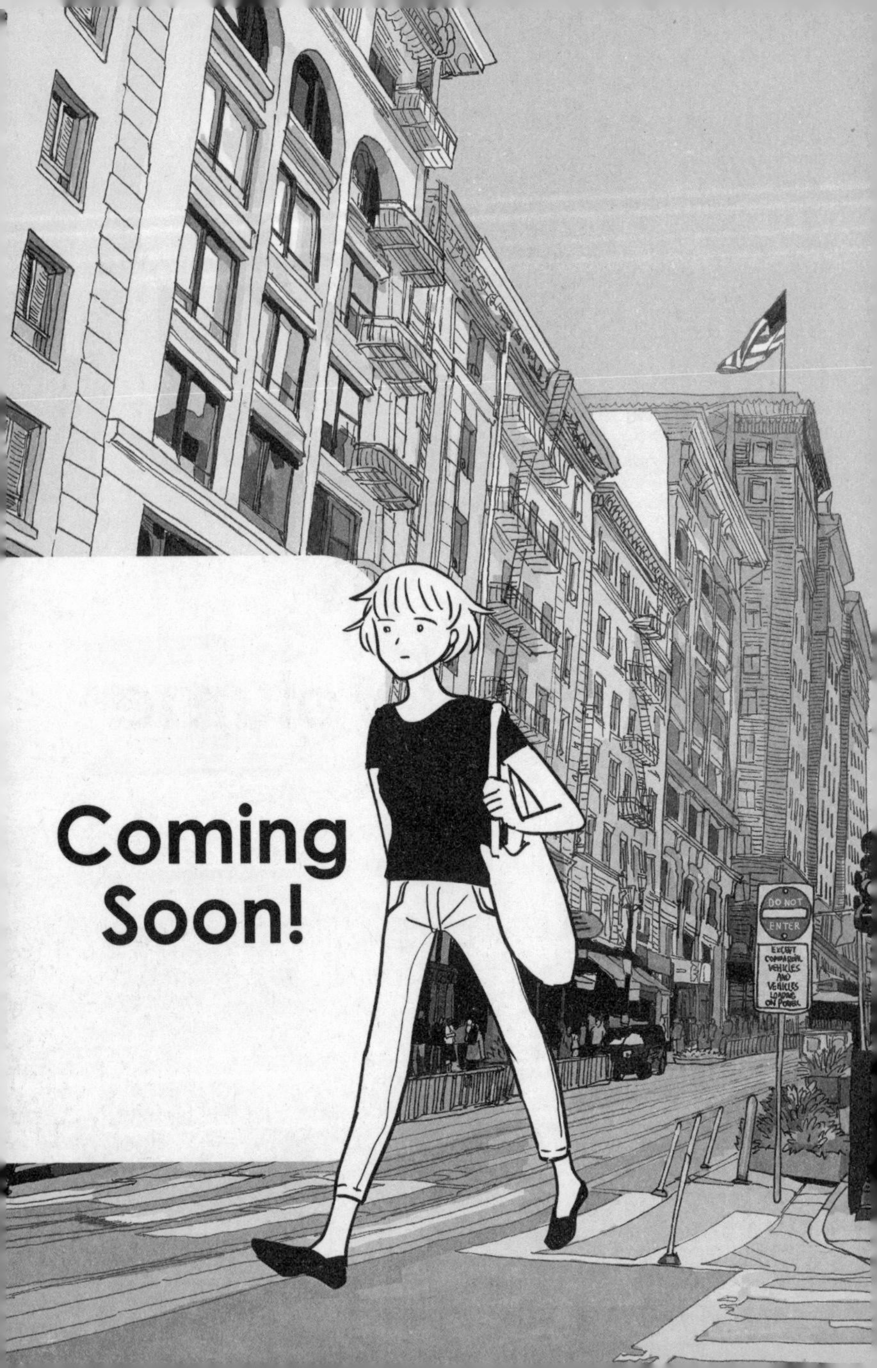
Coming Soon!
DO NOT ENTER

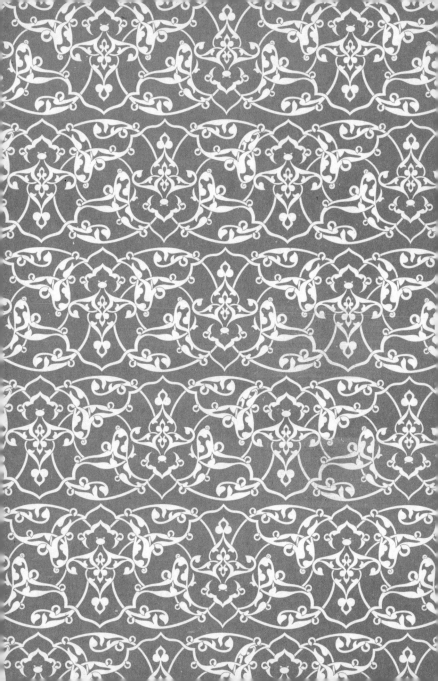

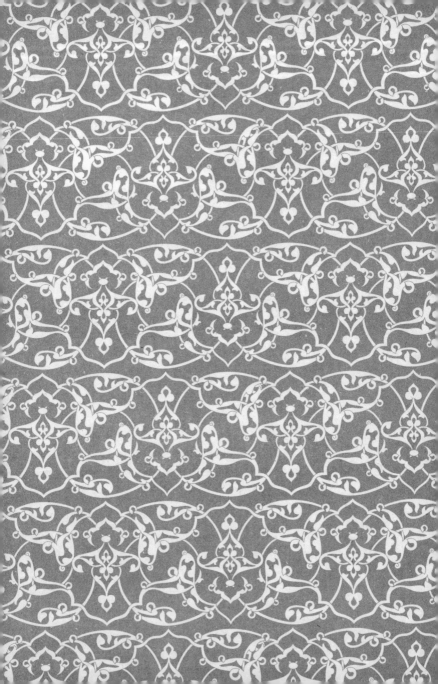

SEVEN SEAS ENTERTAINMENT PRESENTS

SATOKO AND NADA

story and art by YUPECHIKA scr

TRANSLATION
Jenny McKeon

ADAPTATION
Lianne Sentar

LETTERING AND RETOUCH
Karis Page

COVER DESIGN
KC Fabellon

PROOFREADER
Danielle King
Kurestin Armada

EDITOR
Jenn Grunigen

PREPRESS TECHNICIAN
Rhiannon Rasmussen-Silverstein

PRODUCTION MANAGER
Lissa Pattillo

MANAGING EDITOR
Julie Davis

ASSOCIATE PUBLISHER
Adam Arnold

PUBLISHER
Jason DeAngelis

First published in Japan in 2018 by Star Seas Company.
Publication rights for this English edition arranged with Star Seas Company through Kodansha Ltd.,Tokyo.

Seven Seas press and purchase enquiries can be sent to Marketing Manager Lianne Sentar at press@gomanga.com. Information regarding the distribution and purchase of digital editions is available from Digital Manager CK Russell at digital@gomanga.com.

ISBN: 978-1-64275-100-0

Printed in Canada

First Printing: May 2020

10 9 8 7 6 5 4 3 2 1

FOLLOW US ONLINE: *www.sevenseasentertainment.com*

READING DIRECTIONS

This book reads from ***right to left***, Japanese style. If this is your first time reading manga, you start reading from the top right panel on each page and take it from there. If you get lost, just follow the numbered diagram here. It may seem backwards at first, but you'll get the hang of it! Have fun!!

1
2
3
4
5
6
7
8
9

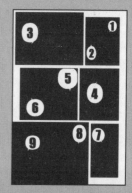